Salvation in the Gospel of Mark

Salvation in the Gospel of Mark

*The Death of Jesus and
the Path of Discipleship*

Gabi Markusse

FOREWORD BY
Paul Middleton

☙PICKWICK *Publications* • Eugene, Oregon

SALVATION IN THE GOSPEL OF MARK
The Death of Jesus and the Path of Discipleship

Copyright © 2018 Gabi Markusse. All rights reserved. Except for brief quotations in critical publications or reviews, no part of this book may be reproduced in any manner without prior written permission from the publisher. Write: Permissions, Wipf and Stock Publishers, 199 W. 8th Ave., Suite 3, Eugene, OR 97401.

Pickwick Publications
An Imprint of Wipf and Stock Publishers
199 W. 8th Ave., Suite 3
Eugene, OR 97401

www.wipfandstock.com

PAPERBACK ISBN: 978-1-5326-0173-6
HARDCOVER ISBN: 978-1-5326-0175-0
EBOOK ISBN: 978-1-5326-0174-3

Cataloguing-in-Publication data:

Names: Markusse, Gabi. | Middleton, Paul, foreword

Title: Salvation in the Gospel of Mark : the death of Jesus and the path of discipleship / by Gabi Markusse.

Description: Eugene, OR: Pickwick Publications, 2018 | Includes bibliographical references and index.

Identifiers: ISBN 978-1-5326-0173-6 (paperback) | ISBN 978-1-5326-0175-0 (hardcover) | ISBN 978-1-5326-0174-3 (ebook)

Subjects: LCSH: Salvation—Biblical teaching. | Bible. Mark—Criticism, interpretation, etc. | Jesus Christ—Crucifixion—History of doctrines—Early church, ca. 30–600. | Christian life—Biblical teaching. | Bible. Mark—Theology.

Classification: LCC BS2585.2 M2 2018 (print) | LCC BS2585.2 (ebook)

All Scripture quotations, unless otherwise indicated, are taken from the Holy Bible, New International Version®, NIV®. Copyright ©1973, 1978, 1984, 2011 by Biblica, Inc.™ Used by permission of Zondervan. All rights reserved worldwide. www.zondervan.com The "NIV" and "New International Version" are trademarks registered in the United States Patent and Trademark Office by Biblica, Inc.™

Manufactured in the U.S.A.   06/20/18

For those of us who see people walking around like trees.
May he touch our eyes again.

Contents

Foreword by Paul Middleton | ix
Preface | xiii
List of Abbreviations | xvii

1 Introduction | 1

Part One: Mark's Theology Highlighted by Narrative Structure | 25

2 Implications of Mark's Narrative Structure | 27
3 The (Im)possible Path of Discipleship | 44

Part Two: Relevant Socio-Historical Background to Mark 8:22—10:52 | 67

4 The Noble Death and the Emotions of Jesus | 69
5 The Divine *Pathos* | 85
6 Mark and Martyrdom | 100

Part Three: Relevant Intertextual Background to Mark 8:22—10:52 | 113

7 Mark's Use of Isaiah's Salvation Narrative | 115
8 Mark's Use of Daniel's *One Like a Son of Man* | 133
9 Mark's Use of Psalm 22's Righteous Sufferer | 153

10 Conclusions | 170

Bibliography | 181
Author Index | 195

Foreword

Paul Middleton

Around the beginning of the second half of the second century, Polycarp, Bishop of Smyrna, stood before a Roman proconsul and large crowd, accused of being a Christian. In common with many other Christians before and after, he was offered a simple choice; he could persist in his confession of Christ and die, or he could save his life by offering a sacrifice to the emperor and cursing Christ. Polycarp's famous response, recorded in what many still believe to be the earliest Christian Martyr Act,[1] confirms that he is prepared to die, rather than deny Christ: "For eighty-six years I have been his servant and he has done me no wrong. How can I blaspheme against my king and saviour?"[2]

In common with Pliny's account of his own dealings with Christians some forty years earlier,[3] Polycarp is given three opportunities to recant, with threats of a tortuous death should he refuse. However, the Bishop explains that to deny Christ in this life will result in a worse fate in the next. So that in response to the threat of execution by burning, Polycarp reasons: "The fire you threaten me with burns merely for a time and is soon extinguished. It is clear you are ignorant of the fire of everlasting punishment and of the judgement that is to come, which awaits the impious."[4] While Roman critics of early Christians thought they exhibited an irrational lust for death,[5] Polycarp's answers demonstrate a logical calculus behind his decision to die rather than deny Christ and save his own life. The proconsul gives up his

---

1. See the important recent challenge to an early dating for *The Martyrdom of Polycarp* by Moss, "On the Dating of Polycarp," 539–74. For response and discussion, see Hartog, *Polycarp's Epistle*, 171–86.

2. *Martyrdom of Polycarp* 9.3. Translation from Musurillo, *Acts of the Christian Martyrs*.

3. Pliny, *Epistles*, 10.96.

4. *Martyrdom of Polycarp*, 11.2.

5. See Middleton, "Noble Death or Death Cult," 207–29.

persuasion and announces: "Three times Polycarp has confessed that he is a Christian."[6] Polycarp is then executed.

A similar situation is found throughout the Christian martyr acts; the dramas often reach a climax when Christians are given a choice to confess or deny Christ accompanied by the threat of torture and execution or the promise of freedom depending on their answer. Early Christian identity was shaped by these experiences—real or literary—of persecution, suffering, and martyrdom.[7] Yet, although the Church could celebrate tales of heroic martyrdom, Christians had to account for both the threat and the actuality of apostasy under pressure. The issue of "the Lapsed" became such a problem in the third and fourth centuries that it would eventually split the Church as Rigorist and Catholic movements collided in their responses, culminating in the dispute between Augustine and the Donatists. Yet, this concern is found in earlier Christian writings, such as the *Martyrs of Lyons* (c. 177 CE).

> Those that were left fell into two groups. Some were clearly ready to become our first martyrs, making a full confession of their faith with the greatest enthusiasm. Yet others were shown to be still untrained, unprepared, and weak, unable to bear the strain of a great conflict. Of these about ten in all were stillborn, causing us great grief and measureless distress.[8]

If successful martyrdom was as important in early Christian identity formation as is generally thought, then denial at the point of trial constituted a hammer blow to the credibility and group cohesion of the church. It is not surprising that early Christian writings stress that death was a better option than facing judgement in future. From the writings of Pliny and Tacitus,[9] it appears that Christians not only denied under pressure, but actually betrayed other Christians to the authorities, reminiscent of Jesus's warning that brother will betray brother to death (Mark 13:12).[10] A warning against denial in a trial setting may also underpin other New Testament sayings, such as the unredeemable apostasy of Hebrews 6:4–6,

---

6. *Martyrdom of Polycarp*, 12.1. Musurillo here has the proconsul announce three times that Polycarp has confessed himself to be Christian, which is also possible.

7. For example, Cobb, *Dying to Be Men*; Castelli, *Martyrdom and Memory*; Boyarin, *Dying For God*; Perkins, *Suffering Self*.

8. *Martyrs of Lyons*, 1.11. Translated by Musurillo.

9. Tacitus, *Annals*, 15.44.

10. Iersel ("Failed Followers," 244–63) makes a direct link between Mark 13:12 and Tacitus's description of the Neronic pogrom. He argues Mark was written to comfort those followers who had betrayed fellow Christians ("brothers") to the authorities. While possible, I am inclined that blood rather than spiritual family is in view here.

the mortal sin of 1 John 5:16, or the unpardonable blasphemy against the Holy Spirit in Mark 3:29.

However, what is noteworthy about the passage from *Martyrs of Lyons* above is the way in which it reverses the categories of life and death, such that to live is to die and to die is to live. Early Christian martyr narratives coalesce around a cluster of themes—confession and denial; saving and losing life; reversing what it means to live and die—that strongly reflect the cross sayings of Jesus, in which he lays out the conditions of discipleship.

> And he called to him the crowd with his disciples and said to them, "If anyone wishes to follow after me, let him deny himself and take up his cross and follow me. For whoever would save his life will lose it; and whoever loses his life for my sake and the gospel's will save it. For what does it profit a person to gain the whole world and forfeit his life? For what can a person give in return for his life? For whoever is ashamed of me and of my words in this adulterous and sinful generation, of him will the Son of man also be ashamed when he comes in the glory of his Father with the holy angels" (Mark 8:34–38).

This collection of sayings, just as the *Martyrs of Lyons* equates denying Jesus to save one's life as death, while losing one's life through confession to win life. Moreover, embracing suffering and death appears to be a *condition* rather than a *consequence* of following Jesus. A would-be disciple has to *first* take up the cross *before* following Jesus.

To be sure, commentators have sought to lessen the impact of this stark saying, arguing that it is metaphorical, and indeed, this is how Luke reinterprets the saying by inserting "daily" (Lk 9:27). However, Mark elsewhere points to the necessity of suffering (8:31; 9:30–31; 10:30, 33–34), and highlights the rejection of suffering as a sign of apostasy (4:17; 8:33). Indeed, so strongly does Mark set up the contrasting roads of the suffering faithful and the denying apostates, that his portrayal of the disciples, especially Peter, who, unlike Polycarp's threefold confession of Jesus, denies him three times (14:66–72) becomes problematic. Instead of denying self, Peter denies and curses Jesus (14:71). If Peter is judged against the conditions of discipleship that Mark has taken the trouble to outline in his Gospel, then he denies Jesus in order to save his life. Consequently, there is nothing he can do to get it back. Mark's "treatment" of Peter and the rest of the disciples is a source of much scholarly debate.[11] While in the main commentators seek to dampen

---

11. The scholarly discussion is clearly laid out in the present volume. I have recently argued for a maximalist understanding of the "rejection" of the disciples in two recent essays: Middleton, "Suffering and the Creation of Christian Identity in Mark," 173–89;

the consequences of their treachery, often pointing to Jesus's promise of post-resurrection restoration, it seems to me puzzling that Mark would lay out the path of apostasy in meticulous detail if the consequences really mattered little when it comes to the disciples. Moreover, despite the prediction of post-resurrection appearances, Mark does not record them, but ends with the women running away saying nothing. The disciples' planned restoration apparently thwarted by the narrator.

In this book, Gabi Markusse tackles the challenges of the necessity of suffering and the failure of the disciples head-on. She argues that salvation is a critical theme that dominates the Gospel. This theme is worked out through Jesus's activity that leads to the cross, which she sees as an outworking of God's plan of salvation. In Mark, Jesus chooses the path of suffering in order to please not himself, but God. It is this pattern of obedience to God that dominates Markusse's reading of discipleship in the Gospel. In order to achieve salvation, disciples must follow Jesus on the road of suffering, being prepared to give up their lives just as Jesus had done. However, this, she notes, proves to be impossible. The disciples fail. However, while the author rejects those accounts that seek to downplay that failure, she argues that Mark builds into his narrative provision for failure, namely the promise of the Holy Spirit promised in Mark 1:8, and whose coming Jesus's death on the cross enables.

This innovative reading takes seriously the themes of suffering and discipleship in the Gospel of Mark, but also brings to the fore the overlooked role of the Holy Spirit. While commentators rightly focus on the first words of Jesus of repentance and the nearness of the Kingdom of God as a key to understanding Mark's purpose, less attention has been given to the first thing said *of* Jesus in the Gospel. John the Baptist announces that he is coming (1:7), and that he will baptize with the Holy Spirit (1:8), a prophecy that finds no obvious fulfilment in the Gospel. Gabi Markusse rectifies this oversight in her bold reading of Mark's Gospel that brings the important themes of suffering and discipleship together in dialogue with a long overdue treatment of the neglected character of the Holy Spirit.

---

and Middleton, "Christology, Martyrdom, and Vindication," 219–37. A more optimistic view is also found in Carey, "'Is It as Bad as All That?'" 3–21. It should also be noted that Gabi Markusse in this volume demurs from my view.

Preface

As a young college student, I sat in class one day listening to Dr. John Perkins speak about the necessity of taking up one's cross to follow after Jesus. He was a guest speaker in a class designed to prepare students for ministry. Our professor, Dr. Bruce Baloian, had done good work before him, and most of us were nodding our heads in agreement with Dr. Perkins. But one question gnawed at my heart: I can accept this way of being a Christian for myself, but what do I say to the homeless women I work with in downtown Los Angeles? They have already suffered so much. What does it mean for them to pick up their cross? I can't remember the answer Dr. Perkins gave to me, but I do remember having lunch with him and his daughter that afternoon, and that he told me that I would always be welcome at their home. I think he liked my question.

This pastoral question remained in the back of my mind throughout the years. The Gospel of Mark is emphatic about the need for those who want to follow Jesus to pick up their cross. But is this really what the Gospel is about? Is it for everybody? Or is it a message only for the rich and privileged? Can I even ethically answer that question? Years later, this inspired the topic of my PhD research.

Half way through my doctoral studies, I decided to quit. I was studying while raising our three daughters and the stress got the better of me. Kent Brower, my supervisor—or Doktorvater as the Germans appropriately say—wisely suggested I just take a break and decide later whether or not I want to continue. After six months, I decided that I needed to know the answer to my question. It had been thirty years since that day I asked the question to Dr. Perkins, and I needed to know the answer for myself. I needed to know if the Gospel message was about *everyone* who wants to follow Jesus needing to pick up their cross to follow him unto death. And so, I resumed my studies and this book is the fruit of my struggle and quest to understand the meaning of the Gospel.

I have become convinced that it was the intent of the implied writer of Mark's Gospel to portray the message that all people are invited to give their lives completely in the hands of God in order to follow Jesus, and face whatever resistance that brings from those who do not understand. This entails great suffering for many people. And yes, this message is not only for me, but also for the homeless and the destitute. But as I delved deeper into the Gospel of Mark, I found that the words about suffering and serving did not stand alone. I began to see that there is a parallel promise that this painful "letting go" of one's life is facilitated by God himself. He never asks us to do it alone. The key to understanding the suffering is tied up with the promise with which Mark begins his Gospel message: Jesus came to baptize the repentant with the Holy Spirit of God. And understanding Jesus's death will bring one to the experiential knowledge of this baptism.

But of course, this work is meant to be academic and not in the first place pastoral. The question that guided this study was whether or not this was the message of Mark's Gospel. The implications of the answer to this question I must leave to others interested in following Jesus in our own time. Although my Doktorvater continually reminded me I was writing for an academic audience, I know that it is often difficult for me to separate the academic from the pastoral. This is a weakness to which I fully admit and for which I take full responsibility.

In the Conclusion, I have allowed my thoughts a bit freer rein to consider some aspects of this message that beg further research. One thing I do not mention there, but which is an aspect of the narrative that I have not yet explored and which is increasingly enticing me, has to do with *love*. Mark does not have the love language that John, for example, uses freely. Yet he does not ignore it either. To the Markan Jesus, the height of obedience is to love God with *everything*, and to love your neighbor as yourself (12:28–34). Could it be that the Markan Jesus hints to this in his conversation with the young man in Mark 10:17–21? The commandments which have to do with loving your neighbor are listed, conspicuously omitting the commands that have to do with loving God. But Jesus adds something: giving up all that the man counts as riches on earth in order to gain riches in heaven, and following Jesus. Could it be that the Markan Jesus is *describing what it means to love God*? When Mark paints the picture of the woman in Bethany anointing Jesus with expensive perfume (14:3–9), he does not speak directly of love. The Markan Jesus does however, describe it as a "beautiful thing" which she does to him. She did what she could do, he says, and her story would be told whenever the gospel would be preached throughout the world. Could this be inferring *love*? Could Mark be saying that the understanding that happens when the death of Jesus is fully grasped is about *love*? Is *love* the mystery of the Kingdom? Feeling or knowing oneself loved by God (cf. 1:11) might be the only motivation possible for the extent of obedience demanded by the Markan Jesus. While I did not include this aspect in my research, this study is incomplete without it.

Finally, I would like to thank all who made this work possible. Thank you to Bruce Baloian who first sparked my interest in Biblical Theology and lived out his teaching of the "upside-down Kingdom of God," to Kent Brower (my dear Doktorvater) and to my family who have been an amazing support and safe place for me in this entire journey. And thank you to the people who have become an inseparable part of my life in the past year who exemplify this message in their lives, many of whom know first-hand what it means to give up family, land, and income because of their loyalty to Jesus. Together we have begun to live out Mark 10:29–30.

Gabi Markusse, August 2017

Abbreviations

ANF	*Ante-Nicene Fathers*
BBR	*Bulletin for Biblical Research*
BEThL	*Bibliotheca ephemeridum theologicarum lovaniensium*
BEvT	*Beiträge zur evangelischen Theologie*
Bib	*Biblica*
BibInt	*Biblical Interpretation*
BJRL	*Bulletin of the John Rylands University Library of Manchester*
BSac	*Bibliotheca Sacra*
BTB	*Biblical Theology Bulletin*
BZNW	*Beihefte zur Zeitschrift für die neutestamentliche Wissenschaft*
CBQ	*Catholic Biblical Quarterly*
CBR	*Currents in Biblical Research*
CTJ	*Calvin Theological Journal*
CTSJ	*Chafer Theological Seminary Journal*
CV	*Communio viatorum*
EQ	*Evangelical Quarterly*
FB	*Forschung zur Bibel*
FTS	*Frankfurter Theologische Studien*
HBT	*Horizons in Biblical Theology*
HeyJ	*Heythrop Journal*
HR	*History of Religions*
HTR	*Harvard Theological Review*
Int	*Interpretation*
IRT	*Issues in Religion and Theology*

ITQ	Irish Theological Quarterly
JAAR	Journal of the American Academy of Religion
JBL	Journal of Biblical Literature
JBMS	Journal of Book of Mormon Studies
JBPR	Journal of Biblical & Pneumatological Research
JECS	Journal of Early Christian Studies
JETS	Journal of the Evangelical Theological Society
JNES	Journal of Near Eastern Studies
JR	Journal of Religion
JSJ	Journal for the Study of Judaism
JSNT	Journal for the Study of the New Testament
JSNTSup	Journal for the Study of the New Testament: Supplement Series
JSOT	Journal for the Study of the Old Testament
JSOTSup	Journal for the Study of the Old Testament: Supplement Series
JTS	Journal of Theological Studies
KBS	Katholieke Bijbelstichting
LCL	Loeb Classical Library
LNTS	Library of New Testament Studies
m. Sanh.	Mishnah Sanhedrin
NIDB	New Interpreter's Dictionary of the Bible.
NIVI	New International Version (inclusive language edition, 1999)
NovT	Novum Testamentum
NovTSup	Supplements to Novum Testamentum
NTS	New Testament Studies
OBT	Overtures to Biblical Theology
Per	Perspective
PTL	A Journal for Poetics and Theory of Literature
RBL	Review of Biblical Literature
RevEx	Review & Expositor
RJ	Rabbinic Judaism
SAJ	Saint Anselm Journal
SBL	Society of Biblical Literature

SBLDS	Society of Biblical Literature Dissertation Series
SBLSymS	Society of Biblical Literature Symposium Series
SBLRBS	Society of Biblical Literature Resources for Biblical Study
SJ	Studia Judaica
SJSJ	Supplements to the Journal for the Study of Judaism
SJT	*Scottish Journal of Theology*
SNT	Studien zum Neuen Testament
SNTSMS	Society for New Testament Studies Monograph Series
SSEJC	Studies in Scripture in Early Judaism and Christianity
ST	*Studia Theologica—Nordic Journal of Theology*
SVTQ	*St. Vladimir's Theological Quarterly*
TDNT	*Theological Dictionary of the New Testament*
ThTo	*Theology Today*
TJ	*Trinity Journal*
TvT	*Tijdschrift voor Theologie*
VT	*Vetus Testamentum*
WUNT	Wissenschaftliche Untersuchungen zum Neuen Testament
ZNW	*Zeitschrift für die neutestamentliche Wissenschaft und die Kunde der älteren Kirche*

1

Introduction

The Gospel of Mark portrays a striking connection between the passion predictions concerning Jesus's fate and Jesus's teaching to his followers. Examining this connection, I discover that Mark approaches salvation not solely as something that Jesus has accomplished for us, but as something that is incomplete without the human response of giving up the rights to one's own life. While Mark portrays the initial failure of the disciples, he stresses the notion of dying to one's self and becoming the servant and slave of all as a necessary component to salvation. This extent of discipleship proves impossible to attain, humanly speaking. Mark's Good News is that through the Holy Spirit even this is possible.

The Death of Jesus and the Path of Discipleship

THE WRITER OF THE Gospel of Mark makes a fascinating connection between the death of Jesus and the path of discipleship. Right in the middle of the narrative, Jesus takes his disciples aside to go on a journey designed specifically to teach them some important things. He doesn't want anyone to know where they are. Experience has taught that when word is out that Jesus is in town, the crowds make it nearly impossible for him to give attention to his own disciples. And right now, he needs to make sure his disciples listen and learn. They tell him that they know he is the Messiah. And then he tells them that he must suffer and die and if they want to continue to follow him, this is also the road that they must take.

In three clearly defined scenes during this journey in the center of the Gospel, Mark combines a prediction of Jesus's passion with teaching about what it means to follow Jesus. In the first of these three discipleship teachings

(8:34—9:1), the Markan Jesus insists that whoever would follow him must pick up their cross and come after him. They must deny themselves and give up their life. For whoever wants to save their life will lose it; only those who are willing to let go of their life will save it. In the second teaching moment (9:35–50), the Markan Jesus speaks of letting go of rights and privileges and of serving the least at whatever cost it might bring to oneself. In the third teaching moment (10:35–45), Jesus combines both of these aspects of discipleship. He implies that being a disciple will entail great suffering in the same way that Jesus himself would suffer. He insists that to be great they must serve and even be a slave to all, using himself as an example of the extent to which this service reaches (10:45). Each of these three teaching moments is attached to a prediction of his own passion and resurrection. According to Mark, the cross of the Messiah Jesus is not sold separately.

Mark introduces and concludes this teaching journey in the same way: with Jesus healing a man's blind eyes. There is a lot to say about this; blind eyes learning to see form a red thread throughout the narrative, indicating an understanding that will lead to salvation. I will pick up on this below.[1] Suffice it for now to say that the eyes of the disciples did not open easily. Jesus was teaching something that was very difficult for them to understand.

The Gospel of Mark is well known for its emphasis on discipleship. It is often referred to as "the Way," echoing "the Way of the LORD" imagery from Isaiah.[2] Mark indeed arranges the teaching material described above in such a way to suggest that this *way* of suffering and service has everything to do with the salvation described in Isaiah as the *way* of the LORD. He also places his entire narrative squarely in the context of God's salvation history with Israel when he begins with the conflated quotation of Exod 23:20, Mal 3:1, and Isa 40:3. And he leads this narrative of God's salvation ultimately to the crucifixion of Jesus. But if Mark presents the cross of Jesus as being God's work of salvation *and* connects the suffering of the disciples narratively to the suffering of Jesus, would that indicate that Mark intends the suffering of the disciples to be understood as also being part of God's work of salvation? This has been the guiding question of this research.

Mark's narrative shows the disciples failing drastically at following Jesus. This forms an interpretive conundrum—for how can this be if their following is so essential to the Kingdom of God? A narrative reading of the Gospel will highlight the promise that is worded by John the Baptist in the prologue: "One is coming after me who is stronger than I; I am not worthy to stoop down to untie the chords of his sandals. I baptize you with water;

---

1. See chapter 7.
2. See, for example, Marcus, *Way of the Lord*.

he will baptize you in the Holy Spirit" (1:7–8).³ Commentators generally agree that this provides an intertextual allusion to the eschatological promise of the Holy Spirit.⁴ However, this promise has largely been ignored by scholars in their studies of the disciples' failure; I propose that it holds the solution to their problem.

Mark's Story of Salvation as the Coming of the Kingdom of God

The message of the Markan Jesus is the nearness of the Kingdom of God (1:15). A basic working assumption in this study is that the essence of *salvation* is to Mark *the coming of the Kingdom of God*. This is what God is moving towards as narrated in Scripture. A related assumption is that salvation is accomplished by God, and cannot be attained without him (see 10:23–27). This is reflected in the background texts that we will look at in Part Three below. In Isaiah, God continually states that *he* is the one who will redeem his people, even when he uses servants to accomplish this. In Daniel 7, only God is able to finally bring a halt to the cruel persecution of his people by the beasts (Dan 7:9–12, 26). All nations are then brought under the umbrella of his Kingdom which will be ruled by his people (Dan 7:14, 18, 27). Psalm 22 also reflects a faith in God as the only one who can help the sufferer, and as the one who ultimately brings relief and vindication.

This Kingdom of God is understood as the realm in which God's ways are lived out, where God is obeyed.⁵ To make this obedience possible, the Holy Spirit was promised to God's people. This is apparent in such texts as Ezekiel 36:27 ("And I will put my spirit in you, and move you to follow my decrees and be careful to keep my laws") which lie at the background of the statement of John the Baptist in Mark's prologue (1:7–8). Mark's use of the term *baptism* in conjunction with the Holy Spirit indicates the connection between John's ministry and that of Jesus, while he focuses on the intensity of the difference. John's baptism in water indicates repentance but Jesus's baptism in the Spirit would actually *enable* a life of obedience. This connection between the Holy Spirit and the ability to obey God, and thus please him, is embodied in the scene immediately following the record of John's message. Jesus is baptized by John and as he arises from the water,

---

3. Texts from Mark are my translation unless otherwise stated. Old Testament and other NT texts are taken from the *NIV* unless otherwise specified.

4. Hooker, *Mark*, 38; Brower, *Mark*, 56; France, *Mark*, 72; Collins, *Mark*, 138–40, 146.

5. See also Colijn, *Images of Salvation*, especially chapter 3.

the Holy Spirit descends upon him and a voice proclaims to him that he is his beloved Son in whom he is well pleased (1:10–11). As the ensuing narrative unfolds, Jesus is portrayed as living out God's will to the utmost. The first activity portrayed after the baptism is the Holy Spirit thrusting Jesus into the wilderness where he undergoes testing by Satan (1:12–13). While Mark does not mention the outcome explicitly as Matthew (Matt 4:1–11) and Luke (Luke 4:1–13) do, it is understood that Jesus passes the testing and remains obedient to God. Mark makes vivid to his audience through the words of John the Baptist that this Holy Spirit will be available to people through Jesus, enabling and even moving them to live a life of pleasing and obeying God even when faced with the testing of the opponent Satan.[6] The background against which my research has been undertaken, is an understanding of the Kingdom of God as the essential Jewish hope that one day all would live in obedience to God.

Although God being King of the Israelites had become "a hope for the future," as R. T. France notes, it was actually "a present fact."[7] From their formation as a nation in the wilderness, they were a people under God's authority. A human could be king only under the authority of God himself. And yet, the realities of daily life—corruption within the priestly offices, kings worshipping other gods, disobedience, etc.—soon shifted what ought to have been a fully realized *present fact* into a *hope for the future*. Not that God was not fully King; he was. But not all recognized nor accepted his authority as King. The prophets reveal that it was those with human authority who had an especially difficult time recognizing God's authority. And yet, Ezekiel (see especially chapter 18) made it clear that part of the communal responsibility as God's people to obey him is the individual's responsibility to obey. No one was exempt from the responsibility to live a life pleasing to God. All of these aspects—and longings for a life as it ought to have been—contribute to the background against which Mark's message of Good News (1:1, 14–15) is revealed.

While the longing for the Kingdom of God to come fully was a recognizable longing in his day, Mark shows Jesus reinterpreting what it means to

---

6. The testing of Jesus by Satan in the wilderness provides a foreshadow of Mark 8:33 where Jesus rebukes Peter, calling him *Satan*. When tempted by Peter to reject the suffering ahead of him, he not only rebuked Peter but provided him with the first tools he would need to resist Satan himself, by explaining what God's thoughts were in the ensuing teaching moment. And then six days later, God underlined this teaching by telling Peter that he must listen to his beloved Son (9:2–7). While understanding God's thoughts would not prove enough to obey them, I will argue below that this understanding will lead to the reception of the Holy Spirit who will make possible the obedience.

7. France, *Divine Government*, 17.

become part of this Kingdom. Living as God's people, with God as King, is more than obeying the commandments (10:19–21), the Markan Jesus says. It has to do with giving up rights and privileges, with being a servant and a slave. Not only a slave to God, but a slave to the least of all people (10:44). It has to do with embracing children (9:35–27 and 10:13–16), but it also has to do with accepting the people that were traditionally thought to be outside of God's circle. Mark shows the disciples wanting to prohibit a stranger from casting out demons in Jesus's name. Jesus insisted they let him be and suggests that God will honor more people than they might expect (9:39–41). Jesus heals the daughter of a Gentile woman after being impressed by her answer to his riddle: even the dogs are allowed to eat the crumbs from the children's bread (7:26–30). After this, he miraculously feeds more than 4,000 Gentiles with only seven loaves of bread and a few fish, leaving seven basketfuls of crumbs (8:1–10). This mirrors the miraculous feeding of more than 5,000 Jews with only five loaves and two fishes, leaving twelve basketfuls of crumbs (6:30–44). There are crumbs enough to feed any who might be hungry, Jew and Gentile alike! To Mark, doing God's will includes accepting radically new and different ways of distinguishing who is *inside* and who is *outside*. Even those friends closest to Jesus could not be guaranteed places of honor in his Kingdom (10:39–40).

To be God's people was a great honor that belonged to the Israelite people. Their traditions, traditions that Mark drew on, included stories of God's Kingdom coming in fullness after times of oppression and suffering when they, as God's people, would have the leadership over all nations. The Markan Jesus draws upon these stories from Daniel in particular. He emphasizes the suffering of the faithful that goes before the glory of leadership. But he describes leadership as service and slavery, to the point of giving one's life for the other (10:42–45). The emotional attitude of the greatest leader in God's Kingdom is described in Mark as *not lording it over* the nations (10:42–43). It is illustrated with the words of the Markan Jesus: "My soul is deeply grieved to the point of death," as he falls to the ground to beg God to take away his impending suffering, and yet ending his prayer with "but not what I want, but what you want" (14:34–36). This is what it means to be God's people, and this service-unto-death way of life is what it means for the disciples to "leave everything to follow [Jesus]" (10:28).

This depth of obedience is the quintessential nature of the Kingdom of God according to Mark. It is impossible for humans to achieve but, according to the Markan Jesus, not with God, for "all things are possible with God" (10:27). When Mark tells his audience that Jesus saw the heavens tear open, and the Spirit descend upon him in 1:10, he is alluding to God's action of salvation which would bring about the fullness of the Kingdom of God. Mark's ideal audience will be longing for this salvation, as they long for God's Kingdom. What they will learn from Mark is that their own role in the coming of this Kingdom may cost a fair bit more than they first bargained for. No different than modern day readers, Mark's first century CE implied audience preferred a life of ease to a life of suffering. But the good news is, God will provide.

Scholarly Context

This study was prompted by a reading of Mark's emphasis on discipleship as a following of Jesus on the way of the cross. Mark couples the giving one's life for the sake of Jesus and of the gospel (8:35) to the impending suffering and death of the Son of Man (8:31). And in these teaching moments, the Markan Jesus is not speaking only to those who will be called on to give their lives, as though it were for comfort for those suffering on his account. This teaching is directed to *any* who want to follow him (8:34: εἴ τις θέλει ὀπίσω μου). The pastoral implications of this coupling are unmeasurably great. It is not often taught in churches that this depth of obedience is the minimum demanded of even the most casual Christian. While this coupling is noted by scholars, most seem to veer away from an interpretation of Mark's message demanding the depths of the cross that Mark speaks of. A survey of those writing on the cross in the Gospel of Mark reveals that scholars generally fail to see the connection between discipleship and the passion predictions as important in understanding the connection between the actual crucifixion of Jesus and the necessary "suffering" of the disciples.

The development of Markan scholarship in the past decades can be seen most clearly in respect to methodology. The past hundred years have shown a movement from historical, through source, form critical and redactional, to narrative studies of Mark's Gospel. Although every once in a while a scholar will still make a contribution in source or redactional criticism, most new studies on Mark concentrate on a narrative methodology. If we look at the themes, insights, and theology revealed in studies on Mark, however, there is little development to be seen. What David Rhoads said in 1982 about the state of Markan discipleship studies rings true today for Markan studies as a whole: "A fascinating question: What is it precisely about each critic's interpretation of Mark—the literary methods involved, the evidence garnered from throughout the story, how the evidence is weighed—which leads to such different conclusions? We are not finished with this puzzle yet."[8]

---

8. Rhoads, "Narrative Criticism," 416.

Perhaps, however, if this study will be received as a viable continuation of studies by Kent Brower, Larry Hurtado, and more recently Paul Middleton on discipleship,[9] the beginning of a development might be taking place. Instead of seeing the failure of the disciples as a toning down of the discipleship requirements in Mark, these scholars take the teaching of cross-bearing seriously as they insist that the Gospel writer intended his audience to be willing to follow Jesus unto death.

Because of my emphasis on the salvific nature of the cross, I will begin with a short review of recent scholarship that concentrates specifically on the cross and salvation in Mark, highlighting areas in which this study either confirms, complements, or critiques the specific work. I will then move on to discuss a few recent contributions to the theme of discipleship in Mark. A fuller interaction with scholarship on the specific research areas of this study can be found in the appropriate places in the chapters below. It is my hope that this brief introductory sketch will provide a rationale for yet another study on the Gospel of Mark, and communicate the importance of this study to a biblical understanding of what it means to follow Jesus.

The Cross and Atonement

Robert Gundry begins his commentary on Mark with a long list of negatives, claiming what the Gospel according to Mark is *not*. His list includes "No 'way'-symbolism for cross-bearing" and "No overarching concentric structure providing a key to meaning at midpoint."[10] He attempts to disprove an emphasis on a central section that might bring together the passion predictions of Jesus with discipleship teachings—on denying oneself, picking up one's cross, and serving the least. Instead he focuses on what he sees as an emphasis on glory surrounding Jesus in Mark's Gospel. Signs of this *glory* emphasis would include the popularity of Jesus among the people, the Transfiguration and the works of power. Even the request of John and James to be afforded the seats of honor next to Jesus when he enters into his glory (10:37) is interpreted as an emphasis on glory which overshadows the suffering inherent in the cross. He states that Mark "dresses up the Passion in colors of fulfilment, decency, dignity, and the supernatural."[11] He refers to Mark as presenting, almost despite the cross, a theology *of glory*. According to Gundry, Mark's portrayal of

---

9. See especially Brower, "'We Are Able'"; Hurtado, "Jesus' Death as Paradigmatic"; Middleton, "Suffering and the Creation."

10. Gundry, *Mark*, 1.

11. Ibid., 1024.

the cross does not lead to a theology of suffering, but to an awareness of glory; Mark presents an *apology* for the cross.

Although I do think that Gundry is right to see a combination of glory and the cross in Mark's Gospel, I do not agree with him that Mark "dresses up the Passion." Mark does not shy away from the messy shame and pain of the realities of the cross. He presents the way to glory as being *through* the filthy, painful, shameful cross. Moreover, he goes beyond the cross of Jesus in his theology of glory. Full glory will be attained only as men and women follow Jesus in the obedience that marks a true child of God, accepting the potentially filthy, painful, shameful suffering of giving up all for the sake of Jesus and the gospel. In putting a *theology of glory* up against a *theology of suffering*, Gundry misses the point that I think that Mark is making. Mark masterfully combines the two. To him, a true theology of suffering *is* a theology of glory, and while there is yet work to be done here on earth, a theology of glory is nothing less than a theology of suffering.

Alexander Weihs, in *Die Deutung des Todes Jesu im Markusevangelium*, defends the "*Fundamenttheologisches*" idea of a substitutionary atonement model. Responding to a (post) modern tendency to do away with the substitutionary atonement model because of the supposed inference that it necessitates an unfeeling or unloving God and the Kantian insight that guilt is something that one person cannot possibly take from another (providing restitution for the other's guilt), he argues that Mark's use of the terms δεῖ and παραδίδωμι indicate that though God wills Jesus to die, Jesus freely chooses to give himself to God's will. This interpretation indicates that God is not a gruesome God, but above all a loving God. He does not fulfil the position of *demander*, but of *giver*. His deep love for Jesus is shown in his allowing him, his beloved Son, to go the way of suffering to bring atonement for others.[12] In this way, God's love for Jesus and for people and the love of Jesus for God the Father and for people all find their highest expression in the substitutionary death of Jesus. Moreover, Weihs insists that "in view of the Soteriology of the Gospel of Mark, it is not possible to speak of a fixation on the cross."[13] According to Weihs, the cross does not represent the core focus of Mark's soteriology; the entire service of Jesus to humanity seen throughout the Gospel is an act of salvation. The cross is merely the consequence, and the extent, of the life of service that Jesus led.

Weihs's purpose is to discover the meaning of Jesus's death in Mark's Gospel. This is a bold ambition while his arguments depend heavily on

---

12. Weihs, *Die Deutung des Todes Jesu im Markusevangelium*, 581.

13. Original: "in Hinblick auf die Soteriologie des Markusevangeliums doch nicht von einer staurologischen Fixierung gesprochen werden kann" (ibid., 583–84; translation mine).

a narrow foundation. Although he insists that he approaches the subject through detailed exegesis of the contexts of each passion and resurrection prediction, he chooses two words from these predictions, and builds his arguments on these. As far as the *context* is concerned, he notes the discipleship teaching moments following each prediction, but does not consider them in his exegesis. In fact, he completely ignores any significance that these teachings may have upon the subject of salvation or the Kingdom of God. His desire, as expressed in his introductory chapters, is to defend a popular atonement model from the demythologization proposed by 20th century German theologians. While he does add (perhaps healthy) nuance to the model, his arguments lack a depth and thoroughness because of his narrow focus. Mark describes following Jesus in terms of *cross* (8:34); a full discussion of the meaning of the cross should take this into consideration. His discovery of the centrality of love and service of God through Jesus to humanity even in the cross, however, is an indispensable reminder that God's love and service provide the context in which the suffering of Markan discipleship must be understood. His findings complement this study in its pastoral implications. Cross-bearing for the disciples cannot be done from any other motivation than love just as Jesus's death on the cross cannot be understood apart from his love for God and for humanity.

In *The Cross from a Distance*, Peter Bolt presents the atonement in Mark as being salvation from the fear of death. He perceives our worse fear as humans as the fear of death. In the death of the innocent Jesus, God in the person of the Son, on an accursed cross, paid the ransom "to free us from the judgment of death" and eternal life for mortals was attained.[14] The fact that Jesus was raised from the dead even though he had died on a cross gives all humans hope that even they may be given eternal life. The cross was so grossly accursed that the idea that one having died on a cross might be acceptable to God was unthinkable. Yet, Jesus did die on a cross and God did accept him because of his innocence.

Bolt says that this fact is comforting: if one who died on a cross is resurrected, surely there is hope for all of us![15] Yet, he also emphasizes the innocence of Jesus as being the reason he was accepted. In dying as innocent, Jesus took all the consequences of sin away. Bolt states that Jesus did not take sin itself away but merely the forensic consequences of sin. In this way, believers can trust in Jesus's death for themselves as they die as sinful

---

14. Bolt, *Cross from a Distance*, 144–45.

15. Bolt's concentration on the resurrection is interesting, given the observation that Mark hardly gives it a prominent place in his narrative.

persons; there will be no consequences awaiting them for their sinfulness at death. They are freed from the fear of judgment.

Mark, however, has very little *sin* language in it. Most telling is the absence of sin language in the references to the impending cross in Mark 8, 9, and 10. The fact that the Markan Jesus lets a wealthy man (10:17ff.) know that even keeping all the commandments is not a guarantee of inheriting eternal life, might point away from the direction that Bolt would have us look. As an obedient Jew, he would surely have few if any consequences of sin to fear! *Sin* does not play a part here, only the giving up of all and following Jesus. Not even during the Passover meal does Mark make reference to forgiveness of sins (cf. Matt 26:28), while Jesus does describe the cup as "my blood of the covenant which is poured out for many" (Mark 14:24). With his concentration on sin and the need to have its forensic consequences removed, Bolt seems to be giving more of a defense of a traditional view of the atonement, than allowing Mark to speak for himself. To Mark, obeying God means following Jesus in giving up all. This is presented as necessary to inheriting eternal life and entering the Kingdom of God (10:17–31) and as impossible for humans, yet made possible by God.

Without going into an in-depth study of Mark's view of sin, we do know that Mark had no Augustine or Calvin or Beza to read. He did, however, have the prophets, which were clearly part of his intellectual baggage. As Abraham Heschel points out, "To the prophets, sin is not an ultimate, irreducible or independent condition, but rather a disturbance in the relationship between God and man; it is an adverb not a noun, a condition that can be surmounted by man's return and God's forgiveness."[16] To see the death of Jesus as being redemptive in the sense that it merely gives freedom from a certain consequence of sin, which in turn would not be removed from the person, could very well be a contradiction in terms to first century CE believers and therefore a foreign concept.[17]

Bolt does note the three main passion predictions in Mark, and he does admit to a connection between the passion predictions and the teachings. However, he mentions it only to say how others have taken this connection to prove that this section in Mark is about discipleship. I agree with Bolt that this very connection indicates that this section is about the cross, and also that it "explains why he *must* die."[18] But I miss a consideration of

---

16. Heschel, *Prophets*, 295.

17. See also Ermakov, "Purity," regarding sin in the context of purity and the contagious holiness of Jesus.

18. Bolt, *Cross from a Distance*, 48. Emphasis in original.

Jesus's teachings of discipleship in reaching his conclusions about the meaning of the cross.

In the volume *Salvation in the New Testament: Perspectives on Soteriology*, Bernard Combrink contributed a chapter on "Salvation in Mark." He points out that although the terms σωτήρ and σωτηρία are not used by Mark, the role of savior is present, and the theme of salvation is seen throughout the narrative from various perspectives. Discussing the theme of salvation as indicated through the conflated quote ascribed to Isaiah in 1:2–3, Jesus's encounter with Satan, and the coming of the Kingdom of God introduced in the prologue and carried out in the narrative, Combrink concludes "that eternal life, kingdom, and salvation function as synonyms in Mark."[19]

Combrink notes that the teaching of suffering and death is placed specifically in teaching moments regarding salvation (8:34—9:1; 10:26–27). In 8:34—9:1, Salvation depends on the honor or shame reaction given in response to Jesus as the Son of Man and *his* suffering and shame.[20] Combrink notes the reference to the good news in 8:35 as an echo of the prologue and states: "The kingdom of God, the time of salvation is at hand, and the salvation of humanity is bound up with this good news and following Jesus."[21] While he affirms a link between the suffering of Jesus with the suffering involved in following Jesus, Combrink emphasizes the distinction between the two. In his discussion of the use of "ransom" in Mark 10:45, he recognizes that it is used in the context of Jesus's teaching on service. However, he immediately disregards the context on the grounds of the word itself: "But it is precisely the presence of 10:45b, the λύτρον [ransom] word, which prevents us from interpreting the saying about Jesus' service as being only exemplary."[22] He proceeds to discuss the phrase in terms of a Righteous Sufferer, the Suffering Servant of Isaiah, and the martyrs of 2 and 4 Maccabees. While this ensuing discussion is helpful, by not including the context of discipleship in the *meaning* of salvation, it is incomplete. Jesus's death is indeed portrayed in Mark as being more than exemplary. But *mimesis* is not the only interpretive option when taking the discipleship context of the teachings into consideration. Mark presents the death of Jesus as making it possible for the disciples to give their own lives in following Jesus. A desire to conserve the uniqueness of the death of Jesus ought not to filter out beforehand all possibilities of the disciples' service being salvific in any way.

19. Combrink, "Salvation," 45.
20. Ibid., 50–52.
21. Ibid., 52.
22. Ibid., 53.

Brant Pitre sees redemption in the Gospel of Mark as the long-awaited restoration of all the tribes of Israel.[23] He supports the use of the Suffering Servant in Isaiah as background to Mark 10:45 by establishing a similar background from Daniel.[24] Within Daniel, he suggests a connection of the Son of Man figure from chapter 7 with the Messiah from chapter 9, pointing towards the suffering and dying of this figure during the eschatological tribulation as bringing about the complete redemption of the twelve tribes of Israel. The suffering and death of Jesus is thus portrayed as the major part of eschatological sufferings which will take place to atone for the sins of all Israel, marking the beginning of full restoration and return from exile. Though he mentions that this suffering of Jesus effects redemption, "along with the other sufferings of the time of trial,"[25] he does not elaborate on the connection between Jesus's suffering and these *other sufferings*, nor even mention it in his conclusions.

In conclusion, while there has been a focus in some recent scholarship on the theme of salvation in the Gospel of Mark, none seem to have taken seriously the path of discipleship in their study of the cross of Jesus. In this study, I will attempt to do justice to Mark's narrative by examining these themes which Mark so tightly knits together, precisely in their relation to each other.

Discipleship

Much of Markan scholarship has concentrated on Mark's discipleship emphasis. Here follow, in roughly chronological order, a few examples of relatively recent works that have concentrated on the subject of discipleship as a whole in Mark.

In *Slave of All*, Narry Santos recognizes the prevalence of an authority-servanthood paradox in the Gospel of Mark. Using reader-response criticism to establish how the intended readers would have understood Mark's message, Santos walks his own readers through the Gospel from beginning to end, pointing out the prevalence of this paradox. His conclusions reflect how he interprets the Gospel's demands of discipleship. In keeping himself bound to a rigid methodology he misses the riches available through intra- and intertextual considerations and a historical understanding of the times in which Mark would have been written.

---

23. See Pitre, "'Ransom for Many.'"

24. See also Manson, *Teaching of Jesus*, 230–31.

25. Pitre, "'Ransom for Many,'" 66. The *time of trial* referred to by Pitre does not refer to Jesus's trial, but to the period of eschatological sufferings.

The readers that Santos envisions seem to have no other background with them than the words that they are given in the specific order of the Gospel. When writing about the authority-servanthood paradox in the sayings about the Son of Man, for example, he does not look to Daniel for any possible background information on this term.[26] While he does keep close to his purpose in walking through the gospel and explicating the said paradox, it would have enriched his interpretation of these passages had he taken an intratextual foreshadow of the death and resurrection of Jesus into consideration. As it is, these form their own textual paradox in his view, but do not add any depth to the paradoxes in the three major passion predictions with their companion discipleship teaching moments.

Santos concludes that Mark's readers are encouraged by example (i.e., Peter's mother-in-law who served Jesus and his disciples after being healed from a fever[27]) to perform acts of service. The life-or-death depth of service is missing in his interpretations. I would agree with him that the paradox he sketches is present from the beginning of the gospel on, though I do not agree to its presence in all the passages where he finds it. Santos stays consistently on the methodological path which he maps for himself, and can be commended for this. This has, however, limited the scope of his contribution to the study of Markan discipleship.

In *Christology and Discipleship*, Suzanne Watts Henderson focuses on the coherence of the Gospel of Mark. She recognizes a tendency in scholarship to emphasize the second half of the gospel to the neglect of the first half. Her aim is "to read Mark's gospel as a unified message that makes sense of both miracle and passion as interwoven strands of Jesus' mission."[28] The wonder-working power of Jesus portrayed in the beginning of Mark is not opposed to the suffering portrayed in the second half. The second is a logical consequence of the first half when the power of the Kingdom of God is not accepted by the ruling authorities. This type of suffering thus also ought to be expected by the disciples of Jesus as they participate in the bringing of the Kingdom of God on earth. Yet, this suffering does not have the last word. It all has its place in the larger work of God who will bring this whole story to a triumph in bringing life out of death. The main task

---

26. See Santos, *Slave of All*, chapter 4, 145–211. See also 249 where once again Santos links the term "Son of Man" to glory with no mention of the suffering of God's holy people as described in Daniel.

27. Santos calls attention to this example of service throughout (*Slave of All*, 21–22, 60, 74, 79–81, 92, 117, 173, 179, 269, 271, 278, 294), while this type of service has nothing to do with the depths of death and suffering described as the necessary service in the discipleship teaching moments.

28. Henderson, *Christology and Discipleship*, 10–11.

of the Markan disciples is not to accept and hold a correct Christological understanding of who Jesus is, but to be present with Jesus and to join in bringing and proclaiming the Kingdom of God. It is not only after the disciples are able to agree to a proper Christology that they can properly serve as good disciples, but even through their failure does God bring about His purposes in bringing the Kingdom. Could it be, however, that Mark intends to convey more than a comfort regarding failure within discipleship? This seems to miss the point of the teaching which insists on a radical *giving up one's life* of the followers. Salvation is, in Mark, not only an entrance into eternal life through death, but is at heart the coming of the Kingdom of God. Henderson notes that the disciples are brought into this mission of the Markan Jesus to bring the Kingdom of God: "Only within this broader horizon—the assertion of God's coming dominion—can we fully grasp not just Jesus's messiahship but also his deliberate involvement of followers in the regime change he institutes."[29] Although my thesis comes close to Henderson's thesis with her emphasis on the presence of the disciples with Jesus in proclaiming and bringing about the Kingdom of God, I will focus more specifically on the relationship between the suffering of Jesus and the following of the disciples unto suffering and death. It is precisely through this obedience that God's Kingdom is brought about. Where she has found that, even in the portrayal of their failure, the involvement of the disciples in the mission of Jesus is presented in Mark as deliberate and indispensable, this study will show that Mark presents a resolution to this tension in his Gospel. Jesus will "baptize in the Holy Spirit" (1:8) and make this depth of obedience possible (10:27). In Henderson's newer book, *Christ and Community*, she also notes that it is the enduring presence of the risen Christ with his followers that makes it possible for them to join in his mission to "repair and restore the world" by "vulnerable sacrifice that works, albeit mysteriously, to undercut the power of the present evil age."[30]

Larry Hurtado, in "Jesus' Death as Paradigmatic in the New Testament," focuses on the portrayal of Jesus's death as not only an inspiration for those disciples who are facing death as a consequence of their faith, but also as a model for the disciples' own commitment of faith, attitude against

---

29. Ibid., 4.

30. Henderson, *Christ and Community*, 219. This book (2015) was published after the research was done for this project (2013), which accounts for my limited interaction with it in this book. *Christ and Community* builds on her earlier work in *Christology and Discipleship*, reaching beyond Mark to include the other Gospels. She finds, as I have, that the Gospel message was meant from the outset to include in its message of salvation a radical form of discipleship that centers around the abiding presence of God with the followers of Jesus. See especially *Christ and Community*, 93–98 and 215–19.

sin, and depth of love for others. He finds references to the death of Jesus as exemplary for disciples throughout the New Testament, including the passion predictions with their companion teaching moments in Mark. Hurtado reflects Mark's theology as he notes that these texts "make heavy intellectual and behavioural demands, but . . . are ignored at great risk to the theological integrity and the efficacy of Christian endeavour."[31]

Hurtado's contribution to the study of the relationship between the cross of Jesus and the following of the disciples is important, and this study should support it. The question arises, however, if the paradigmatic aspects of the cross of Jesus in Mark's theology of discipleship are limited to inspiration and example. In his discussion of Mark 10:42–45, Hurtado is quick to note that "it is not a case of direct replication of Jesus's own unique action, for the preceding exhortation is not to death but to service, and in any case disciples are not able to give their lives as a 'ransom for many.'"[32] He does not define *ransom*, nor explain why disciples are not able to give their lives as a ransom for others. Mark relies heavily on Isaiah in his narrative, and, as will be discussed in chapter 7 below, Isaiah uses ransom language in order to emphasize God's *guarantee* that he will bring salvation to its culmination rather than to accentuate a type of exchange. Moreover, the language of *cup* and *baptism* in the preceding discussion with James and John in 10:35–40 do insinuate that suffering and perhaps even death are what the Markan Jesus has in mind when he speaks of service. Also, a study of Mark's use of the term Son of Man may provide a bit more room to see the way of service, suffering and death for the disciples as part of the whole picture of the coming of God's Kingdom, and therefore of salvation.[33] These aspects of Mark's message will be examined further below.

In his article "'We Are Able': Cross-bearing Discipleship and the Way of the Lord in Mark," Kent Brower notes the tendency of commentators to shrink back from attributing a redemptive factor to the suffering of anyone besides Jesus.[34] The term "ransom for many" in Mark 10:45 is often seen to refer to the unique propitiatory offering of Jesus in his death. Though it is found within a command of Jesus to his disciples to do as he does, it is most often not interpreted as anything more than an example of the attitude of

---

31. Hurtado, "Jesus' Death as Paradigmatic," 414.

32. Ibid., 420.

33. Hurtado's purpose, however, is not to provide an in-depth study of the various texts he mentions; his intention is to discuss the texts just enough to demonstrate the paradigmatic function of Jesus's death ("Jesus' Death as Paradigmatic," 414).

34. Brower, "'We Are Able,'" 179, 198.

service which is to be found in his disciples.[35] Brower argues in this article for redemptive value in the suffering of the disciples.

This redemptive value, however, does not originate from within the disciples, but is a result of their being *in Christ*.[36] According to Brower, Mark's theology includes a new covenant community that is formed around and through Jesus and which participates *through communion with Jesus* in his redemptive suffering and resurrection.

In his article "Suffering and the Creation of Christian Identity in the Gospel of Mark," Paul Middleton focuses on the distinction that Mark makes regarding the insiders and outsiders of God's Kingdom. All those desiring to follow Jesus will face a choice. The insiders are those who are able to stand up against resistance and continue to confess allegiance to Jesus Christ no matter the cost.[37] Middleton concludes, as I do, that there is no option in Mark's Gospel of softening the demands of discipleship on account of the failure of the disciples to live accordingly. Where I differ from his view is in Mark's portrayal of the hope for the restoration of the disciples after they prove themselves outsiders within the narrative. Middleton considers the narrated facts regarding the flight of the twelve disciples at face value, without any intention from Mark to point to hope of restoration. I take, however, the promise of the baptism of the Holy Spirit in the prologue as being programmatic for the hearing experience of the whole, and come to different conclusions.[38]

Much more has been written on the Gospel of Mark than can be mentioned.[39] What my research adds to the library of Markan studies is a narrative study on the relationship between the suffering of Jesus and the suffering of the disciples seen in light of salvation. As mentioned above, the driving question motivating my research has been whether Mark attributes any salvific value to the suffering of the disciples together with that of Jesus. Brower is the only recent Markan scholar I am aware of who has seriously addressed this issue.[40] My research complements his study

---

35. Ibid., 179.

36. Ibid., 191, 201.

37. Middleton, "Suffering and the Creation," 174, 176, 180.

38. See Hooker, "Beginnings and Endings," on the important narrative and theological function of prologue.

39. See the extensive work done by Telford, published in 2009, in cataloguing Markan scholarship: *Writing on the Gospel of Mark*.

40. Manson's work on the Son of Man language in Mark does come to the conclusion that the disciples are *intended* to join Jesus in being the Son of Man in his redemptive suffering even though they do not, and Jesus dies alone. In *The Teaching of Jesus*, Manson writes that the correspondence between the Passion predictions and the

as I move beyond Mark 10:33–45 and consider the narrative development of Mark as a whole. My conclusions reach beyond his as I follow the lead of the prologue and consider Mark's entwining hope into his narration of the failure of the disciples.

This study builds on a great mass of scholarly work on the Gospel of Mark in the areas of salvation and discipleship. In recent years, some have begun to study these themes together and this has opened new windows of light onto Mark's message. Those who find that even in the face of failure, Mark insists on the necessity of the disciples to follow Jesus on the way of the cross, will hopefully recognize support in the research done for this study. I hope that my study of Mark's resolution to this tension created by the narrative story-line and the teaching content will both enhance scholarship and provide background support for those teaching at church-level. It is an essential question that, as Hurtado warned, can only be avoided at great cost to the "Christian endeavour."[41] For, if the cross that the disciples are enjoined to take up is a necessary part of God's story of salvation, why do they fail at doing so in Mark's narrative? This question will be tackled below from the context of the narrative flow of the whole Gospel. Mark's answer to the *why* questions is that they cannot do otherwise. But he does not stop there. I will show in chapter 3 below that he also provides the clue to *how* they can succeed at the high demands of discipleship presented by the Markan Jesus.

Methodology

The methodology used in this research is primarily narrative critical. My attention will be on the text as we now have it, without being concerned which portions are redacted or come from the early Christian community's traditions. My assumption is that the author has consciously chosen what to put together, whether or not it originated from him, in order to communicate with his audience. I will not attempt to find biographical information of the writer of the Gospel, nor the first real audience. As far as the author is concerned, I will speak of the *implied* author (the author implied by the text) and

---

discipleship teaching moments "suggests that what was in the mind of Jesus was that he and his followers *together* should share that destiny which he describes as the Passion of the Son of Man: that he and they *together* should be the Son of Man, the Remnant that saves by service and self-sacrifice, the organ of God's redemptive purpose in the world" (231; *emphasis in the original*). Present day Markan scholars would do well to consider the implications of Manson's work on the Son of Man to the theme of discipleship in Mark. I will refer again to Manson's work below (chapter 8) in the discussion of the intertextual background of Mark's use of the term Son of Man.

41. Hurtado, "Jesus' Death as Paradigmatic," 414.

will refer to him as Mark.⁴² The audience I will speak of is the audience implied by the narrative. In the several narrative techniques perceived, an *ideal* response from the audience will become apparent, and therefore the term *ideal audience* will also be used. It is conceivable that the implied and the ideal audience differ from each other. It could become apparent, for example, that the implied author would like his audience to respond in a certain way (the *ideal* audience), but does not believe they will, and therefore forms his narrative in a way that assumes they are stupid and stubborn (the *implied* audience). In Mark, however, the implied audience generally coincides with the ideal audience. If I use the terms seemingly interchangeably, I purpose to use each term in a way which reflects its own nuance.⁴³

While the historical audience and its community is not of primary concern in this study, the implied audience *is* an audience within history. The implied audience carries intellectual baggage with it that includes a knowledge of and respect for the Jewish Scriptures,⁴⁴ a longing for God's salvation, and aspects of the first century CE Greco-Roman culture in which the Roman empire was saturated. For that reason, my research will include a socio-historical investigation of possible background motifs that may have provided a context to Mark's dealing with the suffering of Jesus and the following of his disciples unto death. While we cannot say for certain which aspects of the culture were chosen and used consciously by Mark to communicate his message, this study will enhance our reading of the Gospel by adding to our understanding of what was "in the air" while Mark prepared his narrative. Because of the deep nature of the Scriptures in relation to the longing for salvation from God, I will also examine aspects of intertextuality between Mark's narrative and the Scriptures which have bearing on the understanding of his message regarding the relationship between Jesus's suffering and death and the following of his disciples.

In taking a narrative approach to understanding Mark's distinct message, it is important to realize that Mark will retain his own agenda in his use of and reference to cultural aspects and texts. For example, in the case of the Socratic Noble Death: several similar elements exist in the Markan

---

42. Schmid, "Implied Author": "The concept of implied author refers to the author-image evoked by a work and constituted by the stylistic, ideological, and aesthetic properties for which indexical signs can be found in the text." For simplicity's sake, and in following s general scholarship, I will use the masculine pronoun when referring to the implied author of the Gospel.

43. See Rhoads, Dewey, and Michie, *Mark as Story*, 138.

44. I will use the term *Scriptures* to denote those writings commonly referred to as "Old Testament" or "Hebrew Bible" to which Mark attributes a certain sacred authority, apparent in his use of them to support and move his story within a salvific context.

account of Jesus's death and his teaching about the necessity of the disciples' following him on this way of "suffering." However, Mark blatantly describes extreme emotion within Jesus in such a way that would shame Jesus in a fully Greco-Roman context. His narrative of Jesus's fear dictates a refusal of the Greco-Roman category. And yet at the same time, a knowledge of this category illuminates precisely that extreme fear which the Markan Jesus admits to. In Mark's use of Scripture, it is equally important to allow his own narrative to guide the way in seeking to understanding his interpretation and use of these older texts.

A narrative reading allows for meaning relayed in the process of dialogue between implied author and implied hearer from beginning to end of the text. As studies have shown that it is probable that what we know as the Gospel according to Mark was prepared and written with the intention of being orally presented to audiences,[45] I will be referring to the implied audience of Mark as hearers, listeners, or audience rather than as readers. I will approach the text as having been prepared specifically to be delivered orally to an audience. This is not meant to imply that Mark had no readers, merely that the audience implied by the narrative consisted of listeners. This nuance highlights portions of the text which speak directly of hearing, such as in 4:3, 9, and 23. Although these admonitions to listen are part of the Markan Jesus's speech to characters within the narrative, they also serve as a direct admonition to the audience to pay extra attention to what is happening and being said within the narrative. As Thomas Boomershine suggests, the text invites the audience to "reflect on the quality of their engagement with the story."[46] This also applies to 13:37, "What I say to you, I say to everyone: 'Watch!'" Any in the audience who may have been tempted to doze off would be jolted to attention when the storyteller spoke these words.

One of the implications of a narrative reading of the text is that the text is approached as a whole. The assumption is that at one point the narrative was meant by a specific author to be a complete story to be told, either read or performed from memory, from beginning to end in one sitting. This allows for the identification of such techniques as foreshadows and echoes to illuminate the story.[47] An example of foreshadows and echoes are the three mentions of Jesus as the Son of God at beginning, the middle and the end of the narrative. When the audience hears the telling of the voice from heaven on the mount of Transfiguration in 9:7, they will be

---

45. Dewey, "Survival of Mark's Gospel." See also Rhoads, Dewey, and Michie, *Mark as Story*; Iverson and Skinner, *Mark as Story*.

46. Boomershine, "Audience Address and Purpose," 133.

47. See Malbon, "Echoes"; Dewey, "Mark as Interwoven Tapestry."

reminded of the voice from heaven that Jesus heard at his baptism in 1:11. This Jesus, whom the disciples at story level and the audience at discourse level are admonished to listen to, has already been established as God's Son, but also as the one through whom God's salvation would come, and the one on whom the Spirit of God had already descended. Including 1:11 in the interpretation of 9:7 will encourage the audience to understand the very difficult teaching of Jesus which they had just heard in 8:31—9:1 in context of the coming of God's salvation. The exclamation from the centurion at the cross at the moment of Jesus's death, identifying him as the Son of God, confirms his death as belonging to God's great work of salvation. This is especially so if we understand the tearing of the temple curtain, also at the moment of Jesus's death, as an echo of the tearing of the heavens in 1:10. As the Gentile centurion recognizes Jesus as the Son of God both scenes in which Jesus was previously confirmed as God's Son will come to mind, each with its own connotations of the coming of salvation and the difficult teachings of suffering and death.[48]

Whether the centurion's confession ought to be seen as a conversion to the God of the Jews, and the recognition of Jesus as his specific representative, or that he recognizes in Jesus a leader appointed by the gods, does not matter to the significance that Mark gives to his statement.[49] Its significance is found both in its function as an echo of the previous two major "Son of God" moments (1:11 and 9:7) and in the fact that it is a Gentile who makes

---

48. There is another reference to Jesus as the Son of God in 3:11. This, however, is a summary statement that records how evil spirits would react when they saw Jesus, and forms more likely an echo of the exorcism in 1:21–28 than that it shares in the positive pattern of 1:11, 9:7, and 15:39. The Markan Jesus forbids these spirits to "tell who he was" (3:12). The statement should be understood as confirming that the spirit world recognizes the true nature and authority of the man Jesus. It should also be understood in light of the conversation that the teachers of the law from Jerusalem have with Jesus about the possibility of him deriving his authority from the prince of demons himself. While the demons bow before him in 3:11, it is not because he is their own prince. As the demons themselves are aware, Jesus's authority comes from the Spirit of God himself (3:29). While this confession in 3:11 can and ought to be included in a full study of *Jesus as the Son of God* in Mark, it does not hold the same significance as the two statements from God (1:11 and 9:7) and the statement from the centurion (15:39).

49. See also Hooker, *Mark*: "Whether Mark thinks that the centurion is aware of the true significance of his words is not clear.... Nevertheless, the centurion stands at this point as the representative of those who acknowledge Jesus as God's son. His words form the climax of Mark's gospel, for they are the words used in the confession of Christian faith, and they are found in the mouth of a Gentile at the moment of Jesus' death" (379). Collins, *Mark* (764–71), notes that although later Christian tradition assumed that the centurion was making a Christian confession and did become part of the Christian community, this is not how Mark portrays him. See Stock, *Mark* (412–15), for an interpretation of the centurion's statement as a confession of faith.

the statement, and recognizes Jesus as his leader. Adela Yarbro Collins suggests that it also functions as an allusion to the "vow of praise" in Ps 22: "All the ends of the earth will remember and will turn to the Lord, and all the peoples of the nations will worship before You, for kingly rule is the Lord's and he is master of the nations."[50] Approaching the narrative as a whole allows for this extra dimension of intratextuality: Mark is not merely recording the confession of the first convert. The dimension of the previous recognitions of Jesus as God's Son, as well as the intertextual allusion to Ps 22 (as an echo to 15:34), all add to the experience of Mark's implied audience as they hear the narration of the centurion's confession.

Other narrative techniques often identified in Mark as useful in interpretation include various concentric forms, such as the *inclusio*, sandwich structure, and chiasmus. Each of these has its own way of highlighting the text. An *inclusio* provides a frame around a unit, suggesting an interpretive key to that unit. An example would be the two blind healings in Mark, forming an *inclusio* around the central teaching section.[51] A sandwich structure is formed when one story is inserted within another story in such a way that the outer story would continue without a break if the inner story is taken away. This structure suggests that the two stories ought to be understood in context of each other, each adding an extra dimension to the other. Chiasmus has proven to be the most controversial of narrative techniques, and therefore calls for a fuller definition and legitimization in being used as an interpretive key to Mark's narrative.

Chiasmus as Interpretive Key to Mark's Narrative

A chiasmus is a literary unit in which two corresponding halves form an inverted parallelism around a center. It is a concentric form in which a movement can be discerned from the beginning towards the center, and then in parallel order from the center outwards to the end. The center is highlighted by the movement towards and away from it. The two halves can correspond to each other either synonymously or antithetically, and be made up of words, phrases, or units of thought.[52] Schematically this is usually documented as ABCXC'B'A', depending on how many elements it entails. The difference between chiasmus and a simple inverted parallelism, or *hysteron proteron* ("the last, first"), is the center.[53] The center forms the climax of the unit, and it will

50. Collins, *Mark*, 771.
51. See chapter 2 for my proposed structure of Mark's Gospel.
52. McCoy, "Chiasmus," 19.
53. See Thomson, *Chiasmus* (14–18), and Stock, "Chiastic Awareness," on the

often, as Ian Thomson says, "enjoy a special prominence, and attention tends to focus on it. As such, these ideas characteristically may have any of three functions: forming the climax of the argument, indicating its purpose, or acting as an apophthegmatic summary of its contents."[54]

Although no scholars deny that chiasmus occurs, how to identify it remains contested in scholarship. Sceptics sigh and proponents enthuse: "once you start to identify chiasmus, you find it everywhere!"[55] Because of the ever-present danger of the Procrustean bed, scholars continue to seek for objective rules for identifying chiasmus.

The use of language in the formation of literature is an art. To a certain extent, time must be taken to get used to seeing something in a new light. Immersion remains essential to appropriating and using language skills at the artistic level. And ancient literature and rhetoric should be approached as art forms. They are different from, and strive for different ideals than modern prose.[56] In ancient rhetoric, for example, parallelism and redundancy thrived. For this reason, John Welch warns that identifying and critiquing chiasmus will be both an objective and subjective exercise.[57]

For objective criteria, Welch suggests that "it is reasonable to require":

- "significant repetitions to be readily apparent"
- "the overall system to be well balanced"
- "the second half of the system should tend to repeat the first half of the system in a recognizably inverted order"
- "the juxtaposition of the two central sections should be marked and highly accentuated"
- "key words, echoes, and balancing should be distinct and should serve defined purposes within the structure."[58]

---

prevalence of *hysteron proteron* in antiquity. Stock, however, does not differentiate between this and chiasmus.

54. Thomson, *Chiasmus*, 43. See also Breck, "Biblical Chiasmus," 70; Breck, *Shape of Biblical Language*, 18–19; Lund, *Chiasmus in the New Testament*, throughout.

55. At an SBL International meeting during the time I was doing research for this project, I had two conversations about finding chiasmus, one with a sceptic and the other with an enthusiastic proponent who both remarked with, in essence, these same words, though one with a sigh and the other with enthusiasm.

56. See Welch, *Chiasmus in Antiquity*, 12.

57. Ibid., 13. See also Welch, "Criteria," 2.

58. Welch, *Chiasmus in Antiquity*, 13. See also Welch, "Criteria," 5–9, for a list of fifteen criteria on which to evaluate a proposed chiasmus.

It will always be difficult to *prove* a chiastic structure longer than a few lines to a sceptic.[59] Chiasmus does exist, however, albeit not everywhere, and therefore can be discovered. In chapter 3 below, I will argue that Mark uses chiasmus at certain crucial points in order to highlight his theological purpose. My goal is not to prove chiasmus; my goal is to understand Mark's message. If that goal is served by taking chiasmus into consideration, as some scholars have proposed,[60] then I will do so.

The Structure of This Book

This study is divided into three parts with a total of ten chapters. The three parts will concentrate on 1) a narrative and structural analysis of Mark and its theological implications; 2) socio-historical background to Mark's message; and 3) intertextual background to key aspects of Mark's message.

In part one of this book, I will discuss the implications for discipleship drawn from a study of Mark's structure. Through a study of the layers of Mark's structure, and some theological implications drawn from them, it will become clear that Mark builds his narrative on a foundation of God's story of salvation and Jesus as the Son of God. While Mark's structure will be seen to uphold the message of the Markan Jesus that discipleship is essential to taking part in God's Kingdom, Mark's narrative displays the disciples as failing drastically. Most recent commentators seem to agree that this serves to comfort Mark's audience that there is always grace available for those failing at discipleship. If this is indeed so, we must come to the conclusion that Mark is communicating that "giving one's life" is not *really* essential to salvation as the Markan Jesus has insisted that it is. I disagree with these commentators and will argue that the very structure upholding the demands of discipleship also point towards a solution to the problem of failure that Mark describes.

In part two, we will look at two broadly known motifs from Mark's socio-historical background in search of a deeper understanding of the connection he makes between the death of Jesus and the cross-bearing of the disciples. Mark's implied author and implied audience are all people within an historical time frame saturated in a specific culture. Both the

---

59. There is very little literature to be found criticizing the study of chiasmus as a whole. Most criticism is directed to specific attempts at finding chiasmus as the macro-structure of full NT books. See, for example, deSilva, "X Marks the Spot?"; Smit, in his review of *Philippians*, suggests that those "who find chiasms all over the place in New Testament literature exaggerate."

60. See, for example, Breck, "Chiasmus as a Key to Biblical Interpretation"; and Scott, "Chiastic Structure."

Greco-Roman culture and Jewish culture and Scripture are part of their background. For this reason, it will be important to discuss the suffering of the disciples following Jesus in his suffering and death with the Greco-Roman motif of the Socratic Noble Death in mind. In the literature of the time, it was not uncommon to model one's death after the death of a hero, and we will discuss whether this motif casts any light on Mark's message. We will also turn to the Jewish idea of God's *pathos*. The suffering that the Markan Jesus endures and that is expected of disciples will be looked at through the perspective of the Jewish God, affected by pain and suffering, being a God who *goes with* his people in bringing salvation.

For the reason of it being a part of Mark's reception history, the phenomenon of martyrdom will also be discussed. Paul Middleton contends that Mark may have encouraged Christians to pursue martyrdom, and Candida Moss has insisted that martyrs believed their deaths would be salvific.[61] The question pertaining to this study will be the extent to which these interpretations reflect Mark's message of discipleship.

The background investigation of Mark's narrative will continue in part three with an intertextual study. Mark is known for his prolific use of Scripture in his Gospel. Mark relies heavily on the Isaiah narrative as he develops his themes of understanding, service, and ransom, all aspects that play heavily into his portrayal of discipleship as following Jesus on the way of the cross. Another key theme used in Mark's portrayal of Jesus's suffering, also in conjunction with discipleship, is the Son of Man. We will look to Daniel 7 as its background. And finally, Psalm 22 will be discussed as it is alluded to in Jesus's desperate cry from the cross, portraying him as a Righteous Sufferer. The starting point for each of these discussions will be Mark's text as it guides its audience to remember these aspects of Scripture.

The final chapter will provide a summary of the relevant background information discussed in the latter two parts as they relate to the focus that Mark provides through his structure discussed in the first part: to God's salvation. I will pull together the research in this study to form a theological conclusion to Mark's perspective on discipleship as an important factor of the coming of the Kingdom of God and how this relates to the death of the Markan Jesus. Finally, a contemporary reading of Mark's narrative will be given, highlighting the way in which Mark speaks hope to the heart longing to be faithful to Jesus in difficult circumstances as an expression of an all-encompassing love for God.

---

61. Middleton, *Radical Martyrdom*; Moss, *Other Christs*.

Part One: Mark's Theology Highlighted by Narrative Structure

THERE WAS A TIME when great scholars insisted that Mark was not a gifted writer. Recognizing Mark's extensive use of *inclusio*—or sandwich type constructions—in order to highlight certain aspects of his message, one scholar suggests that "such contrivances would have been unworthy of a trained writer. But at Mark's level, which is that of the first gropings of a religious literature designed for a public with little education, their use reveals a desire for order and clarity which is the mark of a writer aware of his methods."[1] With his low assessment of Mark's writing skills, it is noteworthy that this scholar calls attention to Mark's "awareness of his methods" and orderly writing. Surprisingly, yet telling for one calling Mark a "clumsy writer unworthy of mention in any history of literature,"[2] he does recognize that Mark formed his narrative purposefully. Whether one agrees that Mark was a creative and gifted writer, one thing that is difficult to deny is his use of narrative techniques to highlight his message.

What did Mark highlight through his structural techniques? What was it that the implied author wanted his audience so desperately to understand? Mark's whole narrative is about salvation. And the point is made early on that understanding leads to repentance and repentance leads to salvation. But he also makes it clear that understanding does not come easily or even naturally. Mark seems to use these techniques in his storytelling to move his audience forward in their search to understand, not unlike a blind man moving from seeing people walking around like trees to being able to see clearly.

---

1. Trocmé, *Formation of the Gospel*, 82–83.
2. Ibid., 72. The development of Narrative Criticism has seen a parallel development in an appreciation for Mark's skills. Moloney has recently described Mark as a "passionate and unified story" ("Writing a Narrative Commentary," 95).

2

Implications of Mark's Narrative Structure

It is no secret that the way in which a story is told can have an enormous effect on how that story is experienced. A scary story told at midnight in a dark tent with a flashlight making strange shadows on the face of the storyteller creates a totally different experience than if the same story were told at noon in a large room lighted by bright fluorescent lamps. Physical circumstances, voice inflection and the movement of plot all make a difference to the storytelling experience.

It has been too long since Mark prepared his manuscript for his first audience for us to know the physical circumstances or even the specific nuances to his voice inflection. We do, however, have the words he used. And this provides us with more information than first meets the eye. Mark used words to enhance other words. He used techniques known to storytellers and audiences in his day which would lead his audience to *experience* his narrative. Not just to see the picture he was creating, but to *understand*. He did not set out to merely give information. He set out to lead his audience in the experience of salvation by following Jesus.

In this chapter, we will take a closer look at a double structure, almost a double storyline, used by Mark to weave together discipleship with the suffering of Jesus. We will first tease out these two important layers of Mark's structure, noting the structural techniques which add a spotlight to specific aspects of the narrative. Finally, we will bring them back together, as Mark has done in the one narrative, discussing the theological implications of their unity.

Mark's Central Focus: Discipleship

The first layer is a concentric focus. Mark sets apart a section in roughly the center of his narrative in which the Markan Jesus spends concentrated time teaching the disciples.¹ This section contains three predictions of the passion and resurrection of the Son of Man, as well as three teachings on what it means to be a disciple. Each of the latter are linked narratively to each of the former, with supporting narrative in between each of the three groups of teachings. Surrounding this section are the only two healings of blind people in Mark. The first, 8:22–26, occurs just outside of Bethsaida. A blind man is brought to Jesus by others and Jesus is begged to heal him. The man is not healed instantly, but first only sees people as trees walking around. Jesus touches him once more and the man is healed fully. The second blind healing account, 10:46–52, shows the blind Bartimaeus being healed instantly by Jesus before commencing to follow him on the way to Jerusalem.

These bookends, or this *inclusio*, are often used to interpret the entire section: Peter *sees* and understands that Jesus is the Christ (8:27–30), but he does not yet see clearly or understand fully. Jesus proceeds to teach that the Son of Man must suffer and die. Peter has difficulty with this teaching (8:32–33). In the Bartimaeus story, Jesus is recognized as the Christ figure, the son of David, and once Bartimaeus's sight has been fully restored, he follows Jesus on the way leading to Jerusalem where the hearer knows that great suffering awaits Jesus. This following is the appropriate response of those who have come to see and understand fully.² This structural technique used by Mark thus highlights the message that suffering and dying are aspects of God's salvation that are difficult to understand, but indispensable. Jesus must suffer and die before he rises again, and his followers must die to themselves and their desires of greatness and success if they truly want to be his followers.

Bas van Iersel recognizes the significance of Mark's arrangement of this material and sees the structure of Mark's entire narrative as having been formed around this section. The significance of this is the resulting focus. All the material before it leads to this section. All the material following it flows from it. Hence, the spotlight effect.³

Title (1:1)

(A´) In the wilderness (1:2–13)

---

1. See especially van Iersel, *Marcus*; Stock, *Mark*, 25–35. Also, Malbon, "Echoes," 214n11. Cf. Hooker, *Mark*, 27–29; Stein, *Mark*, 35–37; and Guelich, *Mark*, xxxvii. These scholars map Mark's structure linearly instead of concentrically, yet do note the section 8:22 (or 27)—10:52 somewhere just beyond the center. Of all the sections noted in various outlines proposed, this center section is rarely debated. See, however, Tolbert who argues for a two-part division following the prologue on the basis of geography: in or around Galilee and in or around Jerusalem (*Sowing the Gospel*, 113–14).

2. Donahue and Harrington, *Mark*, 319–20; Hooker, *Mark*, 253.

3. See also Malbon, "Echoes," 214n11.

first hinge (1:14–15)

(B′) In Galilee (1:16—8:21)

    blindness → sight 1 (8:22–26)

(C) On the way (8:27—10:45)

    blindness → sight 2 (10:46–52)

(B′′) In Jerusalem (11:1—15:39)

second hinge (15:40-41)

(A′′) At the tomb (15:42—16:8)[4]

While the terms van Iersel uses to describe the various sections are spatial or geographical terms reflecting the movement of the plot, these terms also reflect Mark's theology.[5] This is especially true of the center section entitled *on the way*. After his time of concentrated ministry in Galilee, Jesus and his disciples move from Bethsaida to Caesarea Philippi, and then slowly down to Jerusalem in Judea. Mark uses the phrase *on the way* [ἐν τῇ ὁδῷ] in four scenes in his Gospel, and only in this section. It is *on the way* that Jesus asks his disciples who others, and who they, think he is, and Peter confesses him as the Christ (8:27–30). It is *on the way* that the Markan disciples, immediately following the second prediction of Jesus's impending suffering, discuss among themselves who of them is greatest (9:33–34). Immediately preceding the third prediction of his impending passion and resurrection, Mark notes that Jesus leads those following him *on the way* up to Jerusalem amidst astonishment and fear (10:32). And when Bartimaeus is healed of his blindness, he follows Jesus *on the way* (10:52). The theological implication of Mark's use of the term *on the way* has to do with the way of suffering that lies before both Jesus and the disciples. It is the way that God's people must go. And yet it also signifies movement: when one is on the way, one has not yet arrived. The disciples did not have their own blindness healed immediately. After each passion prediction, they showed resistance to the words of the Markan Jesus regarding suffering and service. Even as blind Bartimaeus jumped up to follow Jesus on the way, the disciples had not yet appeared to embrace the way of suffering. But the healing of Bartimaeus will remind Mark's audience of the healing of that other blind man at the beginning of this section. And that man was not healed immediately. That man first saw people walking around like trees. He needed more from Jesus before he finally could see clearly.

    4. Van Iersel, *Marcus*, 69.

    5. See also Malbon, "Galilee and Jerusalem," for the theological and narrative significance of Mark's use of geographical and spatial terms.

And yet, both healing stories finally result in both having their sight fully restored, thus providing Mark's audience with the hope that the disciples—and they—will one day have their own sight fully restored. There is hope that they will be able to understand and be saved.

So, what is the message that Mark so desperately wants his audience to see? A closer observation of the structure of this section may help us to understand.

    A   Peter confesses Jesus as Christ (8:27–30)

1a   Jesus teaches, the Son of Man must suffer and die (8:31–32a)

1b   Peter misunderstands (8:32b–33)

1c   Jesus teaches, whoever wants to follow must pick up their cross and follow (8:34—9:1)

    B   Mount of Transfiguration moment: "this is my beloved Son; Listen to him!" (9:2–8)

    C   Conversation on the way down the mountain about Elijah and SM and suffering (9:9–13)

    D   Other disciples had struggled with healing demonic boy, Jesus heals him in response to prayer of father ("I believe, help my unbelief!"); teaching regarding necessity of prayer (9:14–29)

2a   Jesus teaches, the Son of Man must suffer and die (9:30–31)

2b   disciples do not understand and argue about who is greatest (9:32–34)

2c   Jesus teaches, whoever wants to be first must be last, and the servant of all (9:35–50)

    E   Teaching crowds; Pharisees test Jesus about divorce; Jesus explains man and wife are one (10:1–12)

    F   Children brought to Jesus; Jesus angry at disciples for hindering them; Jesus blesses children (10:13–16)

    G   Jesus and rich man, teaching about giving up all; humanly impossible, with God possible (10:17–31)

3a   Jesus teaches, the Son of Man must suffer and die (10:32–34)

3b   disciples do not understand, James & John ask for seats of honor (10:35–40)

3c Jesus teaches, whoever wants to be great among you must be servant to all, slave to the least, just as the Son of Man has come to give his life as a ransom for many (10:41–45)

The divisions lettered A through G merely provide a brief overview of the narrative in between the combined passion predictions and discipleship teaching moments represented by the three numbered segments.[6] Each of these lettered scenes support and elucidate the teachings found in the numbered segments.

In the numbered segments, a pattern is quickly discerned: teaching by Jesus, misunderstanding of the disciples, teaching by Jesus.[7] The content of the teaching moments also follows a pattern. The first teaching (1a, 2a, 3a) is about the impending passion of the Son of Man. The second teaching (1c, 2c, 3c) is about discipleship. By coupling these two subjects of teaching around the misunderstanding of the disciples (1b, 2b, 3b), and repeating this triptych three times, Mark intertwines the suffering of the Son of Man with discipleship.

In fact, Mark seems to be explaining the need for Jesus to suffer by the fact that the disciples will have to suffer and give up their rights and perhaps even their lives. In the first segment, Jesus responds to Peter's objection to the suffering of the Son of Man with the explanation that only through giving one's life for the sake of Jesus and the gospel can one save one's life. This is curious. Peter was objecting to the suffering of the Son of Man; there had not yet been any mention of suffering for the *disciples*. In this first section, the pattern is clear. Mark explains the need for Jesus to suffer by explaining the need for the disciples to give their lives. A similar move, but the other way around, can be discerned in the third segment as well. Here Jesus explains discipleship in terms of the extent of the suffering of the Son of Man. According to Mark, Jesus must suffer because disciples will have to suffer. And disciples will suffer because Jesus will have to suffer.

Scholars are divided regarding the theme of the entire section: is it about the passion of Jesus and the need for the disciples to understand that the Messiah must suffer and die, or is it about discipleship? I contend that the two must not be separated. Mark has linked them narratively with the

---

6. The B and C could arguably be one section centered around the Transfiguration moment. Elijah appears in both, and both re-emphasize the message about suffering in the previous teaching segment. Exactly how these moments are represented structurally does not change their theological significance within Mark's narrative.

7. Hurtado suggests that the misunderstanding of the disciples at each of these points provides an opportunity for the Markan Jesus to explain himself further ("Following Jesus," 22).

intention that his audience hear and understand the two perspectives in relation to each other.

In each of these three teaching segments, Mark uses similar language. This language will prove to act as a foreshadow as it returns in the scene of Jesus's prayer in Gethsemane. In the first discipleship teaching segment (1c), the Markan Jesus teaches that if one *wants* (εἴ τις θέλει) to follow they must pick up their cross and follow behind him. In 2c, the Markan Jesus teaches that if one *wants* (εἴ τις θέλει) to be the first they must serve the least, embrace the outsider, and, as Morna Hooker summarizes, "accept discipline now, for the sake of entering into life."[8] In 3c, the Markan Jesus explains to all the disciples—after James and John had just announced that they *want* him to do for them what they ask of him (θέλομεν ἵνα ὅ ἐὰν αἰτήσωμέν σε ποιήσῃς ἡμῖν)—that the one who *wants* (ὃς ἂν θέλῃ) to be great among the disciple must serve the others. But he does not stop there; he stretches the service, as it were, to the breaking point with the use of the ascensive καὶ: ὃς ἂν θέλῃ μέγας γενέσθαι ἐν ὑμῖν ἔσται ὑμῶν διάκονος, καὶ ὃς ἂν θέλῃ ἐν ὑμῖν εἶναι πρῶτος ἔσται πάντων δοῦλος. καὶ γὰρ ὁ υἱὸς τοῦ ἀνθρώπου οὐκ ἦλθεν διακονηθῆναι ἀλλὰ διακονῆσαι καὶ δοῦναι τὴν ψυχὴν αὐτοῦ λύτρον ἀντὶ πολλῶν (10:43b–45). Mark seems to be playing with the word *to want*. His audience is encouraged to consider what it is that they want. His audience will want to follow Jesus, just as the disciples do. The crowd is called to join the disciples when the Markan Jesus first says, "if one wants to follow me . . . ." Mark's ideal audience will sense that they, too, are included in the call to listen. They, too, want to follow Jesus. By the time the third teaching moment comes along, the Markan Jesus has had the conversation with the rich man about the need to sell all his possessions before coming to follow him (see section G in the outline above). If Mark's audience had come to the point of understanding that to follow Jesus means forfeiting a life of pleasure, they will be brought one step further when John and James present to Jesus what they want. They want seats of honor in the Kingdom of God. If not in this life, then at least in the next. So, Jesus goes a step deeper in his explanation to them about the shape their lives are to take. Do they want greatness? Greatness in the Kingdom of God is the exact opposite to that in the human realm: it is not lording it over others, but it is service. It is service to the point, and beyond, of relinquishing honor. It is service to the point of giving one's life for another.

Mark intends this teaching to make its impression on his audience. To follow Jesus means to go where he went and do as he did. Nothing less. The seriousness of this is made clear in the three teaching segments

---

8. Hooker, *Mark*, 232.

where it is noted that hanging on to one's life will cause one to lose it, and choosing to sin will cause one to be cast off into the fires of Gehenna.[9] If they want to follow Jesus, then they must do as Jesus did, and be willing to suffer and even give their lives for Jesus's sake. If they do, however, they will inherit eternal life.

Of course, no one *wants* to lose their life. Most people will *want* to save their lives if they have the choice. Yet the Markan Jesus is teaching about God's thoughts here. This teaching will prove a foreshadow of the moment on the outskirts of Jerusalem, just before Jesus is arrested, when he falls to the ground in Gethsemane, deeply distressed, and prays to God about what he actually *wants*, but at the same time praying that not his own *want* be fulfilled, but that what God *wants* be done (ἀλλ' οὐ τί ἐγὼ θέλω ἀλλὰ τί σύ [14:32–36]). The Markan Jesus embodies the answer to the rhetorical questions that lie at the center of the teaching in segment 1c: "For what good is it for you to gain the whole world, yet forfeit your life? For what can you give as exchange for your life?" The answer lies beyond a simple *nothing*. There is more: the key to *not* forfeiting one's life is to do what God wants even if that means losing one's life. God's Kingdom, according to Mark, reaches beyond the normal boundaries of life and death. The suffering and death of the Son of Man would lead to rising again (8:31; 9:31; 10:34). A time will come when the Son of Man comes in the Father's glory with the holy angels. This infers a time of judgment and vindication. The Son of Man will be ashamed of those who were ashamed of him. A positive parallel is not stated in this sentence, but clearly inferred through the earlier verses: the ones who lose their lives for his sake will gain them, even after death. Those who put their wants aside for his sake, will gain life.

Understood together with 14:32–36, the teaching in 8:34—9:1 reaches back to 3:33–35: "Looking around at those sitting in a circle around him, he said, 'Behold! My mother and my brothers! For the one who does the will of God (τὸ θέλημα τοῦ θεοῦ) that one is my brother and sister and mother.'" In Gethsemane, Jesus did what God wanted. In the three teaching segments, by pulling others into this same pattern, Mark shows how Jesus's suffering and death should be understood in terms of God's thoughts. Doing what God wants, giving one's life, going the depths of service in leadership, these are all things that belong to God's Kingdom, and to the way of both Jesus *and* his

---

9. Hooker notes that the valley of Gehenna had once been a place of sacrifice for Moloch, but after the reforms of Josiah (2 Kgs 23:10) had been used as a rubbish dump with fires burning continuously, becoming symbolic for the destruction of the wicked (*Mark*, 232).

followers. Their ways are intertwined. Doing what God wants is the family characteristic of the people of God.[10]

By weaving the teaching regarding the way of true discipleship with the teaching regarding the way that Jesus would go, and repeating this three times and surrounding the entire section with the *inclusio* of the blind healings, Mark masterfully brings the attention of his audience to focus on this coupling. Mark does not treat the suffering of Jesus and the following of the disciples as two different subjects in a generic teaching section. He forms them into one theme. And this unified theme is reinforced in the narratives between the teaching moments.

Mark's Foundational Focus: Salvation

But how do we see that these things belong to God's Kingdom and God's great story of salvation? I suggest that Mark has another important layer of structure that points towards this. However helpful van Iersel's outline is, one simple chiastic structure cannot do justice to Mark's full design. As Joanna Dewey describes, Mark is as an intricately woven tapestry, with various patterns working together to form the whole: ". . . Mark does not have a single structure made up of discrete sequential units but rather is an interwoven tapestry or fugue made up of multiple overlapping structures and sequences, forecasts of what is to come and echoes of what has already been said."[11]

Following Dewey's idea of "overlapping structures and sequences," I suggest a layered structure which both underlines Mark's central section and places Mark's whole narrative in the perspective of God's great story of salvation. My aim is not to present an exhaustive map of the Gospel's intricate structure. The question at this point is how the central teaching section is to be understood in relation to the narrative as a whole.

Setting van Iersel's chiastic structure, described above, aside for just a moment, another pattern emerges in Mark's narrative. Set in the beginning, center and end of the Gospel, we find the following three narrated moments:

1. "And immediately, as he was coming out of the water, he saw the heavens being torn apart and the Spirit as a dove descending into him. And a voice came from the heavens: 'You are my beloved Son, in you I am well-pleased!'" (1:10–11).

---

10. See Brower, "Holy One," on the formation of the new people of God centered around Jesus in Mark (especially 68–70).

11. Dewey, "Mark as Interwoven Tapestry." See also Donahue and Harrington, *Mark*, 47.

2. "And a cloud enveloped them while a voice came from the cloud: This is my beloved Son, listen to him!" (9:7).

3. "And the curtain of the temple was torn in two from top to bottom. And the centurion who was standing across from Jesus saw how he died, and said, 'Surely this man was the Son of God!'" (15:38–39).

The relationship between these three moments in Mark has been noted by various scholars.[12] In the texts quoted above, each includes (a) an action of God, with salvific connotations (b) an acknowledgement of Jesus as God's Son, and (c) an allusion to Elijah in the immediate context. Each of the texts will be considered separately before going on to look at the significance of how they relate to each other for Mark's narrative as a whole. It will become apparent that these texts provide important information to Mark's audience about the nature of salvation from God, and form three foundational pillars upon which Mark's narrative rests. But this structure cannot be understood completely apart from the discipleship structure that we have discussed above. The two structures fit together, and these three texts will also prove to be vital to understanding Mark's teaching on discipleship.

First Foundational Pillar: Mark 1:10–11

The first *Jesus as Son of God* moment is placed in the prologue. It is narrated as an event that only Jesus actually saw happen, but to which Mark's audience is made privy. A prologue is programmatic of the rest of the narrative, and Mark intends his narrative to be understood in light of this event. The action of God narrated here is a tearing of the heavens. Collins notes that the verb used here, σχίζω, is not used in the *LXX*, where "theophanic, epiphanic, or revelatory purposes" are indicated by the idea of the heavens *opening* [ἀνοίγω], not tearing.[13] However, as Joel Marcus points out, the MT of Isa 63:19 (*LXX* 64:1) does use a term that could well be translated as σχίζω, allowing the reading "O that you would rend the heavens and come down!"[14] Donahue and Harrington suggest that this is indeed an allusion to Isa 63:19 (MT) and that this is only part of a medley of Isaiah allusions in Mark that point to God's great work of salvation for all nations coming to fulfilment through Jesus.[15] Mark uses this verb once more in his narrative,

---

12. See, for example, Ulansey, "Heavenly Veil"; Motyer, "Rending of the Veil"; Collins, *Mark*, 762–64; Donahue and Harrington, *Mark*, 452.

13. Collins, *Mark*, 148.

14. Marcus, *Way of the Lord*, 49. Also, France, *Mark*, 77.

15. Donahue and Harrington, *Mark*, 65–68. Also, Hooker, *Mark*, 46; Lane, *Mark*,

at the third moment of this structural layer, for the tearing of the temple curtain at Jesus's death.[16]

The entrance of the Holy Spirit into Jesus (εἰς αὐτόν) as the heavens tear open is a salvific moment in line with the eschatological hopes of salvation from God as worded in Isa 63. This also ought to be understood in light of the intertextuality in the promise that the Markan John the Baptist makes about the one coming after him: "I baptize you in water, but he will baptize you in the Holy Spirit" (1:8). While John's presence in the narrative has already been explained in context of God's great story of salvation, in this statement he points away from himself and towards Jesus. The context of repentance, water, and Spirit strongly suggests an intertextual relationship with Ezekiel 36:25–27: "I will sprinkle clean water on you, and you will be clean; I will cleanse you from all your impurities and from all your idols. I will give you a new heart and put a new spirit in you; I will remove from you your heart of stone and give you a heart of flesh. And I will put my Spirit in you and move you to follow my decrees and be careful to keep my laws." Jesus is presented as the avenue through which the eschatological hope of the presence of the Holy Spirit will be realized, enabling God's people to live according to God's ways. In this context, the goal of salvation is the obedience from the heart that can only be attained through the Holy Spirit.[17]

Behind the words from heaven, "You are my beloved Son, in you I am well-pleased!" lie possible echoes of Gen 22:2; Ps 2:7; Isa 42:1; 62:4.[18] Narratively speaking, Mark prepares the expectations of his audience towards Jesus through the message of John the Baptist. But when Jesus actually appears, it is God himself who presents him to Mark's audience. Jesus is God's own unique and beloved Son, Messiah, the one in and through whom God himself acts out his great work of salvation, and with whom God is pleased. The Markan Jesus, bearer of the Holy Spirit, is the locus of God's presence on earth, and is the one through whom repentant persons will be baptized in the Holy Spirit.

55–56. See also chapter 7 below.

16. A cognate of this verb, the noun σχίσμα, is used in 2:21 by the Markan Jesus in an illustration indicating the incompatibility of the old with the new (cf. 1:27) in the coming of God's Kingdom.

17. This is not to say that there is no aspect of life beyond this life in Mark's presentation of salvation; it is merely to say that the goal of salvation is obedience of the heart. In Mark, God is God of the living not of the dead. The Kingdom of God crosses over the boundaries between life and death.

18. Marshall, "Son of God or Servant of Yahweh?"; Collins, *Mark*, 150–51.

Second Foundational Pillar: Mark 9:7

Six days after Jesus's teaching moment in 8:31—9:1, the Markan Jesus climbs a high mountain with three of his disciples. While alone at the top, Jesus is transformed before the eyes of the disciples, and his clothing turns unearthly white. Elijah and Moses appear before them, in conversation with Jesus. Then, a cloud comes, envelopes them all, and God speaks once again: "This is my beloved Son, listen to him!" (9:7).

Elijah and Moses were the two people narrated in Scripture who had had a revelation of God on a mountain top. It is likely that Mark intends an allusion to both moments, although the theophany experience of Moses related in Exod 24 provides the most parallels. Mark's story includes a specific reference to six days, as does God's revelation to Moses in Exod 24:16, yet with different significance.[19] Mark's time reference serves to connect the Transfiguration story to the teaching moment immediately preceding it in the narrative, while in Exodus, a cloud covered the mountain for six days before God called out to Moses. Moses brought his disciple Joshua with him. Jesus brought the representatives of his disciples with him: Peter, James, and John. A significant element of the theophany in Exodus was the giving of the law. God called Moses up the mountain in order to present him with the law, the words which were to show the people how to live in a way pleasing to God. Mark tells of God's voice affirming Jesus as his Son, and admonishing the disciples to listen to him. This hooks back to the previous teaching moment in which Jesus rebuked Peter for considering the things of men instead of the things of God. The teaching of giving up one's life for Jesus and the sake of the Gospel—of doing what God wants instead of what one wants for themselves—is the message that God wants the disciples to listen to and to heed.

Mark does not negate the law of God given to Moses for God's people, but he also does not consider it the final word on what God wants. He redefines what God wants in the person and message of Jesus. The subject reappears in the narrative in 10:2–12, in the form of a question set before Jesus by some Pharisees: "Is it allowed that a man divorce his wife?" The Markan Jesus explains that even though Moses had allowed for divorce, what God intended was for husband and wife to remain together: "what God has joined together, a person must not separate" (10:9). In other words, if one wants to do what God wants, one will not separate husband and wife. Mark's

---

19. See Lane, *Mark*, 317.

redefinition of being obedient to God has to do with doing what God wants, even when it does not coincide with one's own desires.[20]

Another significance of both Elijah's and Moses's theophanies to this moment in Mark has to do with the formation of the people of God. The law given to Moses on Mt Sinai is intended to form the Israelites into God's people. Elijah is reminded on Mt Horeb that although it may seem to him that he is the only one left of God's people, he is not; there are yet 7,000 who have not left God to worship Baal (I Kg 19:14–18). A mark of God's true people is their faithful obedience to him. In Mark 9:7, Mark is suggesting that the true people of God are formed around Jesus as they listen to what he says.

When Jesus and his disciples arrive on top of the mountain, the focus of the narrative is on Jesus. When God's voice is heard, it is to point again to Jesus. Although there are several points of parallel with the Moses theophany, Mark is not saying that Jesus is a new Moses. Moses carried two tablets of stone down the mountain with the laws of God written on them. In Mark, Jesus *embodies* the will of God.[21] His disciples are to listen to *him*. What he tells them is that they are to live and die *as he lives and dies*—accepting God's will over and above their own wants. This proves in the ensuing narrative to be complex. When Jesus arrives at the bottom of the mountain, he finds his disciples failing in their attempt to cast out a demon. The problem lies in their failure to pray. This again provides a clue to Mark's message: doing God's will is made possible only through God himself. It will also prove to foreshadow Jesus's prayer in Gethsemane and his warning to the disciples to "watch and pray" so they would not fall into temptation (14:38).

The prominence of Elijah in the Transfiguration story is also significant. The audience has already been pointed towards understanding the role of John the Baptist in terms of the eschatological return of Elijah as written in Malachi 3 and 4. Elijah's preparatory role has to do with bringing God's people to obedience. His presence upon the mountain with Moses and Jesus carries these connotations of repentance and obedience (1:4–8) in a salvific context.

---

20. This needs to be seen in light of the flippant ease with which one could use a law to justify selfish behavior. It is God's will that man and woman live together in loving unity, and not that one uses the other merely to satisfy selfish desires until another becomes the object of these desires. This is not a commentary on what to do when one partner is used unjustly by the other.

21 See Ermakov, "Holy Community," 179.

Third Foundational Pillar: Mark 15:38–39

Moving on to the third moment marking Jesus as Son of God brings us to the crucifixion of Jesus. This scene marks the climax of Mark's narrative. Jesus, who is known by the audience to be the Messiah, is portrayed on the cross ironically as the king of the Jews. After he cries out loudly, the temple curtain tears from top to bottom, and the centurion standing by him sees how he dies and exclaims, "Surely this man was the Son of God!" (15:37–39). The scene is full of irony. Jesus is named King of the Jews by those who do not honor him. And indeed, he is king in God's Kingdom. People all around him are attempting to *see* (15:32, 36), but only the centurion in the end truly sees (15:39). The seeing and hearing of the centurion echoes 4:12, especially after the ironic mockery from the chief priests and teachers of the law: "Let the Christ, the King of Israel, come down from the cross now, so that we will see and believe!" (15:32). In 4:12, Mark had coaxed his audience towards truly looking and truly listening. Salvation is found by seeing and perceiving, hearing and understanding. And this is precisely what the centurion does. He hears the cry of Jesus and sees how he dies, and truly understands: the crucified Jesus is the Son of God.

This scene is packed full of Mark's message regarding salvation. It comes by listening to Jesus and seeing how he dies. It is open to a gentile, and a centurion overseeing the crucifixion of the Messiah at that! The tearing of the temple curtain, presumably by God himself (from top to bottom), announces God's salvation. This image is also pregnant with meaning: David Ulansey has pointed out that Josephus describes the outer curtain of the temple as a Babylonian tapestry, with all the heavenly bodies embroidered elaborately on it.[22] Hearing that the temple curtain was torn, Mark's implied audience would *see* in their mind's eye the heavens being torn apart, and be reminded of the Spirit descending as the heavens tore apart in 1:10. But this would not be the only connotation. The audience would also be aware that it was the *temple* curtain which was torn by God; they would remember the stories alluding to judgment upon the temple system and

---

22. Ulansey, "Heavenly Veil," 124. See Josephus, "Wars of the Jews," 5.5.4: "It was a Babylonian curtain, embroidered with blue, and fine linen, and scarlet, and purple, and of a contexture that was truly wonderful. Nor was this mixture of colors without its mystical interpretation, but was a kind of image of the universe; for by the scarlet there seemed to be enigmatically signified fire, by the fine flax the earth, by the blue the air, and by the purple the sea; two of them having their colors the foundation of this resemblance; but the fine flax and the purple have their own origin for that foundation, the earth producing the one, and the sea the other. This curtain had also embroidered upon it all that was mystical in the heavens, excepting that of the [twelve] signs, representing living creatures." See also Ryou, "Apocalyptic Opening."

its leaders earlier in the narrative (11:12–25; 12:1–12), and the allusions to eschatological judgment in the Markan Jesus's use of the term Son of Man (especially 14:62; but also 8:38). The temple was the locus of God's presence, but since Jesus's baptism, the Markan Jesus had become the locus of God's presence. The tearing of the temple curtain would not only be a reminder of the tearing open of the heavens and the descent of the Spirit into Jesus, but would affirm, even in the face of crucifixion, that God's eschatological salvation had come.[23] The promise given by John the Baptist regarding Jesus would also be brought to mind, this time focusing on the crucified Jesus as the key to its realization. This is especially relevant to Mark's teaching on discipleship and will be the focus of the following chapter.

This final scene in the Markan Jesus's life echoes the baptism of Jesus, with his experience of seeing the heavens open and the Spirit descend into him while hearing the voice of God affirming him as his Son.[24] Together these two moments form an *inclusio* to Mark's Gospel. But this moment also echoes 9:2–8 and the voice of God affirming Jesus as his Son, admonishing the disciples to listen to him. Structurally, these three moments with strong salvific connotations work together to form three pillars on which Mark's Gospel rests, and which guide his audience in understanding Mark's message as God's great work of salvation. In the prologue, Mark's audience is presented with Jesus as the locus of God's presence in God's great eschatological work of salvation. In the center of the narrative, the audience is reminded again that God's salvific work centers around Jesus and obedience to his message. Finally, the audience is brought to see how Jesus dies and the Kingdom is affirmed as being formed around Jesus. These three pillars form a firm foundational structure that presents Mark's message as the story of God's salvation.

---

23. Donahue and Harrington, *Mark*, 65–68; Hooker, *Mark*, 46.

24. See also Motyer, "Rending of the Veil," 155. See, however, Lentzen-Deis (*Die Taufe Jesu nach den Synoptikern*, 281) who suggests that the tearing of the temple curtain must be understood as judgment upon the old temple, while the confession of the centurion indicates the eschatological reinstatement of the temple. He disregards any connection to the baptism scene on the grounds that the meaning of the scenes differs. At the baptism, he says, the Holy Spirit comes out of the tear, as does the heavenly voice; whereas at the crucifixion, no one comes out nor enters the tear in the temple, but it is destroyed. I disagree, however, that these two happenings contradict each other. They are two aspects of the same salvific act of God in Jesus. The new people of God are formed around Jesus, with the presence of the Holy Spirit coming to the people (arguably, coming out of the old temple building), and enabling them to *be* God's people, through Jesus as the new temple, rendering the old temple redundant. Mark brings both aspects together in his theology of salvation.

Putting Mark's Layers Together

When this structural layer is added to the structure that we discussed earlier, we see that Mark positioned it so that it serves to underline the central teaching section. The center pillar follows immediately after the first combined teaching moment. As is often noted, Mark makes prolific use of echoing and foreshadowing in his narrative. He is seldom so clear in hooking the attention backwards as he is in 9:7 when the voice of God calls to the disciples to "Listen to him!" He has already joined the two scenes through the use of a temporal link in 9:2 ("after six days . . ."). Another link is provided by the misunderstanding of Peter, and Jesus's harsh rebuke of him: ὅτι οὐ φρονεῖς τὰ τοῦ θεοῦ ἀλλὰ τὰ τῶν ἀνθρώπων. Jesus proceeds to explain what the things of God are, and on the mountain God reinforces his message as he tells the disciples himself that τὰ τοῦ θεοῦ is indeed what Jesus had just taught them. They must listen to Jesus.

Mark intertwines these two layers into one narrative, using one theme to support the other. While much of Mark's structure is balanced, these two layers, though clear and balanced in themselves, do not fit together in a balanced way. One might expect the central *on the way* section to fit evenly around the center *Jesus as Son of God* moment in 9:7, which is placed at nearly exact the center of the narrative. But Mark has tied his first, and not his second, combined passion prediction and discipleship teaching moment to this central pillar. Effectually, at the moment Mark provides his most powerful scene in which the disciples themselves hear the voice of God and see Jesus in full glory and perhaps even understand that Jesus is the key figure in God's whole story of salvation that has included both Moses and Elijah in ages passed, he jars his audience in the midst of their awe back into the reality of the difficult teaching of giving one's life to the point of death. The content of the three teaching moments (8:31—9:1; 9:31-50; and 10:33-45), with their own unique perspective on the same theme, are condensed into this one moment in which the voice of God speaks (9:7): "This is my beloved Son! Listen to him!"

By placing this center pillar moment immediately following the first of the three teaching moments, the content of the teaching is emphasized and highlighted. The combined message of both layers of Mark's structure becomes something like this: God is performing his decisive act of salvation through Jesus, which includes the death of Jesus and the formation of a people around Jesus who will give their lives in service to the point of death, choosing what God wants above what they want and desire for themselves.

A structural map of Mark's Gospel message might then look a bit like this:

- *Introduction: The beginning of the good news of Jesus Christ, the Son of God*

1. **"You are my beloved Son, in you I am well pleased!"**

   A. *the* Son of Man *must suffer and die, and be raised again. This pattern is also to be followed by any who follow Jesus.*

2. **"This is my beloved Son, Listen to him!"**

   B. *the* Son of Man *must suffer and die, and be raised again. This pattern of service is also to be followed by all disciples.*

   C. *the* Son of Man *must suffer and die, and be raised again. This pattern of service is also to be followed by all in God's Kingdom.*

3. **"Surely this man was the Son of God!"**

   - *Conclusion: report of resurrection of Jesus and the promise to see him in Galilee*

As with all outlines, this map does not do justice to the depths of Mark's message. It does, however, provide a quick overview of the relationship between the pillar moments (1,2 and 3) marking Jesus as the beloved of God who is his agent of salvation, and the character of the people of God formed around Jesus. The message of the Markan Jesus is the message of God, Mark says. Salvation looks like this: Jesus, surrounded by all who want to follow him, all doing what God wants instead of what they want for themselves, even as it leads to death.

The Kingdom of God is being formed around Jesus, in spite of resistance and even death. In this way, the obedience of Jesus unto death and the obedience of the disciples unto death are both portrayed as salvific in Mark's gospel. Salvific is understood to indicate being a vital component of God's salvation. In order to understand how this Markan salvific obedience relates to God's salvation and how the obedience of Jesus relates to the obedience of the disciples, we cannot disregard the failure of the disciples within the narrative.

Mark's story shows that doing God's thing will meet resistance both from spiritual powers and from human powers. The spiritual powers all know who Jesus is, and those encountering Jesus are quickly silenced into submission and cast away from those they were hurting. But the *people* who resist Jesus must decide for themselves to submit. In Mark's narrative, this is the biggest struggle. The more one has of power and riches the more resistant one is to this message. But even for those who have given all they had to follow Jesus, to follow to the end proves impossible. The tension that this brings to the narrative is almost too much for the narrative to hold. The message of the necessity of following Jesus unto death is strong, held up by the very pillars of the narrative. And yet, none are able. Contrary to what many scholars claim, the failure of those desiring to follow Jesus in the narrative can do nothing to soften the demands of discipleship.[25] God himself has claimed that to be one of his true people, Jesus and the way of the cross *must* be followed. Therein lie salvation, the Kingdom of God, and eternal life. Mark does not ignore this tension; he drives his audience to look closely and listen intently in search of the key to unlock it.

---

25. See the overview of scholarship in the following chapter on discipleship failure in Mark.

3

The (Im)possible Path of Discipleship

As is reflected in the structure of Mark's narrative described above, Mark's message of salvation insists that the disciples follow Jesus faithfully unto death. As his story develops, however, the disciples fail drastically, revealing the truth of the words the Markan Jesus speaks in Mark 10: πῶς δύσκολόν ἐστιν εἰς τὴν βασιλείαν τοῦ θεοῦ εἰσελθεῖν ... παρὰ ἀνθρώποις ἀδύνατον ("how difficult it is to enter the Kingdom of God ... for people it is impossible" 10:24, 27a; cf. 14:50). And yet, the Markan Jesus continues and reveals that this may not be the final scene to their story: ἀλλ' οὐ παρὰ θεῷ· πάντα γὰρ δυνατὰ παρὰ τῷ θεῷ ("but not for God, for all things are possible with God" 10:27b). It is impossible for them to enter the Kingdom of God; and yet, God will make it possible. In fact, Mark weaves this same promise into his narrative from the beginning, even before the disciples come on stage. Beginning in the prologue, and reinforcing it in the other two pillar moments of his narrative, Mark provides his audience with the expectation initially planted by John the Baptist that Jesus would be the one to baptize with the Holy Spirit. This promise is essential to Mark's message of salvation, and the fulfilment of God's enabling of obedience.

The Markan disciples fail drastically within the confines of the narrative. Why does Mark go to this extent? Is he merely tracing the tragic history of the relationship between Jesus and his chosen twelve, with whom he had shared his authority (3:14–15 and 6:7)? Why does he shed them of honor by drawing such attention to their failure? My theory is that Mark is using them to portray the double truth of Jesus's statement quoted above from 10:27, while pointing his audience to the promise of the Holy Spirit. But what have others said about this?

Review of Scholarship on Discipleship Failure in Mark

While many have noted the importance of the promises of reconciliation or the historical evidence that the disciples had later become faithful followers under persecution, Mark has not yet been understood to point to an actual *solution* to discipleship failure. Some scholars have disregarded the promises of reconciliation altogether (cf. 14:28; 16:7), and have painted a polemical historical situation as explanation for Mark's choice of allowing the disciples to fail blatantly at following Jesus. Another group focuses on Mark's message to his audience and hearers. Some of these scholars suggest that Mark uses a narrative strategy involving reader identification with the disciples or with Jesus which would move them to choose for themselves to be faithful followers of Jesus in their own situations. Others of these approach the message of Mark as a whole, and seek the explanation of the disciples' failure in Mark's overall message. I will briefly sketch the arguments of some of the most prominent representatives of each of these three categories.

Polemical Historical Situation

In "The Blindness of the Disciples in Mark," Joseph Tyson describes Mark as portraying the disciples as blind to the necessity of the cross. This arose, he says, from the historical situation reflected in Peter's speech in Acts 2, in which there was no significance given to the death of Christ. He paints a description of the disciples in the post-narrative times as focusing more on the resurrection than on the death of Jesus, and hoping for a royal Messiahship at his return, with prestigious positions for themselves.[1] Theodore Weeden is similar, though a bit harsher, in his description of the historical situation to which he believes Mark was writing. In his article "The Heresy that Necessitated Mark's Gospel," he describes Mark's opponents as holding to a *theios anēr* Christology, while Mark held to a *theologia crucis*. According to Weeden, Mark's depiction of the failure of the disciples is crafted carefully in order to "disgrace and debunk" them and their position as well as "their successors, the Marcan opponents."[2]

While there have been a few interpreters who have continued to look for a historical explanation for the depiction of the disciples in Mark,[3] an awareness of literary strategies in the Gospels has shifted the attention

---

1. Tyson, "Blindness," 264, 266.
2. Weeden, "Heresy that Necessitated Mark's Gospel," 91.
3. See, for example, van Iersel, "Failed Followers." Kelber, *Oral and the Written Gospel*, argues that Mark used the failure of the disciples to depict the breakdown of the oral tradition by depicting the breakdown of its representatives, thereby proving the need for the written gospel: "In other words, the gospel articulates the *raison d'être* for its own written existence by dramatizing the breakdown of the mimetic process. The emergence of thoroughgoing textuality and the gospel's narration of the failure of oral transmission are rigorously complementary phenomenon" (98).

of scholars away from a reconstruction of the historical situation and towards the message of the Gospel in its entirety and its purpose intended by the author.

Reader Identification

Robert Tannehill writes in his 1977 article, "The Disciples in Mark: the Function of a Narrative Role," of the importance of taking the whole story into consideration when interpreting the function of a character or character group such as the disciples. One of Tannehill's arguments against the polemical picture drawn by Weeden is that he does not consider the positive attention that Mark gives to the disciples.[4] As Tannehill explains, "Our surest guide to the implied author's evaluation of the disciples is to follow the shifting relationship between Jesus and the disciples, noting where they are in concord and where they are not."[5] Taking this into consideration, the promise of restoration to the disciples cannot be overlooked: "Even if the reconciliation is temporarily frustrated (see 16:8), it remains the intention of Jesus (and the author)."[6] This portrayal of the disciples in both positive and negative ways, builds a reflective bond of the reader with the disciples. The reader is encouraged to identify with the disciples as they follow along with Jesus,[7] and when confronted initially with the disciples' difficulties in following, the reader is reminded of his or her own similar difficulties. Yet, as these difficulties develop more fully into failure, the readers are moved to separate themselves from their own failures, and search for a "new self who can follow Jesus faithfully as a disciple."[8] Tannehill's thesis is that the readers would be subtly brought to be involved in a story "in which they will first recognize themselves and the positive qualities of their own self-image and then be led to self-criticism."[9]

While Tannehill suggests that Mark intended the readers to find the resolution of the frustrated identification with the disciples within themselves, David Rhoads suggests a different resolution. As the narrative proceeds and

---

4. Tannehill, "Disciples," 394.

5. Ibid., 391.

6. Ibid., 394.

7. Ibid., 398: "In [the first part of Mark's Gospel], the author goes out of his way to make the disciples attractive figures, both by stressing their close association with Jesus and by contrasting them sharply with negative groups."

8. Ibid., 395.

9. Ibid., 398. See also Klauck, "Die erzählerische Rolle der Jünger," 1–26, for a similar interpretation. Klauck suggests that the narrator teaches the readers to trust Jesus and his offer of salvation even in the painful drama of the failure of the disciples.

the disciples begin to show signs of not being able to give their lives for Jesus, but rather betray and deny him, the readers shift their identification to Jesus himself. Identifying with Jesus as he suffers and dies empowers the readers with courage to face the same persecution without fear, says Rhoads: "by going through Jesus' death vicariously in the experience of the narrative, they face with courage the fears that might otherwise paralyze them."[10]

Both of these interpretations attribute an enormous responsibility to Mark. But does Mark's narrative reflect the expectation to be the catalyst of faithfulness within a person? The disciples within the narrative had the opportunity to live with Jesus, travel with him, experience his power and his fear and his faithfulness firsthand. They were there, albeit at a distance, when he suffered in the court of the high priest. And yet, it was there that Peter denied even knowing him. Rhoads suggests that although the disciples had difficulty understanding Jesus, they had "eventually accept[ed] his teachings."[11] By the time of the betrayal and crucifixion, the Markan Peter had realized that Jesus was the promised Messiah (8:29), had heard the voice of God claiming Jesus as his Son (9:7), and although he feared for his and for Jesus's life, he did follow Jesus into Jerusalem (10:32), and did promise him that Passover evening to die with him if necessary (14:29, 31), apparently thinking he had overcome his fear. The narrative itself provides evidence that mere closeness to or identification with one or more of the characters, even Jesus himself, could not bring about faithfulness in the hearts of Jesus's followers. Even after accepting Jesus's teaching, those intending to follow are not able to. It is not a logical conclusion that the implied author considered his narrative to have even more power, and would be able to enact this fundamental change within the hearts of his audience.

The Failure "Serves the Message of the Whole"

A third group of scholars has suggested that the disciples' failure must be integrated into Mark's theological message. Failure is suggested to be par for the course, and that Mark's narrative is meant to encourage those followers of Jesus who have also experienced such failure in their own discipleship.

Elisabeth Struthers Malbon interprets Mark's choice of portraying the misunderstandings and the fallibility of the disciples as flowing from a pastoral concern to tell his readers that although "anyone can be a follower, no one finds it easy."[12] Ernest Best suggests that the knowledge of Mark's readers

---

10. Rhoads, "Losing Life for Others," 366.
11. Ibid., 359.
12. Malbon, "Fallible Followers," 46. While her determination to take the positive

that the disciples who had failed in the narrative had later become pillars in the church would be an encouragement to those who had themselves failed. Not their own failure, but "God's love and strength" and the ability to finally triumph would have the last word in their discipleship.[13]

Best suggests, moreover, that in all master-disciple relationships, the failure of a disciple would provide the master with a teaching opportunity. He points out that Mark does not condemn the disciples, rather uses them as a foil. Their failure to understand gives Jesus an opportunity to

> ... give further and fuller instruction; their fearfulness is brought out in order that Jesus may show them the source of calm and courage; their desire for positions of importance is stressed in order that Jesus may teach them about the meaning of service.... Any apparent attack on them normally ends, not in the negative side of their failure, but in positive teaching on the part of Jesus which will assist Mark's community.[14]

Mary Ann Tolbert claims similarly that the failure of the disciples provides the author with the opportunity "through both the narrator and the character Jesus to explain, repeat, and elaborate upon important teachings and issues."[15] She disagrees with the tendency to attribute to Mark certain literary techniques designed to hook readers into identifying with certain characters, claiming that in ancient writing characters would not be used for this purpose. Characters were used as tools to support a specific message.[16]

According to Tolbert, the heart of the message that Mark was trying to get across to his readers was the message found in his two longest parables:

---

portrayal of the disciples throughout Mark's narrative seriously is to be applauded, this conclusion does not take either the demands of discipleship or the failure of the disciples seriously enough. According to the Markan Jesus, the one who chooses to save his or her own life will lose it, while only the one who loses it for the sake of Jesus and the gospel will save it (8:35). Mark's message is that there are serious consequences attached to failure.

13. Best, "Role of the Disciples," 399.
14. Ibid.
15. Tolbert, *Sowing the Gospel*, 221. See also Hurtado, "Following Jesus," 9–10. Hurtado states, moreover, that the negative portrayal of the disciples provides Mark with the opportunity to portray Jesus as the "model of discipleship" (25). According to Hurtado, withholding a proper understanding of Jesus until after the crucifixion points to the cross as the key to understanding both Jesus and discipleship. The disciples as a character group provide a warning "of the dangers that readers must avoid," while Jesus's death is portrayed as the paradigm for discipleship (25). See also Hurtado, "Jesus' Death as Paradigmatic."
16. Tolbert, "How the Gospel of Mark," 349. See also Tolbert, *Sowing the Gospel*, 223–24 and 295–99.

the Sower in 4:3–9, 14–20 and the Tenants in 12:1–12. The message of the Tenants parable indicates the apocalyptic nature of Mark's Gospel, that God will bring his Kingdom through Jesus no matter what the response.[17] The message of the Sower (4:3–9, 14–20) illustrates the faithless and hardhearted responses of "most of humanity" to Jesus's message. Mark then "dramatizes those responses through the characterization of all the groups and individuals around Jesus throughout the narrative."[18] The disciples are represented in the parable by the stony ground, which Tolbert considers a pun on the nickname that the Markan Jesus had given to Simon, Andrew's brother: "Every time Peter's name is used throughout the Gospel of Mark, the listening audience is reminded of that shallow ground that cannot withstand trouble."[19] Provided with various characters representing the various types of soil within the narrative, Mark's readers will finally ask themselves the question which sort of soil they represent.[20] According to Tolbert, it is the message of Mark that causes the readers to ask themselves this question, and not an identification with the disciples.

James Hanson also interprets the failure of the disciples in Mark as being a support to Mark's message. The Markan Jesus's conflicts with the religious leaders and with the disciples are to be understood as conflicts with the power of Satan in this world.[21] Mark shows Jesus put to death by the religious leaders and allows the disciples to fail drastically, but at the same time tells that Jesus was raised from the dead and that Jesus gave promises that demonstrate that God's purposes of redemption and reconciliation are more powerful than the power of Satan. According to Hanson, the tension created thus in the narrative is not resolved by Mark and is characteristic of Christian existence.[22] The readers are to understand that the promise of God's salvation is not dependent on the faithful following of the disciples.[23]

This movement towards seeing the failure of the disciples in Mark's narrative as supporting his message has been an important move. It takes Mark seriously as implied author of the text, respecting the various aspects of the narrative and trusting them to make sense as a whole. In approaching the subject from this perspective, Malbon, Best, Tolbert and Hanson have

17. Tolbert, "How the Gospel of Mark," 350–51.

18. Ibid., 351.

19. Ibid., 353. See also Rhoads, Dewey, and Michie, *Mark as Story* (129), for this interpretation regarding Peter's name.

20. Tolbert, *Sowing the Gospel*, 299.

21. Hanson, *Endangered Promises*, 224–48. See also Hanson, "Disciples in Mark's Gospel."

22. Hanson, *Endangered Promises*, 245.

23. Ibid., 247.

made important contributions to the discussion on discipleship as they have allowed the tension created in this failure to add to the understanding of the message of Mark. None of these, however, has noticed that Mark also provides a key to the resolution of this tension.

The Present State of the Issue

The main consensus that has developed in the past fifty years is that Mark was not necessarily writing a polemical document in which he portrayed those he disagreed with as the disciples of Jesus who utterly failed to live up to the standards which Jesus had demanded of those who followed him. Most scholars do agree that the failure of the disciples provides some sort of motivation to Mark's audience. When interpreted together with the demands of discipleship and the promise of restoration in 14:28 and 16:7, their failure either provides Mark's audience with hope that they may one day also overcome their failures and be welcomed back as followers of Jesus, or at least that they may find comfort in that Jesus's first followers were also not able to follow flawlessly.

Mark, however, is unwavering in the demands of following Jesus that he portrays. The message, through the mouth of Jesus, is harsh to those who do not follow: "For if one wants to save their life, they will lose it" (8:35a); "For if one is ashamed of me and my words in this adulterous and sinful generation the Son of Man will be ashamed of them when he comes in his Father's glory with the holy angels" (8:38); "How difficult it is for those with riches to enter into the kingdom of God" (10:23b).

What Mark shows in his narrative supports and elucidates the words of the Markan Jesus.[24] When Mark sets the scene of his Gospel, he shows immediately that Jesus is God's Son, whom he loves, and sets his ministry in context of the long-awaited salvation promised by the prophet Isaiah. He consistently portrays Jesus positively as God's beloved Son (cf. 12:1–12; 15:39), even through the narration of conflicts with the religious leaders and his death.[25] Aligning Jesus with God is one of the ways that Mark indicates his agreement with the message spoken by the Markan Jesus. Jesus's teaching on the demands of discipleship is central to Mark's Gospel. If Mark then

---

24. An example of this relationship between the words of the Markan Jesus and the narrative could be seen in 11:1–6 and 14:13–16. In both cases, Jesus tells his disciples to do something, explaining exactly what will happen as they do so. The narrative then shows that it happens just as Jesus had said it would.

25. See Roskam, *Purpose of the Gospel of Mark*. See also Klauck, "Die erzählerische Roller der Jünger," 20.

proceeds to show the disciples as failing to live up to these demands of Jesus, then this failure must somehow not detract from these demands at all. The apparent inconsistency combined with the conviction that the Markan Jesus's words are trustworthy moves Mark's hearers to search for a resolution to the inconsistency in the form of hope for the disciples. This hope is found perhaps most clearly in the promise of reconciliation worded by the Markan Jesus in 14:28 and repeated by the messenger at the tomb in 16:7. Yet, for those who look and listen more intently, there is more to find.

Mark 16:7 provides an often overlooked Markan clue to understanding the relationship of the failure and the reconciliation: after repeating the promise that Jesus will go before them into Galilee, the angel adds the information that the disciples will *see* Jesus in Galilee. This has been the problem all along. They had not yet been able to fully *see* and understand.[26] Mark surrounds his central message with the inclusio of the conspicuously different blind healings (8:22–26 and 10:46–52) which indicates the process of beginning to *see* and understand that takes place within the disciples. However, the narrative indicates that full seeing had not yet taken place, even after the healing of Bartimaeus in Jericho who follows Jesus to Jerusalem. The promise that the disciples will *see* Jesus in Galilee in 16:7 indicates that their own "blind healing" will be made complete when they meet him there. The implication is that once they *see* Jesus in Galilee, they will be able to follow him to the cross. Mark first plants the seed of this expectation in his prologue. His ideal audience will have noticed it, and as they hear the story of the disciples unfold, will gradually understand its significance to Mark's message.

Mark's Theme of Hope Woven Into His Salvation Focus

Mark opens his narrative with John the Baptist baptizing those who confessed their sins, and announcing, "One is coming after me who is stronger than I; I am not worthy to stoop down to untie the chords of his sandals. I baptize you with water; he will baptize you in the Holy Spirit" (1:7–8). Mark intends this reference to the Holy Spirit to indicate his solution to the discipleship problem. Though scholars rarely, if ever, mention the Holy Spirit, let alone this verse, in their treatment of the discipleship problem, there is evidence in Mark's narrative that he intends this verse to indicate a solution to the problem he presents.[27]

---

26. See chapter 7 below, where I discuss the theme of *seeing* from the perspective of intertextuality with Isaiah.

27. See, however, Powery, "Spirit and Political Dissent." Powery interprets obedience

Very simply stated, as discussed above in chapter 2, Mark's narrative structure is held up by three foundational pillars in which Jesus is referred to as the Son of God—at the beginning, middle and end of the narrative. The first pillar is Mark's prologue, the second is the Transfiguration moment, and the third pillar is the crucifixion scene. While the most obvious binding factor of these three pillars is the reference to Jesus as God's Son, the context of each also plays a part in its significance. In each section, God takes an active role, and Elijah enters the narrative either specifically mentioned or as a strong allusion.

In what follows, each of these foundational passages of Mark's narrative will be looked at anew from a different perspective. I will show that each of these passages also indicates the fulfilling of expectation created in 1:8 that the baptism in the Holy Spirit will be realized through Jesus, enabling those who would to follow Jesus on the way of the cross. While the Gospel does not have much Holy Spirit language—and only here and in Mark 13 as available for others than Jesus—Mark coaxes his hearers forward to search for and understand the significance of this promise of John the Baptist in light of the teaching and death of Jesus.

The first and third pillars seem to be designed chiastically. The second pillar clearly points to a teaching moment by the Markan Jesus which also appears to be poured into a concentric mold. Observing Mark's use of chiasmus at these moments will not lead to a different interpretation compared to that found in the previous chapter, but to an extra dimension and heightened emphasis.

First Foundational Pillar

A   The beginning of the gospel of Jesus Christ [the Son of God] (1:1).

B   Just as it was written in Isaiah the prophet, 'Behold, I send my messenger before you who will make ready your way. The voice of one crying out loud in the wilderness, "Prepare the way of the Lord! Make his paths straight!"' (1:2–3).

C   John the Baptist appeared in the wilderness, proclaiming a baptism of repentance towards forgiveness of sins. And all the countryside of Judea came to him and all the inhabitants of Jerusalem. And they were baptized by him in the Jordan river, confessing

---

of the disciples as "political dissent," and recognizes the Holy Spirit as enabling this dissent.

their sins. And John was clothed in camel hair and a leather belt around his loin, eating grasshoppers and wild honey (1:4–6).

X   And he proclaimed, saying, "One stronger than I am is coming after me; I am not fit to bow down and loosen the tie of his sandals. I baptize you with water, but he will baptize you in the Holy Spirit!" (1:7–8).

C`   And it happened in those days Jesus came from Nazareth in Galilee and was baptized in the Jordan by John. And immediately as he was rising up out of the water, he saw the heavens tearing and the spirit like a dove descending into him. And a voice came from the heavens, "you are my beloved Son; in you I am well pleased" (1:9–11).

B`   And immediately the Spirit throws him out into the wilderness. And he was in the wilderness forty days, being challenged by Satan. And he was with the wild animals, and the angels served him (1:12–13).

A`   And after John was arrested, Jesus came into Galilee, proclaiming the good news of God, and saying that the time was at hand and the Kingdom of God has been brought near, repent and believe in the good news (1:14–15).

In ancient writing and rhetoric, the prologue would hold vital information about what follows, and the scene would be set against which an entire narrative could be understood.[28] Referring to Mark's prologue, Morna Hooker says:

> In a few short verses, Mark provides us with a great deal of theological information: scripture is being fulfilled, the expected prophet has prepared the way of the Lord, Jesus has been identified as God's Son by a heavenly voice, God's Spirit is at work, and Jesus has confronted Satan in the company of wild beasts while angels lent him support.[29]

---

28. Hooker, "Beginnings and Endings." See also Quintillian, *Institutes of Oratory*: "In giving an exordium at all, there is no other object but to prepare the hearer to listen to us more readily in the subsequent parts of our pleading. This object, as is agreed among most authors, is principally effected by three means: by securing his good will and his attention, and by rendering him desirous of further information. These ends are not to be kept in view throughout the whole pleading, but they are pre-eminently necessary at the commencement, when we gain admission, as it were, to the mind of the judge in order to penetrate still farther into it" (IV, 1.5; Watson). Mark's purpose was also to render the audience "desirous of further information."

29. Hooker, "Beginnings and Endings," 189.

Hooker is right to indicate the information in Mark's prologue as "theological information." One thing that Hooker does not mention in her list of information, however, is the indication that Jesus would baptize in the Holy Spirit. Seen through the lens of chiasmus, this is precisely the information that Mark intended to emphasize.

At the center of the prologue lies 1:7–8, the promise of the Holy Spirit. As noted in the Introduction, the center of a chiasmus indicates a structural spotlight on this segment of the text. We will come back to this center after looking at how the other layers correspond to each other, and the context that they provide for this central text.

The outer sections (**A** and **A`**) refer to the "good news", **A** refers to Mark's entire narrative as the beginning of the good news of Jesus, **A`** refers to the good news of God that Jesus began to preach after John the Baptist was removed from the scene. Because of the verbal parallel of the good news and the relation of 1:15 to the rest of the prologue through the mention of both Jesus and John the Baptist, 1:1 and 1:15 are understood as the outer boundaries of the prologue.

In the next layer (**B** and **B`**), **B** refers to a scriptural eschatological promise that a messenger would come as a voice in the wilderness to prepare the way for the Lord, and **B`** describes a spiritual battle played out in the wilderness between Jesus and Satan, with the help of angels for Jesus. The apocalyptic type of language in **B`**—being *thrown* out by the Spirit, a spiritual battle between the Son of God and evil, and a reference to the wild beasts—could remind the audience of the eschatological salvation that God has promised in the texts referred to in section **B**. Later in the narrative (in Mark 3), section **B`** will prove to be a foreshadow of the statement of Jesus regarding the necessity of binding the strong man before his house could be plundered, and Jesus's inference that it is by the Holy Spirit himself that he casts out demons.[30] The two sections of this layer correspond to each other with the verbal echo of the wilderness, and by presenting salvation on the one hand and the struggle inherent to its coming on the other. This is a theme that is central to the Jewish story of the Exodus, and one that will prove to be central to Mark's message.

The inner layer (**C** and **C`**) is bound together by the content centering around baptism. Section **C** refers to John as Baptizer, portraying him as one of the prophets—intimating that he is the eschatological prophet Elijah who is preparing the way for the Lord and his salvation. John's baptism is one of repentance and the forgiveness of sins. Section **C`** shows us Jesus being

---

30. See also Collins, *Mark*, 151–53. She notes a similarity between 1:12 and 13 (my **B`**) to Ps 91 (especially verses 11–13) as received at Qumran, where the Psalm was understood in connection with exorcism.

baptized, the heavens opening as the Holy Spirit descends on him and the very important voice from Heaven proclaiming him as the Son of God. We see here the narrative outworking of the center of the chiasmus: on the one hand John baptizing with water, on the other hand God baptizing Jesus in the Holy Spirit. Jesus is at once the receptor of this baptism and the one who comes after John, who will *do* the baptizing.[31]

The center of this chiasmus exhibits the only words spoken by the Markan John the Baptist: "One is coming after me who is stronger than I; I am not worthy to stoop down to untie the chords of his sandals. I baptize you with water; he will baptize you in the Holy Spirit" (1:7–8). Technically, this section forms the hinge between the *promise of salvation* and John the Baptist as the forerunner of the one coming, and the *beginning of the coming of salvation* and Jesus as God's beloved Son. Theologically, it provides insight into what this salvation is all about: the baptism in the Holy Spirit.

Commentators agree that this text refers back to the promise of the outpouring of the Spirit found in the Hebrew prophets Isaiah, Joel and Ezekiel, though without bringing it into the context of discipleship. The parallels with Ezekiel 36:25–27, however, are striking:[32]

> I will sprinkle clean water on you, and you will be clean; I will cleanse you from all your impurities and from all your idols. I will give you a new heart and put a new spirit in you; I will remove from you your heart of stone and give you a heart of flesh. And I will put my Spirit in you and move you to follow my decrees and be careful to keep my laws.

Here we find the water bringing about cleansing and forgiveness, just as John's water baptism of repentance and forgiveness, together with the gift of God's own Spirit. In Ezekiel, the gift of the Spirit of God is directed specifically towards enabling the people to "follow God's decrees and to be careful to keep God's laws." Mark's hearers would know that the ability to obey is the goal of the eschatological gift of God's Spirit. Obedience to God emerges in the narrative as a major concern of Mark's, notably in Mark 3 where, when told that his mother and brothers were looking for him, the Markan Jesus looks around him, and says, "Behold! My mother and my brothers! For the one who does the will of God, that one is my brother and sister and mother" (3:33–34). In Mark 14, in the garden of Gethsemane, Jesus wrestles with his own desires until he can pray, "not what I want, but what you want" (14:36).

---

31. See Hooker, *Mark*, 38–39.

32. Hooker, *Mark*: "the two ideas had already come together in Ezek. 35:25–27, where cleansing is the preliminary step to the gift of God's Spirit" (42).

The identification of a chiasmus in Mark's prologue does not influence the interpretation of the actual information that it gives; it merely indicates Mark's spotlight. The words themselves would be effective for Mark's ideal audience because of their importance to the subject of salvation. Collins suggests that Mark divides this event into two parts: the cleansing through the ministry of John the Baptist, and the filling of the Holy Spirit through the ministry of Jesus. According to her, this is not consonant with Ezekiel where it is presented as one "event" or "process."[33] But is this really diverging from Ezekiel? Both aspects are part of the whole work of God. Ezekiel speaks from the perspective of God; Mark shows God doing this through John and Jesus. But there is a third party in Mark's statement: those to whom John spoke. Mark purposefully includes all three. John prepares the way, Jesus accomplishes it, and all who are repentant will experience it and live out the obedience that is enabled. Mark binds all three parties together in a pattern that will continue to emerge at the foundational moments of his narrative.

The nature of a prologue is to provide information that will serve as a background and hermeneutic to understanding what follows. By highlighting the promise of the Holy Spirit in a statement that includes each of the three parties mentioned, Mark begins his narrative with the implicit promise that the ability to do God's will is in sight. His narrative then illustrates the problem of failure to do God's will in those who do actually want to obey. But the promise of a solution has already been given to the people who had come out to be baptized by John. These are the characters with whom Mark's audience, who have come to listen to the beginning of the good news about Jesus the Christ, will identify.

As Mark's narrative continues, the audience will search for the key that activates the promise given. This search will lead to Mark's following pillar scene, and the teaching moment that it highlights. At this moment, when the demands of discipleship are given clearly, Mark provides once again a reminder that the power to obey will one day be available.

Second Foundational Pillar

Mark's central teaching section is given extra force by a voice from heaven, insisting that the disciples listen to what Jesus has to say. In this scene, Jesus is on a high mountain together with Peter, James, and John. Jesus is transformed before their eyes, his clothing becoming radiant white, and Elijah and Moses appear and begin to converse with him. And then, a cloud

---

33. Collins, *Mark*, 146.

descends on them, and a voice from heaven is heard saying, "This is my beloved Son, listen to him!" (9:7).

As discussed above in chapter 2, these words point to the narrative immediately preceding this scene. Jesus had just announced to all his disciples that the Son of Man must suffer and die at the hands of the elders, chief priests, and teachers of the law, and then be raised again after three days (8:31). Peter had rebuked him for saying such things—to which Jesus responded with a very sharp rebuke: "Get behind me, Satan!" he said. "You are not thinking God's thoughts, but human thoughts!" (8:32–33). Jesus then pulls the crowd together with his disciples to continue: "If someone wants to come after me they must deny themselves and take up their cross and follow me. For if one wants to save their life, they will lose it, but whoever loses their life for me and for the gospel will save it" (8:34–35).

This is what the voice of God on the mountain is pointing to when it insists that Peter and the others listen to what Jesus, God's beloved Son, says.[34]

According to Mark, to do God's will is to deny oneself and follow Jesus on the way of the cross. And, again, this is precisely what Mark shows the disciples NOT doing in the rest of the narrative. But Jesus embeds a promise within this teaching moment: the final sentence reads, "Truly I say to you, there are ones standing here who will not taste death until they have seen the Kingdom of God having come with power" (9:1). In my interpretation, this is an echo of the promise of 1:8.

In Mark, the power of the Kingdom of God is revealed in service and powerlessness.[35] The height of the greatness and power of the Kingdom of God is found on the cross. As Michael Bird says,

> The crucifixion that expresses the zenith of disempowerment, degradation, and death becomes the vehicle for the expression of the kingdom's salvific power. It is by renouncing power to save oneself that the power to save others is unleashed with formidable force. This is intimated in the ransom logion (10:45) and reaches its stunning climax in 15:31–32 where the high priest and scribes mock Jesus because he is not 'powerful' enough . . . to save himself, and therefore, not a king. . . . However, the same

---

34. See Puig i Tàrrech, "Glory on the Mountain," 160. Though he concentrates on the announcement of the suffering of Jesus rather than on the discipleship teaching moment, he does see these two scenes as clearly connected through both the "six days later" and the words of the heavenly voice indicating that God's will is what Jesus had just been teaching the disciples.

35. See also Brower, "Mark 9:1"; and Bird, "Crucifixion of Jesus."

power that pillaged the demonic realm (cf. 1:24; 3:11; 5:7) is now displayed in the apex of human weakness and suffering.[36]

When Mark uses the term *to see*, he is usually encouraging a salvific understanding. So when the Markan Jesus speaks of some not tasting death until they *see* the Kingdom having come with power, this could be interpreted as meaning that they will not need to give their lives for him (taste death) until they have understood and experienced the power of the Kingdom of God through the crucifixion of Jesus. The Kingdom coming with power need not indicate coming in its eschatological fullness.[37] In Mark the coming of salvation is accompanied by the descent of the Holy Spirit on Jesus, enabling him to live according to the will of God. The promise of the Holy Spirit in 1:8 is embedded in a narrative of the fulfilment of Scripture as people come for baptism to John with repentance. Salvation is understood as the baptism in the Holy Spirit. When Jesus, in 1:15, announces the nearness of the Kingdom of God, he is announcing salvation and the fulfilment of Ezekiel 36:27 of which John spoke in 1:8. The *power* of the Kingdom of God is the *power* to obey God. Mark 9:1 points towards an understanding of the crucifixion of Jesus as the decisive moment of the availability of the Holy Spirit, confirmed in the tearing of the temple curtain (as we will see below), and echoing the promise of 1:8.

A look at 9:1 in its narrative context may elucidate this interpretation.[38] Verbal indicators in the teaching moment from 8:34b–9:1 suggest a concentric pattern to at least 8:35–38. This is represented in the schema below as **B X B`**, with the emphasis indicating the Greek verbal parallels.

- A   "If someone wants to come after me they must deny themselves and take up their cross and follow me" (8:34b).

- B   "For if one (ὃς γὰρ ἐὰν) wants to save their life, they will lose it, but whoever loses their life for me and for the gospel will save it" (8:35).[39]

- X   "For what (τί γὰρ) good is it for you to gain the whole world, yet forfeit your life (τὴν ψυχὴν αὐτοῦ)?

  For what (τί γὰρ) can you give as exchange for your life (τὴν ψυχὴν αὐτοῦ)?" (8:36, 37).

36. Bird, "Crucifixion of Jesus," 31.

37. See chapter 8 below, and the discussion of the context of Mark 13:26.

38. Brower, "Mark 9:1," 32.

39. Here and elsewhere when referring to an unidentified person regardless of gender, I have translated the Greek masculine singular pronoun with an English "they," taking a singular verb to avoid unnecessary gender implications.

B` "For if one (ὃς γὰρ ἐὰν) is ashamed of me and my words in this adulterous and sinful generation, the Son of Man will be ashamed of them when he comes in his Father's glory with the holy angels" (8:38).

A` "Truly, I say to you, there are those standing here who will not taste death until they see the Kingdom of God having come with power" (9:1).

This chiasmus revolves around the need to give up one's life in order to follow Jesus. The center is comprised of two rhetorical questions, tied together by verbal parallels at the beginning and at the close of the questions and by their content. Layer B corresponds to layer B` with again a verbal parallel and a parallel in content. B` paints a vivid picture of the first half of B: "those who want to save their life will lose it": when these people choose their life and deny Christ instead of admitting to be a follower and dying for it, they will in turn be "denied" when the Son of Man returns in glory. The positive side of B is not mentioned in B`, but is, however, implicitly present in the mention of the Son of Man. For, as will be discussed in chapter 8 below, the Son of Man represents the ones who were faithful in the face of persecution.

And now we turn to the layer A and A`. This layer is not bound by a similar verbal parallel. But it is clearly part of this teaching moment. Section A provides a forceful introduction to the teaching, telling the extent of what it means to follow after Jesus: Jesus provides the pattern for those who follow in his suffering and death.[40] A` provides a conclusion to the teaching moment. The solemn introductory words to the conclusion (καὶ ἔλεγεν αὐτοῖς· ἀμὴν λέγω ὑμῖν) indicate its importance.[41] The Markan Jesus proceeds to say that there were those standing there who would not taste death until they had seen the Kingdom of God come with power. If this statement is understood to indicate that the parousia would come while some of those listening were still living, then Mark was mistaken. This is thus also the conclusion of some commentators.[42]

---

40. Mark's ideal audience would be aware that Jesus had died through crucifixion.

41. Hooker, Mark, 211.

42. See ibid., 211–13. Hooker warns against forcing an interpretation merely because one does not "dare" admit that Jesus could have been mistaken. She suggests that Jesus was mistaken, and that this is a logical possibility in relation to the human limits inherent in the doctrine of the incarnation. However, she also sees the essence of this text as an encouragement to Christians that "God's final intervention was at hand" (212). In light of the persecution facing the Christians, the followers of Jesus "could take comfort from his assurance that, whatever tribulations might lie in store, the Kingdom of God would eventually be established" (213).

But Mark was not mistaken about a time frame.[43] As Brower and Bird both argue, his focus is elsewhere.[44] His writing is theological here. In no uncertain terms, the Markan Jesus spells out that those who want to save their lives, and do not let go of them in order to hold to the confession of Jesus, will lose them. This is exactly what we see the disciples doing as the crucifixion of Jesus becomes reality. Mark's message is that it is impossible for humans to be saved in light of this demand (10:27a). If layer **B`** forms the end of the story, with the news that the end were coming quickly, this would not be good news. But the Markan Jesus's message is also that with God all is possible (10:27). Those that lose their lives will save them (**A**), but in order to do so the followers will need the help of God himself. In Gethsemane, Mark demonstrates through Jesus how to remain faithful: "Watch and pray so that you will not fall into temptation. The spirit is willing, but the body is weak" (14:38).[45] He also demonstrates how not to: the disciples fall asleep rather than pray, and flee when Jesus is arrested (14:39–41, 50).

If **A`** corresponds to **A**, it could be indicating the positive counterpart of the scenario painted in **B`**: they will indeed lose their life and thereby gain it, for they would have seen and understood the crucifixion of Jesus, and have received power to obey by the Holy Spirit. This will be the scenario which is painted clearly in 13:11. When brought to trial, the Holy Spirit will provide the words to say. The followers who see and understand what is happening at the moment of Jesus's deepest service (cf. 10:45) would experience the Kingdom of God coming with power. The time frame in which the followers would see would in any case be before they are faced with the opportunity to take up their cross, and to give their life. Interpreted in this way, 9:1 echoes the promise given in 1:8 regarding the Holy Spirit. The eschatological promise of the Holy Spirit would enable God's people to live according to his laws. In Mark, Jesus is presented as God's "law" (cf. 9:7).[46] To live according to this law is to follow Jesus on the way of the cross. We will see that at Mark's third pillar moment, the fulfilment of this promise is reflected once again.

---

43. See also Brower, "Mark 9:1," 39.

44. See Brower, "Mark 9:1," and Bird, "Crucifixion of Jesus," throughout.

45. In light of my argument, the "spirit" in 14:38 very likely refers both to the Spirit of God, willing to enable, and to the willing human spirit that is unable to be stronger than the human body and its desires. Cf. Collins, *Mark* (681), and Hooker, *Mark* (349), who interpret it as referring to the human spirit.

46. See the discussion above.

Third Foundational Pillar

Moving on to the third pillar of Mark's narrative, we come to the scene of the cross. After experiencing the failure of the disciples to hold true to their intent to stand by Jesus even in the face of death, and realizing the promise of power in the powerlessness of the cross promised in 9:1, Mark's hearers will be alert when hearing the narration of the crucifixion.

The depth of the narrative lies in the heart-cry of the Markan Jesus: "My God, my God, why have you forsaken me?!" (15:34). The pain of the moment is heightened, if possible, by the blatant and crude misunderstanding narrated immediately after the cry. The bystanders misunderstand Jesus's words and think he might be calling out to Elijah to take him down from the cross. Some want to give him some vinegary wine on a sponge, and suggest they leave him alone to see if Elijah actually does come. Jesus cries out again, and releases his spirit. The temple curtain is torn from top to bottom, and a Roman centurion standing near sees him die, and exclaims, "surely this man was the Son of God."

This death scene is narrated in the form of a chiasmus.[47] The corresponding layers indicate the different actors in the scene: God, Jesus, and the bystanders. **D** forms a conclusion to the scene, and exhibits the centurion as the actor.

> **A** And at the sixth hour, darkness came over the whole earth until the ninth hour (15:33).
>
> **B** At the ninth hour Jesus cried out in a loud voice, '*Eloi, Eloi, lema sabachtani?*'—which means, 'My God, my God, why have you forsaken me?!' (15:34).
>
> **C** And when some of those standing by heard, they said, 'Listen! He calls Elijah!' (15:35).
>
> **X** Someone ran, filled a sponge with sour wine, put it on a stick, and gave it to Jesus to drink [Psalm 69:21] (15:36a).
>
> **C`** Saying, 'Now leave him alone so that we can see if Elijah comes to take him down' (15:36b).
>
> **B`** But Jesus, letting out a loud cry, breathed his last (15:37).
>
> **A`** And the curtain of the temple tore in two from top to bottom (15:38).
>
> **D** Seeing how he died, the centurion standing opposite him said, 'Truly, this man was the Son of God' (15:39).

---

47. Adapted from Brower, "Elijah," 89–90.

This scene, including the significance of the allusion to Ps 69:21 at its center, will be discussed more fully in chapter 9 on the significance of Ps 22 as background to the passion narrative. In our discussion of the first pillar moment, the pattern that Mark establishes that incorporates John the Baptist, Jesus, and those following was mentioned. Throughout his narrative, Mark has reinterpreted this pattern in terms of suffering. We will discuss this pattern of suffering more fully below in chapter 9. It is enough to note now that this pattern will come to mind as Mark's audience hears mention of Elijah.[48] But this is not all. The mention of Elijah here will also remind Mark's audience of the message of John the Baptist as Elijah *redivivus*: "One stronger than I am is coming after me; I am not fit to bow down and loosen the tie of his sandals. I baptize you with water, but he will baptize you in the Holy Spirit!" (1:7–8).

At the cross, intertwined in the narrative of Jesus's death, Mark reminds his hearers of both the pattern of suffering necessary for them to follow, and the promise of the Holy Spirit who would make obedience possible. The Holy Spirit had descended upon Jesus (1:10), and Mark's narrative shows him preaching, healing and casting out demons while the resistance rises from the religious leaders of the day. The Markan Jesus was aware that his obedience to God would cause resistance and ultimately his death. But, empowered by God's Spirit from the beginning on, he was able to continue to live pleasing God (cf. 1:11; 9:7) and finally was able to face the cross (cf. 14:32–41). Ezekiel 36:27, alluded to in Mark 1:8, had come to its ultimate fulfilment. However, Mark had given his allusion a twist: God's Spirit would come to those longing to be God's people, through the mediation of Jesus. Mark wanted his audience to see their own future scenario reflected in Jesus's death.

With the promise of the Holy Spirit in mind, Mark's audience might also be reminded of another story as they hear the narration of the Elijah misunderstanding. Several scholars have found in Mark's Gospel various allusions to the prophets Elijah and Elisha of I and II Kings;[49] more specifically, an allusion to the assumption of Elijah in Mark's narration of the crucifixion.[50]

---

48. See chapter 9 below.

49. Roth, *Hebrew Gospel*, is probably the most extreme in his thesis that Mark used the Elijah-Elisha narrative as a literary model in creating his entire Gospel. His arguments, however, are not convincing.

50. Brown, *Death of the Messiah*, 2:1101; Daube, *New Testament and Rabbinic Judaism*, 22–23. See also Bligh, "Typology in the Passion Narratives." I disagree, however, with Bligh's contention that Jesus quoted Ps 22 as a "prayer of confidence" (306) and his argumentation is not appropriate for us as he combines references from the Gospels of

Elisha knew that his forerunner was going to be taken away by God. He asked Elijah if he would allow him to inherit a double portion of his spirit, to which Elijah answered: if you *see* me taken up, that will be a sign to you that your request will be granted. Elisha did *see*, and did receive the double portion of Elijah's spirit.[51]

If Mark intended an allusion here, it would reinforce what he had already led his audience to expect. The story of Elisha receiving a double portion of Elijah's spirit after *seeing* him taken up would encourage his hearers to look closely, so that they would see and perceive, and receive the Spirit that was in Jesus.

As we have discussed above, Mark 9:1 indicates that the power to follow Jesus on the way of suffering even in the face of death would come to the disciples as they understand the power of the Kingdom expressed through Jesus's death on the cross. Immediately after Jesus's last breath, the temple curtain tore from top to bottom. For the alert hearer of Mark's Gospel, Jesus's baptism would immediately come to mind: Jesus *saw* the heavens tear open and the Holy Spirit descend upon him, while he heard the voice of God saying that he was his beloved Son, in whom he was well-pleased. Would this opening of the temple indicate to Mark's hearers that the Spirit of God would now descend upon even them? It was through the Spirit that Jesus was enabled to suffer and give his life. Now they, too, would be enabled through the Spirit to follow after Jesus and give their lives in suffering and service.

Mark had provided his hearers from the start with the expectation that his narrative would present the key to understanding the coming of the Kingdom of God through Jesus. His hearers would have been conditioned to look for and expect an offering of the Holy Spirit providing the possibility to obey God and remain faithful to him in giving up all on account of Jesus. The key to understanding which leads to salvation was presented in 4:12 as *hearing* and *seeing*. These motifs are emphasized throughout the Gospel narrative. This is especially clear as Mark uses the blind-healings to represent understanding the necessity of the way of the cross. These aspects would be in the minds of Mark's ideal audience as they hear the markers

---

John, Matthew, and Mark in order to make suggestions as to what the historical Jesus could have meant.

51. Another aspect of the allusion could be the parallels between 2 Kgs 2:2, 4, 6, and Mark 14:29, 31. Elisha insists three times that he will not leave Elijah. He does not, and is there to see him taken up and to receive the double portion of his spirit. In Mark, the disciples insist that they will not leave Jesus, even if it would mean to die with him. However, they do leave him (and Peter denies him three times), and they are nowhere to be seen at the moment when Jesus breathes out his spirit.

that might bring to mind the story of Elijah and Elisha. Immediately after the cry of Jesus when he breathed out his spirit, the temple curtain tore from top to bottom. This same pattern can be seen in the Elisha/Elijah narrative. Elisha *sees* Elijah taken up, and tears his clothing apart. There is no need for the old cloak, for he now has Elijah's cloak. In Mark, at the death of Jesus, the temple curtain is torn. There is no need for the temple building, for the Spirit of God which had once been in the temple and was in Jesus throughout Mark's narrative, is now available for those who *see* and will follow after Jesus. The Kingdom of God has come with power.

Conclusions: Jesus's Death as Enabling the Path of Discipleship

Mark begins his Gospel with the words "the beginning of the good news of Jesus Christ" (1:1). His ideal audience would have been anticipating the coming of the Kingdom of God, which he shows Jesus announce in 1:15, as precisely that good news promised by Mark in his opening sentence. These ideal hearers of his Gospel will have longed for the Kingdom of God to come as God's long-awaited salvation. As they hear the description of John the Baptist, they begin to see that Mark means to describe him as the one coming to prepare the way for the salvation of the Lord. He was the one to come who would prepare the hearts of the people for obedience. And then they hear John's message: that after him, one more powerful than he would come and would baptize them with the Holy Spirit. The Holy Spirit would enable them to do the will of God, a necessity to taking part in the Kingdom of God. This would be good news to the ears of Mark's ideal audience.

However, half way through the narrative, Mark has this same Jesus describe what it means to obey God. This is not clearly good news. To obey God would mean for them to give their lives for Jesus and the gospel. If they chose not to give up their lives in the face of persecution, they would be shamed from the community of God's people. But then Mark's Jesus goes on to promise his disciples, and implicitly Mark's ideal audience, that they would yet experience the power of the Kingdom of God in their lives—before they would taste death. Mark's ideal hearers would slowly be made aware by the teachings of Mark's Jesus that this power of the Kingdom of God is manifested in powerlessness, and in the giving of one's life. The power to give one's life would be found in the giving of life.

And this is what Mark's ideal audience would encounter while they listen intently to the crucifixion story. Jesus is hung on a cross as a righteous sufferer, feeling the depths of despair. His powerlessness is magnified by the retorts of those around him, jeering at him and challenging him to step down from the cross if he is so powerful. But this is the moment of powerlessness—the moment in which Mark's Jesus gives *his* life completely, in obedience to the Father. At this moment, Mark's ideal audience is brought to remember the promise made earlier, at 9:1, that the power of the Kingdom of God—the power to obey, to give one's life, to be powerless—would be seen. Mark's ideal hearers will long for the same Spirit that was in Jesus to fill them so that they, too, will be able to obey and give their lives when their time comes to taste death. They will find comfort as they remember the promise from Mark's prologue—that they would receive the Holy Spirit through the power of this Jesus. And as they hear of the tearing of the temple curtain, they will know that now the Holy Spirit is ready to descend into them, just as he had descended into Jesus in Mark's prologue, and had enabled Jesus to give his life.

Mark's ideal hearers just might begin to be concerned for the fate of the Markan disciples, for none of them, besides a few women, were looking on to see and understand for themselves. But Mark is not quite done with his narrative yet, for on the third day the women come to the grave which is empty, and are given a message to pass on to Jesus's disciples: Tell them, and Peter, that Jesus will go ahead of them to Galilee. There *they* will *see* him!

If Mark meant for 1:8, the promise of baptism in the Holy Spirit through Jesus, to provide a solution to the discipleship problem, then this is how Mark's Gospel could be heard. And it would then truly be the *beginning* of the good news of Jesus for his ideal audience, for their own life of obedience to God's will through the Holy Spirit would be just beginning as Mark's narrative closes.

A close observation of Mark's structure leads to an understanding of his message as follows: *Those seeking to obey God, and be a part of his Kingdom, will need to follow Jesus unto death, looking to please God rather than themselves. This is not possible to do as a human. However, with the Holy Spirit, in whom the one seeking repentance is baptized through the death of Jesus, it is made possible.*

Mark's structure has shown us that this is an indispensable aspect of Mark's message of the coming of the Kingdom of God. The disciples failed because it is not humanly possible to follow Jesus in this way. However, they are promised that when they understand fully through the Holy Spirit, they will be able to follow. This provides some answer to the question why they failed within Mark's narrative. However, this also raises more questions. What is the meaning of the relationship between the disciples and Jesus? Those soaked in evangelical reformed tradition might ask how it can then be that God brings his salvation in a way that involves humans so intimately? Does Mark's fast-moving story really intend to communicate such far-reaching theological implications? In what follows, we will look at some aspects of the culture in which Mark prepared his narrative with the aim of understanding the relationship of the death of Jesus to the death of his followers more fully. Mark's ideal readers will have also been seeped in this culture and this will have had influence on their own interpretive process while hearing the Gospel.

Part Two: Relevant Socio-Historical Background to Mark 8:22—10:52

IN PART TWO, WE will be looking at aspects of the socio-historical background in which Mark developed, in the hope of gaining understanding of the coupling that Mark makes of the way of Jesus and those who would follow him. No text is written in a vacuum, and therefore it is vital to the understanding of a text to be familiar with as much as possible of the environment and culture in which it was written.

Mark was written in the first century CE. It goes beyond our purposes to suggest an exact year, but most scholars agree that it was written between the late sixties and early seventies.[1] Discussing her own preference to place the Gospel in the context of the traumatizing destruction of the temple in 70, Morna Hooker states, "whatever one decides on this particular point, the evidence points to a date just before or just after the events of AD 70."[2] One aspect stands out: suffering and death are not merely concepts which one could hold at a safe distance during this time.

We will discuss first a Greco-Roman motif of dealing with this issue, the Socratic Noble Death. Then will we move on to the divine *pathos* as a motif that Mark could have had in mind as he describes the suffering involved in the faithful obedience of Jesus and the disciples. The vehicle that Mark uses to express this motif is the metaphorical family of God. Finally, we will look at Mark's message from the perspective of the martyrs of the early Church. Each of these aspects of Mark's culture will help us to understand how Mark meant his message about salvific suffering to be understood.

---

1. Collins, *Mark*, 14; Donahue and Harrington, *Mark*, 46; Evans, *Mark*, lxiii; Hooker, *Mark*, 8; Lane, *Mark*, 17.

2. Hooker, *Mark*, 8.

4

The Noble Death and the Emotions of Jesus

> *"Take, for example, Scipio, the father-in-law of Gnaeus Pompeius: he was driven back upon the African coast by a head-wind and saw his ship in the power of the enemy. He therefore pierced his body with a sword; and when they asked where the commander was, he replied: 'All is well with the commander.' These words brought him up to the level of his ancestors and suffered not the glory which fate gave to the Scipios in Africa to lose its continuity. It was a great deed to conquer Carthage, but a greater deed to conquer death."*[1]

SOCRATIC NOBLE DEATH ACCOUNTS were presented in Mark's time as examples to be emulated by those desiring to live and die nobly. There are scholars who suggest one or other New Testament death account of Jesus as either falling in the category of the Socratic Noble Death tradition, or as having been at least influenced by this tradition. According to David Seeley, Paul presents the death of Jesus in his letters as a form of Noble Death.[2] Greg Sterling suggests that the tradition of Noble Death fits neatly into the background of Luke's portrayal of the death of Jesus.[3] Mark presents the death of Jesus as a pattern which his disciples ought to follow. Could this indicate that the Greco-Roman category of Noble Death is part of Mark's deliberate background? This possibility warrants a closer look at both the Greco-Roman category and Mark's portrayal of Jesus's death. While we will see that Mark's portrayal of Jesus's death is very different from Noble Death accounts, we will also see that an understanding of the Noble Death

---

1. Seneca, *Ad Lucilium*, XXIV.9–10.
2. See Seeley, *Noble Death*.
3. See Sterling, "*Mors philosophi*."

category does illuminate our understanding of Jesus's death as well as our understanding of the connection between Jesus's death and that of his followers, and how this pertains to salvation in Mark.

Although there are similarities in Mark to Noble Death texts, there are also vital differences. The first question that will need an answer is that of what actually makes up a Noble Death account. A look at Mark's account of Jesus's passion will follow, holding it up to the mirror of Noble Death to see if it fits the pattern of the motif. A short comparison with the passion narrative in the Gospel of Luke may also provide insights into some of the early reception history of Mark's account. This will lead us to some important insights into Mark's purposes in his portrayal of the death of Jesus.

The Socratic Noble Death in Relation to Greco-Roman Culture[4]

In the Greco-Roman world in which the Gospel of Mark came into being, the attitude towards honor and death as reflected in the quote from Seneca at the beginning of this chapter, was a commonplace among the Stoic philosophers. In a letter to his friend Lucilius, Seneca refers to these well-known noble death examples. Guessing that his friend will not be easily impressed, Seneca writes: "'Oh,' say you, 'those stories have been droned to death in all the schools.'"[5] Men who would be wise were admonished to emulate the courage and calmness with which those who had gone before them had faced pain and death.

Socrates was portrayed by Plato as having sent his emotional wife away from the prison where he sat with his visiting friends, casually awaiting the moment when he would be administered the poison which would take his life.[6] Others were praised for having emulated Socrates in their own death: "But why should I not tell you about Cato, how he read Plato's book on that last glorious night, with a sword laid at his pillow? He had provided these two requisites for his last moments, the first, that he might have the will to die, and the second, that he might have the means."[7] Sometimes these Noble Death accounts are just a few sentences embedded in a larger treatise; some-

---

4. The tradition of writing up accounts of the deaths of noble men pertains to a broad category of ancient literature. For our purposes, I will be looking at the category of Noble Death that has been influenced by the accounts of the death of Socrates. My research has included writings of Plato, Seneca, Italicus, Plutarch, and Epictetus.

5. Seneca, *Ad Lucilium*, XXIV.6.

6. See Plato, *Phaedo*.

7. Seneca, *Ad Lucilium*, XXIV.9.

times they are the treatise. But always there is the element of encouraging the other to face suffering and death head on without fear, as Seneca says to his friend Lucilius, "I am not now heaping up these illustrations for the purpose of exercising my wit, but for the purpose of encouraging you to face that which is thought to be most terrible."[8]

This Noble Death category flows naturally from the Stoic philosophy that is reflected in much of the literature ranging from Plato through Seneca and Epictetus and beyond. The opening verses of 4 Maccabees, place this text right alongside the philosophers of its day:

> The subject that I am about to discuss is most philosophical, that is, whether devout reason is sovereign over the emotions. So it is right for me to advise you to pay earnest attention to philosophy. For the subject is essential to everyone who is seeking knowledge, and in addition it includes the praise of the highest virtue–I mean, of course, rational judgement. If, then, it is evident that reason rules over those emotions that hinder self-control, namely gluttony and lust, it is also clear that it masters the emotions that hinder one from justice, such as malice, and those that stand in the way of courage, namely anger, fear, and pain. . . . I could prove to you from many and various examples that reason is dominant over the emotions, but I can demonstrate it best from the noble bravery of those who died for the sake of virtue, Eleazar and the seven brothers and their mother. All of these, by despising sufferings that bring death, demonstrated that reason controls the emotions. (4 Maccabees 1:1–9)

Through the description of the "noble bravery" of these martyrs, the writer of 4 Maccabees desires to demonstrate that "devout reason is sovereign over the emotions." This Jewish piece of literature reflects well the Greco-Roman culture.

A similar attitude is found in a narrative about Regulus, told by Silius Italicus. He describes Regulus's former companion Marus tending the battle wounds of Serranus, Regulus's son. Marus tells Serranus how his father, while marching back to the ship that would take him to certain death, had calmly requested that Marus keep him from any signs of affection from his young wife and children. Upon hearing this story, Serranus broke down and spoke "with a deep groan and starting tears."[9] The young man, now grown, could not understand why his father had left his family without so much as a kiss or a hug ("How much lighter my present wounds would be, had I

---

8. Ibid., XXIV.9.
9. Italicus, *Punica*, 313.

been allowed to carry to the grave the undying memory of your embrace, O worshipful father!"[10]). In answer, Marus continued his story of Regulus's heroic decisions and actions, ending with:

> Nor would I essay to tell you how the people of Carthage behaved with the cruelty of wild beasts, if mankind had ever seen in any part of the world a nobler example than was set by the splendid courage of your father.... You too, dear youth, must still think yourself worthy of such a glorious descent, and check those starting tears.... Weep no more, young man. That endurance is greater than all triumphs. His laurels will be green throughout the ages, as long as unstained Loyalty keeps her seat in heaven and on earth, and will last as long as virtue's name is worshipped.[11]

Serranus is finding it difficult to bear his battle wounds. To encourage him, and help him to face his own suffering, Marus holds up his father's courage and *Noble Death* to him as an example to emulate. The idea of an embrace, a kiss, or a touch, through which perhaps courage might pass from father to son, is suggested by Serranus as an alternative to the rational refusal to show emotion, and is quickly brushed aside by Marus. The rational victory over the emotions is presented as the ideal of courage. A Noble Death is an *apathetic* death.

Epictetus is recorded as teaching his students what it means to be noble with the example of Diogenes:

> "It is difficulties that show what men are.... And now we are sending you to Rome as a scout, to spy out the land. But no one sends a coward as a scout, that, if he merely hears a noise and sees a shadow anywhere, he may come running back in terror and report, 'The enemy is already upon us.' So now also, if you should come and tell us, 'The state of things at Rome is fearful; terrible is death, terrible is exile, terrible is reviling, terrible is poverty; flee, sirs, the enemy is upon us!' we shall say to you, 'Away, prophesy to yourself! Our one mistake was that we sent a man like you as a scout.'
>
> Diogenes, who before you was sent forth as a scout, has brought us back a different report. He says, 'Death is not an evil, since it is not dishonourable'; he says, 'Ill repute is a noise made by madmen.' And what a report this scout has made us about toil and about pleasure and about poverty! He says, 'To be naked

---

10. Ibid.
11. Ibid., 321.

is better than any scarlet robe; and to sleep on the bare ground,' he says, 'is the softest couch.' And he offers as a proof of each statement his own courage, his tranquillity, his freedom, and finally his body, radiant with health and hardened. 'There is no enemy near,' says he; 'all is full of peace.'"[12]

The Noble Death motif cannot be separated from the honor-shame culture in which it flourished. Just as important as living a noble life, was dying a noble death.[13] A rational control over one's emotions was an essential characteristic of people deserving of honor. As Plutarch writes: "But the disposition of the wise man yields the highest degree of calm to his bodily affections."[14] To show oneself afraid of pain and death was shameful.

It was against this cultural background that Celsus wrote his treaty against Christianity. In *Against Celsus*, Origen takes up the challenge of refuting this work. Origen quotes Celsus as writing:

> ... how much better it would have been if you had chosen as the object of your zealous homage some one of those who died a glorious death, and whose divinity might have received the support of some myth to perpetuate his memory! Why, if you were not satisfied with Hercules or Aesculapius, and other heroes of antiquity, you had Orpheus, who was confessedly a divinely inspired man, who died a violent death. But perhaps some others have taken him up before you. You may then take Anaxarchus, who, when cast into a mortar, and beaten most barbarously, showed a noble contempt for his suffering, and said, "Beat, beat the shell of Anaxarchus, for himself you do not beat,"—a speech surely of a spirit truly divine.... What saying equal to these did your god utter under suffering? If you had said even of the Sibyl, whose authority some of you acknowledge, that she was a child of God, you would have said something more reasonable. But you have had the presumption to include in her writings many impious things, and set up as a god one who ended a most infamous life by a most miserable death. How much more suitable than he would have been Jonah in the whale's belly, or Daniel delivered from the wild beasts, or any of a still more portentous kind![15]

---

12. Epictetus, *Discourses*, 1.24.
13. Droge and Tabor, *Noble Death*, 18.
14. Plutarch, "On Tranquility of Mind," 476, 231.
15. Origen, *Against Celsus*, VII.53. While both Celsus (second century CE) and Origen (third century CE) are later than the Gospel of Mark, the literature from just before and during the first century CE reflects the same deep cultural value for the

Origen, interestingly, does not proceed to refute the idea that honor is to go only to those who bear up under suffering. That idea is treated as a given. His arguments for Jesus's honor agree with this culture. They are based on Jesus's silence to his accusers and his eventual acceptance of the suffering due to come his way, as he carefully avoids mention of Jesus's fear or incessant desire to avoid the pain that lie before him. Indeed, he even agrees that Celsus is right to recognize Anaxarchus as noble![16]

This example demonstrates the wide acceptance of this cultural definition of nobility. Paul Middleton points out that while some ancient Christian writers used the Noble Death ideal to accentuate the greatness of the martyrs (notably, John Chrysostom, *Homily IV on I Cor. 1.18–20* and Tertullian, *Ad Martyras* 4), pagan writers actually point out the despicable emotional behavior of these Christian martyrs.[17] While some of these examples have been taken from the centuries following Mark, they portray the same attitude towards the showing of emotion that are described by Plato (around 427–347 BCE) in his narration of the death of Socrates.[18] The preference for a rational victory over emotions in Mark's cultural environment should be taken into consideration in any discussion of Mark's passion narrative.

David Seeley, in *Noble Death: Graeco-Roman Martyrology and Paul's Concept of Salvation*, describes five characteristics of a Noble Death: vicariousness, obedience, a military setting, the overcoming of physical vulnerability, and, in some instances, the presence of sacrificial metaphors. Seeley writes that where at least the first four of these five components are present in the portrayal of a death, one can speak of a Noble Death.[19] If we follow Seeley, would Mark's passion narrative fit the mold of a Noble Death account?

Is Mark's Portrayal of the Death of Jesus Meant to Reflect a Noble Death?

Each of the five characteristics described by Seeley are present in Mark's passion narrative. However, Seeley has overlooked the very foundational characteristic of the motif: the stoic rational victory over emotions.

Mark paints a picture of a suffering Jesus who experiences the depths of pain. He shows Jesus "deeply grieved to the point of death" (14:34),

---

rational control of emotion.

16. Ibid., VII.54.
17. Middleton, *Radical Martyrdom*, 120–23.
18. Plato, *Phaedo*.
19. Seeley, *Noble Death*, chapters 5 and 6.

begging God that the cup of suffering be taken away from him (14:36), and screaming out his abandonment by God at the moment of death (15:34). According to the Greco-Roman culture, Mark trespasses on Jesus's honor in two ways in the passion narrative: he allows Jesus to show his emotions of *not wanting to suffer*, and he shows Jesus accepting, albeit with obvious negative emotion, a death on a cross. According to Seneca, it would be more honorable to kill oneself before succumbing to crucifixion.[20] Without attempting to escape from his impending death, Jesus is portrayed as actually being terrified by what lies ahead of him and begging God that the suffering be taken from him.

Stein suggests that the terror that the Markan Jesus experienced was *not* due to the horror of human suffering. He claims that Jesus he had become sin on the cross, and was experiencing God's wrath. However, Mark's narrative does not support this.[21] The Markan Jesus experienced and expressed the depths of human emotions and fear of death.[22] The Noble Death tradition pointed to exemplars who did not allow their souls to be overwhelmed with sorrow, but to those who have the soul of a philosopher, as Socrates says in Plato's *Phaedo*, "bringing about a respite from these emotions, following reason and being always engaged in it, contemplating the truth, the divine and . . . being nourished by it."[23]

If one would take only the five aspects of Noble Death which Seeley mentions and hold the Markan portrayal of the suffering of Jesus up to them, one could find elements of each aspect. That Jesus's death was vicarious, or as Seeley says, a death that is "of benefit to others"[24] can be seen in Mark 10:45, where the Markan Jesus describes his pending death as a

---

20. Seneca, *Ad Lucilium*, CI.10–15. He retorts regarding Maecenas who prayed that he might live, even though it would mean hanging on a cross: "I should deem him most despicable had he wished to live up to the very time of crucifixion" (CI.12). After describing the horrors of crucifixion in detail, he says: "I think he would have many excuses for dying even before mounting the cross!" (CI.14). Droge and Tabor note that Plato recognizes three circumstances in which it would be permissible to take one's own life: "(1) if one has been ordered to do so by the *polis*; (2) if one has encountered devastating misfortune; and (3) if one is faced with intolerable shame" (*Noble Death*, 22). Crucifixion would be "intolerable shame," and could therefore be avoided honorably by killing oneself first.

21. See Stein, *Mark*, 663. Stein supports his interpretation with texts from 2 Corinthians and Galatians, not from Mark's own narrative. To discuss Paul's theological interpretation of the crucifixion goes beyond our purposes here, but in any discussion Col 1:24 ought to be taken into account.

22. Brower, *Mark*, 367–68. Hooker, *Mark*, 348. See also the discussion of Ps 22 in the crucifixion narrative in chapter 9 below.

23. Plato, *Phaedo*, 84b.

24. Seeley, *Noble Death*, 13.

ransom for many. His obedience becomes clear in the divine necessity of his death (δεῖ, Mark 8:31) and his acceptance of the will of God in his prayer in Gethsemane (Mark 14:36). The Romans who did the actual crucifying and the centurion who confessed at Jesus's death that he was indeed the Son of God (Mark 15:39) provide the military context.[25] The aspect of overcoming physical vulnerability is present in the garden where Jesus stays awake and prays in contrast to his weary companions (Mark 14:36). The sacrificial aspect can be found in the last Passover meal which Jesus shared with his disciples, and the words regarding the cup of wine which they shared being his "blood of the new covenant, which is poured out for many" (Mark 14:24). According to Seeley, if these aspects are present, one can speak of a Noble Death.[26] Does Mark indeed intend to portray the death of Jesus through the motif of a Noble Death?

As we noted above, Seeley has missed a vital element of a Noble Death found in the classic literature of the time: rational control over the emotions. When read against the background of this cultural ideal, Mark's narrative screams out the emotions of Jesus and the shame of the cross. In her article, "From Noble Death to Crucified Messiah," Adela Yarbro Collins points out the atrocities of the crucifixion, and uses Celsus's objections to the Christian faith to illustrate the fact that in the Greco-Roman world, not only would it be unthinkable to portray the Jewish Messiah as crucified, but any show of emotion by a *noble* person facing death would prove him ignoble.[27] It seems plausible to conclude that Mark consciously chose to highlight specifically these unseemly characteristics of Jesus's death. Mark wants his audience to know that Jesus suffered deep pain, loneliness, and shame.

Luke: Early Difficulty with Mark's Portrayal of Jesus's Emotion

We have noted above Origen's reaction to Celsus's argument that Christians honored a dishonorable man. Origen accepted fully the cultural idea that a rational control over emotions is honorable above a show of fear, and he attempts to explain away Jesus's emotions by calling attention to his courage. In the Gospel of Luke, we see a similar movement. Greg Sterling, in his article, "*Mors philosophi*: The Death of Jesus in Luke," compares Luke's passion narrative with that of Mark, and points out several passages in which

---

25. Seeley's category of "military context" does not require that the hero die in war. The presence of military in the narrative account is enough to fulfill this category.
26. Seeley, *Noble Death*, 82.
27. Collins, "From Noble Death," 482.

Luke blatantly differs from Mark. According to Sterling, "the differences between the Markan and Lukan passion traditions are so stark that the specific model had to have been different."[28] He concludes that it is probable that the Socratic traditions influenced Luke's choice of material. Three motifs within the narrative motivate his conclusions: "the Calmness of Jesus," "An Innocent Man," and "A Paradigm."[29] It is especially the first motif, "the Calmness of Jesus," which reflects the difference between Luke and Mark's passion narratives.

In the Gethsemane scene, Luke re-orientates Jesus's struggle apparent in Mark, to become the disciples' struggle, resulting in a much calmer Jesus. He drops texts which reflect a struggle or anguish on Jesus's part such as, "'and he began to be disturbed and agitated' (Mark 14:33); . . . 'My soul is distressed, even to the point of death' (Mark 14:34); and the first part of the prayer, 'If it is possible, let this hour pass from me' (Mark 14:35)."[30] Another change that Sterling points out is that Jesus "falls to the ground to pray" in Mark, while in Luke, he "gets down on his knees to pray" (Mark 14:35; Luke 22:41).[31] Luke also adds little remarks regarding the disciples which point to a struggle on their part: As Jesus moves on to pray privately, in Luke he says to his disciples, "Pray that you are not put to the test" (Luke 22:40). When Jesus finds his disciples sleeping, Luke adds that they were sleeping "out of distress" (Luke 22:45).

One exception to this line of de-emotionalizing the passion narrative, is Luke 22:43–45, which portrays Jesus praying, in anguish and sweating drops like blood, with an angel to strengthen him. This text, however, provides a known textual problem, with mainly Western witnesses who include these verses, and Alexandrian witnesses who exclude them. There have been several scholars throughout the ages (evidence from the fourth century and on) who have wrestled with this, taking position that scribes either added or excluded these verses purposefully.[32] Bart Ehrman and Mark Plunkett make an interesting observation: Luke 22:40–46 forms a chiasmus when the verses 43 and 44 are taken out:

A   On reaching the place, he said to them, "Pray that you do not fall into temptation" (22:40).

B   He withdrew about a stone's throw beyond them (22:41a)

---

28. Sterling, "*Mors philosophi*," 394.

29. Ibid., 395, 398–99.

30. Ibid., 395.

31. Ibid., 396.

32. See Ehrman and Plunkett, "Angel and the Agony," 404–7, for a summary of the evidence for and against the exclusion of these verses.

C   knelt down (22:41b)

D   and prayed, "Father, if you are willing, take this cup from me; yet not my will, but yours be done" (22:41c–42).

C′ when he rose from prayer (22:45a)

B′ and went back to the disciples (22:45b)

A′ he found them asleep, exhausted from sorrow. "Why are you sleeping?" he asked them. "Get up and pray so that you will not fall into temptation" (22:45c–46).[33]

Verses 43 and 44, which show a deep emotional suffering in Jesus, disrupt the chiastic form of this passage.[34] This could support the position that these verses were added later on in Luke's textual history.

Sterling takes the position that the passage is most likely not originally from the author of the gospel because of its inconsistency with the rest of Luke's choices: "If the evangelist penned the episode, he undid what he had just so painstakingly accomplished. . . . The best explanation is that a second-century scribe included it to accentuate Jesus' humanity over against those who might have used the absence of Jesus' emotions in this text to call his humanity into question."[35]

At the scene of the crucifixion, Luke deviates again from Mark's narrative. Instead of the heart-wrenching cry of Jesus on the cross, "*eloi, eloi, lama sabachtani?!*," from Psalm 22:2, Luke has Jesus quoting Psalm 31:6: "Father, into your hands I entrust my spirit" (cf. Mark 15:34–37; Luke 23:44–46). Although he admits to the possibility of other explanations for this change, Sterling sees it as part of the overall removal of any signs of emotional struggle within Jesus.[36]

As we noted above, the stream of philosophers who were greatly influenced by Socrates's death in their ideas of the Noble Death, were clear on the need to, above all, control one's emotions. Sterling quotes from Plato's *Phaedo* in which Socrates states: "The true practitioners of philosophy

---

33. Ibid., 413.

34. This does happen at times, according to Ehrman and Plunkett, "Angel and the Agony." They point as example to Eph 5:28b–33a, with 29a as intruding phrase. However, "[t]here are noteworthy differences between the structural problems of the two passages. . . . Eph 5:29a consists of a parenthetic explanation at the fringe of the chiasm made in the context of discourse; Luke 22:43–44 is a substantive addition to a narrative, an addition that shifts the entire center of gravity of the chiasm away from the focal point of the pericope (Jesus' prayer)," (415).

35. Sterling, "*Mors philosophi*," 396.

36. Ibid., 396–97.

practice dying and death as less fearful to them than for any others."[37] To show any form of anxiety or emotional struggle in the face of death was a proof of cowardice to these philosophers. If Luke were to portray Jesus in emotional turmoil, he would be portraying a coward in the context of the Greco-Roman cultural ideal of a Noble Death. Instead, he chose to eliminate those remarks that Mark used in his passion narrative which were not appropriate to the cultural ideal.

Sterling concludes that although Luke did not use the Socratic example explicitly in his passion narrative, he does seem to have used it implicitly, "to remind the hearer/reader of Socrates, the paradigmatic martyr of his society."[38] It is not our purpose to attempt a reconstruction of Luke's reasons for using the Socratic Noble Death as one of the several models for his passion narrative. However, if Sterling is correct, then his view offers an indirect confirmation that Luke chose a different route than Mark, namely to place Jesus's death in a positive—or at least, less negative—light within the Greco-Roman society and time in which he lived.

Mark's gospel was also written in a time when the Greco-Roman philosophers were encouraging each other with words such as those quoted above from Plato's *Phaedo*, and the schools were full of examples of those who allowed reason to rule over their emotions, even in the face of death. Even 2 and 4 Maccabees portray the deaths of the Jewish martyrs Eleazar and the mother with her seven sons in culturally noble terms. Luke chose not to use most of the references that Mark did use to describe the suffering and anguish that Jesus went through leading up to, and on, the cross.[39] If this idea of what an honorable, noble death constitutes was truly such a pervasive part of the culture of the first century CE, then it is reasonable to suggest that Mark also must have made a conscious choice to present Jesus as feeling and expressing the depths of fear and sorrow, and experiencing the shame of crucifixion. To make a conscious choice away from the culture of the day, and to present salvation from God in terms that were embarrassing to his hearers, was a daring choice. The choice to do so, however, may have been motivated by the use of a different motif.

---

37. Plato, *Phaedo*, 67e, quoted by Sterling, "*Mors philosophi*," 397.

38. Sterling, "*Mors philosophi*," 401.

39. Of course, the death of Jesus by crucifixion, however ignoble in Roman eyes, could not be denied by Christians. Luke does not deny that Jesus suffered, but he portrays his suffering in terms comparable to those in a Noble Death account. For more on how Luke may have constructed his *theologia crucis*, see Doble, *Paradox of Salvation*.

The Emotions of Jesus as Related to the *Pathos* of God

A more fruitful context may be found in A. Y. Collins's suggestion that the passion narratives could have been formed with the idea of God's *pathos* in mind as a motif for the portrayal of Jesus with such deep emotions.

The divine *pathos* could provide a way of explaining the death of Jesus in a time when most Greco-Romans would be looking for a rational victory over the emotions as a noble quality in a leader facing death. Collins refers to Abraham Heschel's description of the prophets who portrayed God as a God of *pathos* and explains: "God is not revealed in abstract absoluteness, but in a personal and intimate relation to the world. God does not simply command and expect obedience, but is also moved and affected by what happens in the world. This *pathos* is not irrational, but the result of decision and determination."[40]

The possibility of this *pathos* as a motif for the passion narrative stems from the phenomenon that cultures tend to determine what makes an ideal human being in terms of how they see their god. Thus, a culture with an apathetic view of their god will idealize their heroes as apathetic. But a culture who believes in a god of *pathos*, will produce a picture of ideal humanity as those who experience suffering and pain, and even dare to complain and to pray for rescue as Jesus did.[41]

Collins surprisingly brushes this possibility quickly aside, with the objection being the role of fate in the final hours of the passion. God seems to recede, she says, as the "impersonal force of Scripture controls the events."[42] Even the voice of God which twice in Mark's narrative emphasizes Jesus's relationship to God is replaced by a centurion who announces at Jesus's death that he was surely a Son of God. This forsakenness by God is central to the terror that Jesus experiences in the passion. And yet, as is shown in his prayer in Gethsemane, he freely agrees to face it. Collins concludes that the necessity of portraying the terror of the passion lie not in the *divine pathos* as motif, but in Mark's desire to highlight Jesus's "freely chosen obedience": "The acceptance of the divine will expressed at the end of the prayer suggests that the purpose of the description of Jesus' distress and the request to let the cup pass is to magnify the choice to submit to death."[43]

---

40. Collins, "From Noble Death," 484. See Heschel, *Prophets*, especially part II.
41. Collins, "From Noble Death," 485.
42. Ibid.
43. Ibid., 486.

Collins helpfully notes the freely chosen submission of Jesus. This obedience to God's will above one's own will was described above (in chapter 2) as the essence of what it means to be God's people. However, she might be too quick to suggest that it is fate to which he submits. Mark does not have God recede from the picture as Jesus suffers because of fate. Jesus's submission is to God himself, and to God's Spirit who enables him to obey.

Jesus is portrayed consistently throughout Mark as being in line with God and with his will, not as passively accepting fate. His prayer in Gethsemane affirms this theme in his life as he proves that even in the midst of deepest suffering, he will continue to act together with God and in line with his purposes. God chooses to enter into the deepest human suffering while bringing salvation. And Jesus chooses to have God do this through him. This could be an expression of the divine *pathos*.

The significance of this notion of divine *pathos* is supported by the Jewish principle of solidarity. Rachel Rosenzweig, in *Solidarität mit den Leidenden im Judentum*, claims that though there is a development in the portrayal of the character of God reflected by Israel's thinkers, the portrayal of one characteristic of God which grew consistently stronger over time was "his identification and solidarity with his people."[44] God is a God who goes with his people, not a God who delivers from a distance:

> In order to redeem them, it would not have been necessary for him to go with them. He could have done that from on high, with great display of power. But YHWH is a God who goes with his people, just as Moses went with his people into the wilderness, or as Jeremiah would go with his people into exile.... Moses does not pray for redemption, but for participation, solidarity, that carrying of the burden together (cf. Num 11:12–15).[45]

Mark knits the themes of the identity of Jesus as Son of God and that of suffering together in his narrative. The theme of Jesus as the Son of God is foundational to Mark's basic structure.[46] Through the flow of the plot, the theme of suffering and dying are brought into the intimate relationship of God and Jesus so much so that it is precisely through Jesus's death and suffering that he is finally recognized by another human being as the Son

---

44. Rosenzweig, *Solidarität*, 87 (*translation mine*).

45. Ibid., 92: "Um sie zu erlösen, wäre es nicht nötig gewesen, daß er mit ihnen ging. Das hätte er von der Höhe herab, mit großer Macht tun können. Doch JHWH ist ein Gott, der mit seinem Volk geht, wie Mose mit seinem Volk ins wüste Land geht, oder wie Jeremia mit seinem Volk ins Exil gehen wird.... Keine Erlösung erbittet Mose, sondern Teilnahme, Solidarität, das gemeinsame Tragen der Last (vgl. Nu 11, 12–15)" (translation mine).

46. See chapter 2 above.

of God. It is not uncontrollable fate that drives the plot on in Mark, but the relationship of God to Jesus, Jesus's divine identity. It is because Jesus is *God's Son* that he suffers and dies.

The terrifying suffering of death is, as Collins points out, facing "the great enemy of God" and "to die means to be utterly forsaken, abandoned even by God."[47] The Markan Jesus experiences the depths of this suffering, and cries out on the cross, "My God, my God, why have you forsaken me?!" But this is not a narration of a literal abandonment. In Mark's narrative, Jesus's cry is a cry of emotion, not a movement of plot.[48] He *experienced* the depths of human suffering. Mark has placed his narrative in the context of the Jewish salvation story as reflected in the prophets. In the discussion in chapter 7 below on Isaiah as background to his narrative, we will see that Isaiah portrays God working through servants to accomplish his redemption acts. What his servant does, is done by God. It is conceivable that when Mark portrays Jesus as joining in the suffering of God's people (see chapter 9), it is because God does not retreat from his people in their pain and suffering.

As noted earlier, the rending of the heavens in 1:10 and the rending of the temple curtain in 15:38 likely allude together to the prophetic cry for salvation in Isa 64:1: "Oh, that you would rend the heavens and come down."[49] Mark's allusion to this text creates the expectation that God was doing just that in Jesus, his Son. The announcement from the centurion that Jesus was truly the Son of God after he *saw how he died* (Mark 15:39), supports the idea that the suffering and death of Jesus are meant in Mark to be the saving act of God. God does not recede in the narrative of Mark.[50] Mark, as a talented

---

47. Collins, "From Noble Death," 486.

48. Cf. Heschel, *Prophets*, 57: "How deeply Hosea must have sensed the pathos of God to have been able to convey such dreadful words against his own people whom he loved so deeply. These words, however, were neither a final judgment nor an actual prediction. Their true intention was to impart the intensity of divine anger. And yet that anger did not express all that God felt about the people. Intense is His anger, but profound is His compassion. It is as if there were a dramatic tension in God." In a similar way, this cry of dereliction is an expression of the intensity of suffering and fear experienced by Jesus and need not be interpreted as a literal fact. It is an expression of the *pathos* in the moment, which creates the dramatic tension of the Son of God experiencing God-abandonment.

49. Hooker, *Mark*, 46; Guelich, *Mark*, 32; France, *Mark*, 77; Witherington, *Mark*, 75; Donahue and Harrington, *Mark*, 65.

50. See also Bolt, *Cross*: "In the end, the cross displays 'God with us'" (136) and "God the Son, suffering for the many sinners in this world under the shadow of death, in perfect harmony with Father and Spirit; God, experiencing the wrath of God on behalf of the many" (141). See also Brower, "Elijah," who suggests that the whole death scene is structured to emphasize that this is God's action in Christ: "Rather than being

storyteller, invites the hearers to discover for themselves God's salvific presence in the depths of Jesus's suffering, as did the centurion. Just as God does not recede from the ugliness of suffering, neither do his people.

Conclusions

Mark concentrates on the relationship between Jesus and his disciples when it comes to the cross. Jesus, although he clearly did not want to, accepted death by crucifixion. According to the Markan Jesus, his disciples were to follow his example. This narrative relationship between a dying exemplar and his followers was also found in what Seneca called a *commonplace*: in the Noble Death narratives. David Seeley suggests five characteristics for identifying a Noble Death narrative. If we apply these five characteristics of Noble Death to Mark's passion narrative, we might come to the premature conclusion that it indeed fits within the Socratic Noble Death tradition. However, we also noted that Seeley overlooked the significance of the glorification of the rational above the emotional within the Noble Death accounts. The Markan Jesus is portrayed soaked in emotion to the point of plausible embarrassment to Christians.

While Mark's narrative was formed in the Greco-Roman world of its time, the Socratic Noble Death could not have formed a model for the relationship that he proposes of the suffering of Jesus and the following of the disciple. This was made clear as early as the second century when Celsus wrote his famous attack on the Christian beliefs. Origen quotes him as writing that faith in Jesus as Messiah was ridiculous precisely because he "was shamefully bound, and disgracefully punished, and very recently was most contumeliously treated before the eyes of all men."[51] Jesus's death was regarded by Celsus as not even coming close to being *noble*.

The Gospel of Luke has striking differences when we look at the specific instances where Mark describes the strong emotions of Jesus. Sterling points out that Luke seems likely to have purposefully veered away from several references to Jesus's emotion in the Markan passion narrative in order to portray his death as, at least implicitly, fitting the tradition of the Socratic Noble Death. Collins is even more radical in her study: beginning with references to Greco-Roman sources, she quickly dispenses with any idea of nobility in any of the passion narratives. In searching for a model, or genre, she concludes that the Gospel passion narratives must be doing something new.[52]

---

absent from the death scene, God's action is observable from start to finish" (94).

51. Origen, *Against Celsus*, VI.10.

52. Collins, "From Noble Death," 487.

While the Markan passion narrative, combined with the distinct call to follow Jesus in suffering and death, seems on the one hand to incite the idea of a Noble Death, the glaring emotions of the Markan Jesus quickly eliminate all likeness to these Greco-Roman death accounts. Reading Mark's account through the grid of the Socratic Noble Death tradition even highlights Jesus's emotions. It is the depth of Jesus's suffering in human emotion that separates the Markan passion narrative from Greco-Roman death accounts of noble men. But Mark may have had a more important purpose than to suggest to Greco-Roman ears that Jesus was a noble man.

Collins mentions in passing the possibility of the divine *pathos* having something to do with this uninhibited show of emotion, only to disregard it. Instead, she thinks God recedes in the Markan passion narrative. A closer look at the evidence, however, is justified. The text tells its audience from the beginning of the Gospel that *God is bringing salvation through his beloved Son*. God does not recede from the stage while Jesus suffered and died. He was very present—even in the Godforsakenness experienced by Jesus. Hearing Mark's narrative with the Greco-Roman ideas of Noble Deaths in mind accentuates the human suffering and fear that Jesus experiences. Mark's ideal audience, as we have seen in Part One above, understands that discipleship is part of God's larger salvation narrative. They will also know that their own experience within this narrative is intimately connected to that of Jesus and may be intensely fearful and painful. But an awareness of the Jewish culture of solidarity may also inform their understanding. The very depths of emotion and shame that the Markan Jesus experiences may actually form a reflection of God's presence. God was known to be a God who went with his people in bringing salvation. The following chapter will consider the divine *pathos* as motif for Mark's portrayal of the suffering involved in Jesus's death and in the following of disciples.

5

The Divine *Pathos*

In all their distress, he too was distressed,
and the angel of his presence saved them.
In his love and mercy he redeemed them;
he lifted them up and carried them
all the days of old.
Yet they rebelled and grieved his Holy Spirit.
So he turned and became their enemy
and he himself fought against them.

Isa 63:9,10

Pathos denotes, not an idea of goodness, but a living care; not an immutable example, but an outgoing challenge, a dynamic relation between God and man; not mere feeling or passive affection, but an act or attitude composed of various spiritual elements; no mere contemplative survey of the world, but a passionate summons.[1]

The Divine *Pathos*

As we have seen above, the intensity of suffering and pain the Markan Jesus experiences shouts out from the narrative, especially when read or heard within the context of the Greco-Roman world of the first century. Mark places his narrative from the beginning in the context of the promised salvation from God. In this chapter, we will discuss how the suffering of Jesus and his disciples—within this context of salvation—can be understood as an

1. Heschel, *Prophets*, 289.

expression of the divine *pathos*. Included in this discussion will be Mark's use of the family metaphor to describe the relationships both between Jesus and God, and Jesus and those obedient to God. The idea of the *pathos* of God will be informed by the Jewish belief discussed in the previous chapter that God is a God who goes with his people while saving them.

In stark contrast to the gods of the Greco-Roman world who were self-centered and bound to fate,[2] the God of Israel is portrayed throughout Scripture as a God who is intimately involved in the business of people. Isaiah claims that Yahweh loves his people, and his actions are influenced by intimate interaction with them. Though anger, happiness, the aching of betrayed love, and hurt are words that describe human feelings, these portray a quality of life that is moved by a loving relationship with another. Although, as the prophet Isaiah says, the thoughts and ways of God are higher and different from those of humans, a human image of God painted by the prophets involves these feelings. Rather than use the human description of emotion, this is what Heschel describes as the *pathos* of God.[3] This *pathos* is not fate to which God is bound, nor is it random passionate action, which overtakes him. The divine *pathos* is intentional action, "depending on free will, the result of decision and determination."[4]

Walter Brueggemann describes God's passion as something new that happens in him when the relationship with his people is stretched beyond what is acceptable. At the moment that it would be fully justifiable for God to retract from the relationship, "at the moment of ominous deciding, Yahweh refused to act in self-regard, because Yahweh found in Yahweh's own internal life a depth of devotion to the well-being of Israel that was not, until that moment of crisis, available to Yahweh."[5] God's passion is two-fold, exhibiting a depth of feeling as well as an intense commitment to solidarity: "a propensity to suffer with and suffer for, to be in solidarity with Israel in its suffering, and by such solidarity to sustain a relationship that rightfully could be terminated."[6]

Justice and righteousness are an integral part of who God is. Unlike other gods, the God of Israel is "personally committed" to justice and

---

2. Collins, "From Noble Death," 485.

3. See also Brueggemann, *Theology*; and Fretheim, "Theological Reflections." Schlimm ("Different Perspectives on Divine Pathos") discusses nuance differences between Brueggemann, Fretheim, and Heschel, but he notes that each agrees that God is affected or moved by his relationship with his people.

4. Heschel, *The Prophets*, 290.

5. Brueggemann, *Theology*, 299.

6. Ibid.

righteousness.[7] And these are not merely values, but are "God's part of human life, *God's stake in human history*."[8] Justice denotes "not only a relationship between man and man, it is an *act* involving God, a divine need."[9] Because of his intimate involvement with humanity, and the fact that he *is* just and righteous, the injustice and unrighteousness that occur in humanity's relationships are deeply painful for him, and go against his work in history. As Heschel says, "Man's sense of injustice is a poor analogy to God's sense of injustice. The exploitation of the poor is to us a misdemeanor; to God, it is a disaster. Our reaction is disapproval; God's reaction is something no language can convey."[10]

And yet, God does not condemn his people lightly: "Do I take any pleasure in the death of the wicked? declares the Sovereign LORD. Rather, am I not pleased when they turn from their ways and live?" (Ezekiel 18:23). His wrath is led by his *pathos*. He has committed himself to human history, and will bring it to its climax of salvation, even if this involves pain on account of injustice. As Terence Fretheim says, "God's anger . . . is always exercised in the service of God's more comprehensive *salvific* purposes for creation."[11]

The salvation narrative in Scripture is full of suffering. The prophets portray the anguish of God when his people do not obey. But the narrative also portrays the suffering of God's people. In Isaiah, God uses servants to bring about his salvation, and they suffer painful resistance in doing so. In the dream of Daniel, the people of God suffer greatly at the hand of the beastly leaders. In the Psalms, righteous sufferers cry out to God for vindication. In Part Three below, these three instances will be discussed more fully in their own context as background to Mark's salvation narrative.

This study is concerned with the suffering that is portrayed by Mark as belonging to a faithful obedience to God. I will argue in this chapter that the pain and suffering that Jesus and the disciples experience is an expression of God's *pathos* in his determination to bring salvation to this world. The relational context that Mark provides for God, Jesus and the disciples is the metaphorical family of God. This family metaphor could provide a natural vehicle through which to portray Jesus and the disciples in terms of God's *pathos*. According to Brueggemann, "[i]t is not surprising . . . that the rhetoric required to narrate such a new emergent in Yahweh's own life requires

---

7. Heschel, *Prophets*, 255.
8. Ibid., 253 (emphasis in original).
9. Ibid. (emphasis in original).
10. Ibid., 365.
11. Fretheim, "Theological Reflections," 25 (emphasis in original).

the metaphors of relationship between husband and wife and between parent and child, for no other images carry such intensity, both positive and negative."[12] Perhaps Mark also, fully consistent with the Jewish tradition, reaches to the intensity of family relationships to describe the expression of God's Spirit in his commitment to bringing salvation. By looking at the evidence of how Mark describes the relationships of God to Jesus and Jesus to disciples, I hope to show that this suffering of Jesus and his disciples is indeed an expression of the divine *pathos*.

Jesus as God's Son

As we have seen in chapters 2 and 3, the relationship that God has with Jesus as his Son is foundational to Mark's whole story. Moreover, the three major announcements that Jesus is God's Son indicate that this theme is intimately connected to Mark's theme of salvation. Although the third announcement is made by a Centurion while the first two are spoken by God, several studies have shown that the first and the last form an inclusio to Mark's narrative, and thereby combine with the central announcement by God in Mark 9 to form this structure of three. The context surrounding all three of the announcements, and thereby the background against which the entire narrative is heard, is the context of salvation. The Markan avenue through which God brings this salvation is Jesus as God's Son.

Aside from the introductory statement in 1:1, the first instance in which Mark's hearers are confronted with the news that Jesus is the Son of God is when God tears open the heavens, the Holy Spirit descends on Jesus, and Jesus hears the voice of God telling him that he is God's beloved Son. Mark's audience is shown that in the spiritual dimensions, there is no doubt about Jesus's identity as the Son of God (cf. 1:34). But to the crowds and the people surrounding Jesus, the Markan Jesus prefers to keep silent about his identity. Mark expects his audience to develop their understanding of Jesus's identity through their experience of him throughout the narrative. To this end Mark provides several clues along the way.

Many commentators suggest that Ps 2:7 is alluded to in God's announcement that Jesus is his beloved Son.[13] In the Psalm, the king of Israel is portrayed as being God's Son. II Samuel 7:14–15 may also significantly inform this allusion.[14] David wants to build a house for God, but instead

---

12. Brueggemann, *Theology*, 299.

13. Hooker, *Mark*, 47; Brower, *Mark*, 60; Collins, *Mark*, 150; France, *Mark*, 80. Witherington, *Mark*, 75.

14. See also Hurtado, "Christology."

God says that *he* will build a house for David (II Sam 7:11). David's son will be the one to build the house for God (II Sam 7:13). In Mark's narrative, just before Jesus arrives in Jerusalem, he passes through Jericho and the blind Bartimaeus calls out to him: "Son of David, Jesus, have mercy on me!" (10:47–48). Later on, in Jerusalem, during a day of debates with the Pharisees and teachers of the law, Jesus poses a riddle: How can the Son of David also be David's Lord? (12:35–37). The Markan Jesus leaves this question unanswered, and doing so, Mark has answered it. Jesus is the Son of David who would be God's Son, whose house would be built by God, and who would build God's house. This is affirmed ironically by the sign on the cross: The King of the Jews (15:26).

Mark's narrative suggests an ultimate fulfilment of this double promise found in II Sam 7: Jesus gathers around himself the true people of God, who together with him, become the locus of God's presence in the world.[15] In other words, as Son, he builds the house of God. By giving his Spirit to Jesus and offering his Spirit to those who follow Jesus, God builds the house of David.

Mark presents Jesus as a human being who does not separate himself from the realities of daily life but joins in and is affected emotionally and physically by others and their choices. He knows both rejection by his leaders and the misunderstanding of those closest to him. He experiences his soul being "overwhelmed to the point of death" (14:34); he is beaten (14:65), bound (15:1), flogged (15:15), mocked, spit upon, repeatedly struck with a staff (15:19), and crucified (15:24). The Markan Jesus is a human being who faces the depths of human suffering.

And yet, without explicitly saying that Jesus is divine, Mark also bestows characteristics of God on Jesus. The Markan Jesus displays a power over sickness and evil spirits, an authority that Mark intimates has been given him by God (11:27–33; cf.1:10; 3:22–30). He also forgives sins, and claims the authority to do so (2:5). He calms the wind and the sea (4:39). Echoing the manna provided by God in the wilderness, he miraculously multiplies loaves and fish to feed thousands (6:41–43; 8:6–8). And, perhaps most confounding of all, he walks on water[16] and refers to himself with *I am*, echoing God's self-reference (6:48–50).[17] In Mark 10, when the rich man falls to his knees before Jesus, and calls out "Good teacher, what must I do to obtain eternal

---

15. See Brower, "Holy One," 57–75.
16. Cf. Job 9:8.
17. See also Brower, "'Who Then Is This?'" 295–96; Guelich, *Mark*, 351; Donahue and Harrington, *Mark*, 213; and Witherington, *Mark*, 221. Hooker, *Mark*, 170; and Lane, *Mark*, 235–37, recognize various ways of interpreting this, but find the divine reference likely, or at least appropriate to the context. But contra France, *Mark*, 273n71.

life?", the Markan Jesus responds with "Why do you call me good? No one is good except God alone" (10:17–18). This may be Mark's way of triggering his audience to consider why indeed Jesus is portrayed as having characteristics of God. Hooker suggests that while the Fathers often explained this verse as pointing towards Jesus's divinity, this interpretation is a by-product of doctrinal issues at the time of the Fathers themselves, and not relevant to Mark's message.[18] Whether or not it reflects doctrinal issues current to the time of the Fathers, however, such an interpretation also reflects Mark's own purposes in presenting Jesus as God-with-us.

True to his style, Mark is not interested in making dogmatic statements about the nature of Jesus. By characterizing Jesus as God's Son, and developing this characterization to include both intensely human characteristics and divine characteristics, he has done more than a dogmatic statement could do. He invites his audience to discover for themselves that the human Jesus is the Son of God, bringing God's promised salvation as a human being *and* as God-with-us.

This aspect of Jesus as God-with-us being a part of Mark's characterization of Jesus as the Son of God will need to be discussed more fully. But first we will look at another aspect of the family metaphor in Mark that is of direct relevance to the question of how Jesus relates to the disciples and their obedience or disobedience to God.

The Disciples as Jesus's Brothers and Sisters

Mark portrays Jesus consistently in relationship with his disciples. The first action of the Markan Jesus was to call the two sets of brothers to follow him (1:16–20). In 3:14–15 (cf. 6:7) he appoints twelve followers to share his unique authority. Just as Jesus's ministry consisted of preaching, driving out demons, and anointing and healing many sick people, so did their ministry (6:12–13; cf. 1:34, 38).

As we have already seen, Mark's narrative is highlighted by the insistence that Jesus's followers also share in his suffering. Sandwiched between the commission of the disciples to go out and minister in Jesus's pattern of teaching, healing and casting out demons (6:7–13), and their return to report all they had taught and done (6:30), is the story of the beheading of John the Baptist (6:14–29). While it is common to see this story as

---

18. Hooker, *Mark*, 241. Cf. France, *Mark*, 402, and Witherington, *Mark*, 282. For recent studies on the early worship of Jesus and it being consistent with Jewish monotheism, see Bauckham, *God Crucified*, and Hurtado, *Lord Jesus Christ*.

pointing forward to the death of Jesus,[19] it also points to a pattern that is to include the disciples. But not all agree on why Mark placed it exactly here, interposed within the commissioning of the disciples. Although Hooker says that it is inserted artificially at this spot without reason,[20] I think that Mark purposefully interposed this story within the story of the disciples' ministry to also point forward to what lies before *them*.[21] John the Baptist, as the one who came to prepare the way of the Lord (1:2-4), was killed; Jesus who came bringing God's salvation would be killed; and all those who would follow him on the way would be called to pick up their crosses, and to give up their lives (8:34-35). Not only the successful teaching and healing ministry was shared by both Jesus and his disciples, the giving up of their lives would also be shared.

Mark uses the family metaphor in describing this close relationship of Jesus and his disciples. In 3:31-35, the mother and brothers of Jesus come to the house where Jesus was and send someone in to call him. When word gets to Jesus that his mother and brothers are outside looking for him, he answers with "who are my mother and my brothers?" He then looks at "those seated in a circle around him" and says, "Here are my mother and my brothers! Whoever does God's will is my brother and sister and mother."

Although for the family members waiting outside to speak to Jesus, this would have been a very painful thing to hear, the Markan Jesus is not denying all physical family ties here.[22] There are too many passages in Mark that affirm family relationships to permit an interpretation of this text as a denial or denouncement of human family (cf. 5:19; 7:9-13; 10:9).

A closer look at some intratextuality may help us to interpret the meaning of Jesus's words in 3:33-35. This text is part of a larger literary construction. It is the conclusion of a story about the mother and brothers of Jesus who, after hearing that the crowds that came for him were so great that he and his disciples were not even able to eat, come to "take charge of him" because they think he is out of his mind (3:20-21). Sandwiched within this story, is a conversation with the teachers of the law who had come down from Jerusalem (3:22).

---

19. Hooker, *Mark*, 158-59. See also Guelich, *Mark*, 328-29; Lane, *Mark*, 215; France, *Mark*, 255.

20. Hooker, *Mark*, 158.

21. See Edwards, "Markan Sandwiches," 196: "The technique is, to be sure, a literary technique, but its purpose is theological. . . . Moreover . . . *the middle story nearly always provides the key to the theological purpose* of the sandwich. The insertion interprets the flanking halves" (emphasis in original).

22. See also Ahearne-Kroll, "'Who Are My Mother and My Brothers?'" 19; and Barton, *Discipleship and Family Ties*, 122.

These teachers accused Jesus of being possessed by Beelzebub, and of driving out demons by the prince of demons himself (3:22). Jesus answered their accusation in parable form, saying that a house or kingdom cannot stand if divided against itself; the house of Satan was being plundered now because Satan was bound. He went on to accuse them of blaspheming against the Holy Spirit,[23] which was an eternal sin.[24]

Further on in Mark's narrative, when Jesus and his disciples come into Jerusalem, he is again in conflict with these same teachers of the law (see 11:27; the ones in Galilee in 3:22–30 had come from Jerusalem), together with the chief priests and the elders. Jesus tells them a parable of the vineyard (12:1–12), planted by a man and rented out to farmers. This parable reflects Isa 5, in which the vineyard imagery is used in an oracle of judgment against the leaders of Israel. After each servant who had been sent to collect some of the fruit had been mistreated or even killed, the farmer finally sent his own son. The qualifying statement "whom he loved" reflects Mark 1:11 and 9:7 and points the alert listener to the interpretation of the parable. Jesus is the son, and God himself is the owner of the vineyard. This son is in turn recognized as rightful heir and consequently killed by the tenant farmers. After this, the owner takes away the vineyard and gives it to others to care for. The Jerusalem leaders know that the parable is spoken against them (12:12) and, in their anger, they look for a way to arrest Jesus. The irony is that in doing so, they fulfil the role of the tenants in the parable.

These Jewish leaders know that the condemnation described in Jesus's parable is applicable to them.[25] In the conversation that Jesus had earlier with these teachers of the law in 3:22–30, Jesus says in response to their accusations that he has an evil spirit, that whoever blasphemes against the Holy Spirit is guilty of an eternal sin. He does not say directly that they fall into this category, but the conclusion is not difficult to make.[26] The conver-

---

23. Note that "woe to those who call evil good and good evil, who put darkness for light and light for darkness, who put bitter for sweet and sweet for bitter" (Isa 5:20), is part of the oracle against the people in the song about God's vineyard in Isa 5 (cf. Mark 12:1–12). Calling the ultimate good, the ultimate evil is the essence of blasphemy.

24. Cf. Isa 22:12–14.

25. See also Heschel, *Prophets*, 259–60. In the context of Israel as the vineyard of the Lord in Isa 5, he quotes among other texts Hos 5:1, which is conspicuously close to Mark's wording in this passage: "Hear this, O priest! Give heed, O house of Israel! Hearken, O house of the king! For the judgment pertains to you." Mark has Jesus speaking to the religious and societal leaders, who after hearing Jesus's words, "knew he had spoken the parable against them" (Mark 12:12). Jesus, in line with the prophets, is clearly judging the leaders of the people for not leading the people in God's justice and righteousness.

26. Hooker, *Mark*, 117. Cf. Brower, *Mark*, 114–15, 118.

sation is significantly sandwiched by the story of Jesus's family coming to collect him, and Jesus's statement that his family actually consists of those men and women around him who do the will of God. The Markan Jesus does not speak words that straightforwardly condemn these men personally, for Mark's purpose is not to seal the fate of the Jewish leaders. Rather, the Markan Jesus paints a picture that remarkably resembles their attitude, and they respond. These men were teachers of the law. In chapter 2 above, it was noted that in Mark 9, Mark presents Jesus as the embodiment of God's law. Now he communicates the same message from another perspective. Those who do the will of God are defined in terms of their relationship to Jesus; they are his brothers and sisters and mother.

In Mark 10, Jesus uses similar language to that in Mark 3. Here, the context is a conversation with his disciples that flowed out of a conversation with a wealthy man. This man had come to Jesus asking what he must do to be saved. When he claimed to have kept the law since his youth, Jesus challenged him to sell all he owned, give the money to the poor, and to come and follow him. This advice was difficult for the man to take and he went away sad. Jesus then sighed, "How hard it is for the rich to enter the Kingdom of God!" (10:23b).

This statement astonished the disciples. They were puzzled and wondered who could *ever* enter God's Kingdom. Jesus replied that it would be impossible, were it not for God. Peter then reminded Jesus that he and the others had left everything behind to follow him. In response, Jesus tells the disciples that if they give up everything that sustains and informs one's life—family and means of living—they will find that they enter into an even greater family, though they will also encounter persecution, and that they will inherit eternal life.

"Giving up all" is the will of God that ultimately determines who is his child and who is not. The teachers of the law could no longer assume to be God's children if they would not obey him. Mark conspicuously leaves out a reference to fathers in his list of family members that will be received in turn by those who give up all. God alone is Father of this new family. Jesus is his beloved Son, and all who follow him, giving up all for his sake, are the brothers, sisters, and mothers.

What does this have to do with both the cross of Jesus and the path of discipleship belonging to the salvific purposes of God? And with the promise of the Holy Spirit who would make discipleship possible? Mark uses the intimacy of family language in describing the relationship between God and Jesus. But he also uses the same motif in describing the relationship between Jesus and all who obey God. God is Father of this family which is based on doing God's will. He is also the one who through his Spirit makes it possible for the humans to do this will, and therefore *be* members of the family. If this is so, then it is quite possible that Mark expects the family members to take on the mission as well as the identity of the Father. And that includes the divine *pathos*. The suffering of Jesus in God's movement of salvation marks the path of obedience expected of the rest of the family. This salvific suffering is an expression of the divine *pathos*. This conclusion is supported further by the solidarity of family identity expressed in the contested phrase *corporate personality*.

The Family of God: A Corporate Personality

There are two aspects of Mark's use of the family motif that are important to note. The first aspect is the special place that is reserved for Jesus. He is the only one in the narrative directly claimed by God as Son. The other aspect is the prerequisite of obedience to the will of God for the family status of all those sitting around Jesus.

Within God's family, Mark reserves a special place for Jesus. He is not just one of the rest. First of all, he is the only one who is directly claimed by God as Son within the narrative. Mark connects this Sonship of Jesus to the giving of the Holy Spirit (1:10–11). This is also directly connected to the promise that Jesus would baptize in the Holy Spirit (1:7–8). As we have noted in chapter 3 above, Jesus is the only one who lives obediently and pleasing to God through the Holy Spirit during the story time of Mark's narrative. Yet, the narrative also points to Jesus being the one through whom the Holy Spirit would become available to those longing to be obedient. While on the one hand Mark narrates a special role for Jesus, at the same time he indicates that this role has everything to do with the others following Jesus in the same way of obedience and bringing pleasure to God.

It is not clear within Mark's narrative how he intends the divine characteristics of Jesus to relate to the disciples once they are fully obedient. There is no indication that Mark intends the disciples to one day be able to say *I AM* while walking on water. However, Mark does indicate that the faithful followers of Jesus will one day be included in what it means to be the Son of Man (see chapter 8 below) and through Jesus, being "baptized in the Holy Spirit" (1:8), they will one day form together with Jesus the "house for God" (II Sam 7, see above), the locus of God's presence on earth.

The family was an immensely important institution in ancient Israel, central to the identity of all individuals.[27] In his doctoral dissertation, Jur-

---

27. Di Vito, "Old Testament Anthropology" (225), describes the individual as being *embedded* in the family, or the house of the father.

rien F. Mol presents a definition of Corporate Personality in Ancient Israel in terms of the family.[28] Mol is aware of the difficulties with the definition of *Corporate Personality* as developed by Wheeler Robinson in the early 20th century. He observes, however, that the term is still being used and suggests that it should therefore be redefined. His dissertation defines the idea of Corporate Personality in terms of the family.

In 1911, Wheeler Robinson coined the phrase *Corporate Personality* to describe the effects of the phenomenon of Jewish solidarity.[29] His suggestion was that this concept would provide an important key to understanding Hebrew thought. He used the term to describe the thinking of so-called primitive peoples in which the differentiation of the individual is not yet fully developed. Each individual gains his or her identity from the group, whether present or throughout time, in such a way that to think of oneself as an individual could be likened to thinking that a human arm was an entity of its own separate from the body. Though the individual was aware of being just one person, living his or her own life, the corporate, not the individual, forms the personality. Yet, each individual could also act as a representative of the whole: "The whole group, including its past, present, and future members, might function as a single individual through any one of those members conceived as representatives of it."[30]

So many scholars had at one point taken over Robinson's concept that J. R. Porter was led to remark in 1965 that it had become somewhat of a commonplace in scholarship.[31] However, as noted above, the concept also began to attract serious criticism. J. W. Rogerson proposed to drop the term altogether.[32] Robinson based at least part of the concept on anthropological studies of Lucien Lévy-Buhl which, by the time of Rogerson, had been outdated and critiqued by more sophisticated investigations.[33] Moreover, according to Rogerson, the tension between the individual and the community in several aspects of Hebrew thought which Robinson sought to ease with his concept, does not need to be explained as a symptom of primitive mentality.[34]

---

28. Mol, "Collectieve en Individuele Verantwoordelijkheid."

29. Robinson, *Christian Doctrine of Man*, 8.

30. Robinson, "Hebrew Conception of Corporate Personality," 25.

31. Porter, "Legal Aspects," 361. See also Kaminsky, *Corporate Responsibility*, who states that the term became somewhat of a cure-all to patch up "a host of interpretive problems in the Hebrew Bible" (17).

32. Rogerson, "Hebrew Conception," 14.

33. Ibid., 9–10.

34. Ibid., 15–16.

J. S. Kaminsky, in *Corporate Responsibility in the Hebrew Bible*, argues especially against Robinson's emphasis on the corporate as primitive. He finds, for example, that in various passages in Deuteronomy which show an appreciation for the individual, this is not set against an older appreciation for the communal, but rather elucidates the communal idea.[35] Finding the concept of a corporate personality present in the texts he examines, he argues against dropping the term altogether, and calls for a renewed attempt to "understand the internal logic of these ideas on their own terms," this time, "within a more critical and nuanced reading."[36]

Mol takes up Kaminsky's challenge, and in his study of individual and corporate responsibility in Ezekiel 18 and 20, Mol finds a Corporate Personality reflected in the context of the family of God. He suggests that the *family of God*, at least in Ezekiel, is more than a metaphor, it is the basic social structure.[37] While the family at any given time is held responsible as a unit for obedience (to God), within the family each generation is held responsible for their actions and decisions and, in turn, each member is individually held responsible by the head of the household, i.e. the father. The family forms a Corporate Personality, in which both corporate and individual levels of responsibility are active.

According to Mol, Ezekiel 18 and 20 are often seen as either conflicting in their ideas of communal and individual responsibility, or showing a development in Hebrew thought from the communal to a more individualistic view. Mol studies these two chapters and comes to a different conclusion. He finds a concept of a Corporate Personality active in both chapters, but of a different essence than that described by Robinson. The respective roles do not contradict each other, nor do the two chapters show a development in Hebrew thinking from a more primitive collective consciousness to more of an individual awareness. It is within the framework of the collective that the individual is confronted with his or her own responsibility.[38] Mol states:

> The family and the members of the family do not exist separate from each other; the collective and the individual are inseparably bound to each other. The individual receives his [sic] identity from the collective. The concept of personal identity that is mirrored in these texts differs radically from our own in (post-)modern western society. Our modern conceptions regarding the individual and his [sic] individuality with regards

---

35. Kaminsky, *Corporate Responsibility*, 136–37.
36. Ibid., 22, 179–80.
37. Mol, "Collectieve en Individuele Verantwoordelijkheid," 251.
38. Ibid., 243.

to responsibility cannot be applied to the individual within the family structure as it is found in the chapters 18 and 20. Individual responsibility is constituted within the community, namely in the family.... The constituent family structure is the 'reason of existence' of collective responsibility and solidarity. In Ezekiel, this relates to the whole people because of the application of the family structure to the relationship between the Lord GOD and his people, the house of Israel.[39]

Di Vito, like Mol, says that in Ezekiel, "righteousness is defined in terms of the demands which come with membership in the community of Israel."[40] In the Gospel of Mark, we find the same principle reflected: *God's will* "is defined in terms of the demands which come with membership" in *the family of God*.

In Mark, the essence of being a member of the family of God is expressed in the coupled obedience of Jesus and of the disciples in giving up their own will to obey God fully unto death. T. W. Manson refers to this connection in his work on the Son of Man in the Gospels, suggesting that Jesus and his disciples *together* are to be the "remnant that saves by service and self-sacrifice, the organ of God's redemptive purpose in the world."[41] Manson later nuanced his interpretation to include the unique position of Jesus: "We should be prepared to find that this corporate entity is embodied par excellence in Jesus himself in such a way that his followers, who together with him constitute the Son of Man as a group, may be thought of as extensions of his personality."[42] Mark's audience is led to Jesus in order to find God's help in obedience. Jesus is God's Son and representative, and Jesus gathers who ever will, around him to do as he does and be his brothers and sisters and mother. Together they constitute the family of God. But in Mark, it is first Jesus who is the Son of God. It is only together with him, and as we have seen in chapter 3 *through* his obedience, that the disciples have membership in this family.

Mark uses various metaphors and allusions to Hebrew thought and Scripture to elucidate his meaning. While, as Manson states, the use of the term Son of Man encourages us to understand the unity between Jesus and his disciples as being together this "organ of God's redemptive purpose in the world," Mark's use of Isaiah suggests that it is indeed God who is the

---

39. Ibid., 254–55 (translation mine).
40. Di Vito, "Old Testament Anthropology," 225 n33.
41. Manson, *Teaching of Jesus*, 231.
42. Manson, "Son of Man," 191. The corporate aspects of the Son of Man in Mark's narrative will be discussed further in chapter 8.

actor behind the work of his servants.[43] Mark's use of the metaphor of the family of God incorporates both of these ideas. Through his family, God enters into the nitty-gritty of human life and suffering in bringing salvation. The *pathos* of God as Father forms the character of his entire family.

Conclusions

God, as Rosenzweig notes, goes *with* his people while bringing them salvation.[44] Applying Mol's concept of Corporate Personality, the individual follower is called to follow after Jesus and to be a member of that family unit that lives out the Kingdom of God through service and giving oneself in obedience to God even as the deepest suffering is involved. This family of God does not merely reflect God's *pathos*, but is the avenue of God's *pathos*. In the Markan Jesus, God experiences the depths of human suffering while bringing salvation. Those who will obey God and follow Jesus on the path of suffering, do so only through God's Spirit, and thereby join him in this mission. The interpretation of the family of God in Mark as a corporate personality presents us with a dynamic metaphor. As fully obedient Son, pleasing to the Father, Jesus is the expression of the Father in Mark's narrative. As Jesus brings his "brothers, sisters, and mother" into the family through the crucifixion, they, too, begin to reflect the character of the Father.

But there is another implication of the family metaphor as expression of God's *pathos*: his commitment to bring salvation to his people. As Brueggemann notes, the Hebrew prophets used family language in depicting the intensity of God's intentional commitment to the relationship. He also notes that *pathos* entails new depths of commitment that find expression in refusing "to act in self-regard"[45] at the *moment suprême*, when leaving the relationship would be justifiable. In Mark, the disciples together with Jesus are not only the avenue of God's *pathos*, they are the recipients of his *pathos*. At the moment in which they are not able to obey, and abandon Jesus, God offers to them, through the intense suffering of Jesus, his Spirit in order to be able to obey and to thus remain in relationship with him. It is his *pathos* that moves him to do so.

In Mark's portrayal of God's story of salvation, the way for Jesus and those who would follow him is to obey God even unto death. This death, as Mark's audience will be aware, is not meant merely figuratively. Everyone

---

43. See chapter 7 below.

44. Rosenzweig, *Solidarität*, 92. This is reflected in Mark's use of Ps 22, as will be discussed in chapter 9 below.

45. Brueggemann, *Theology*, 299.

who openly comes out for Jesus and his teaching is liable to persecution leading to death (8:38). Mark does not waste words in his portrayal of how difficult this is: it led to extreme fear and agony for Jesus, and finally shameful death by crucifixion. This is not what one would normally expect in a culture where the Noble Death accounts were commonplace. We have discussed that this is an expression of God's way of doing things—his *pathos* in dealing with people. He is affected by people and their actions, and is moved to choose to join with them in solidarity, as he leads them in his salvation story. Mark presents Jesus as reflecting God's character in his identity as Son. In his suffering, he *goes with* his people while saving them, just as God does. As family of God, his brothers and sisters and mother will do the same.

This begs the question: *In what way is this obedience salvific?* The death of Jesus has been observed to be salvific for his followers—seeing and understanding his crucifixion and *how* he died in obedience leads to the baptism in the Holy Spirit as promised in 1:8—but how is the faithful obedience of the followers to be understood in the context of God's story of salvation? A look at some early reception history of the Gospel of Mark may elucidate this aspect of my thesis. Those writing about the early martyrs believed their deaths to be salvific. This will be the topic of the next chapter.

6

Mark and Martyrdom

I write to the Churches, and impress on them all, that I shall willingly die for God, unless ye hinder me. I beseech of you not to show an unseasonable good-will towards me. Suffer me to become food for the wild beasts, through whose instrumentality it will be granted me to attain to God. I am the wheat of God, and let me be ground by the teeth of the wild beasts, that I may be found the pure bread of Christ. Rather entice the wild beasts, that they may become my tomb, and may leave nothing of my body; so that when I have fallen asleep [in death], I may be no trouble to any one. Then shall I truly be a disciple of Christ, when the world shall not see so much as my body. Entreat Christ for me, that by these instruments I may be found a sacrifice [to God].

IGNATIUS[1]

IN THIS QUOTE FROM Ignatius's letter to the Romans, we see a Christian leader longing for a martyr's death. Paul Middleton shows that such radical martyrdom does not represent merely a few isolated instances at the fringes of Christianity during the first few centuries of the Common Era. Christians throughout the Roman Empire were not only persecuted, but many sought to seal their devotion to Christ by actively seeking martyrdom.[2] In this chapter we will be looking at not only how Mark's ideal audi-

---

1. Ignatius, "Letter to the Romans," ch IV.
2. Middleton, *Radical Martyrdom*, especially chapter 1. See also Moss, *Myth of Persecution*, 18. While Moss admits that there were Christians who actively sought death, she does not agree that they were actively persecuted on account of being Christian.

ence was to respond, but also at how some Christians in the first centuries CE may have interpreted Mark's message of the necessity of following Jesus even unto death.

Tertullian, in his epistle *To Scapula*, attempts to warn Scapula (proconsul of Carthage) of the guilt he, and all Carthage with him, had incurred by persecuting Christians. He feels obliged as a Christian to warn him that he will be punished for his sin of persecution, although the Christians, he assures him, are not really sorry for these persecutions. They do not feel constrained in any way to rush into the cruelties as they do, but do so freely: they "even invite their infliction."[3] Tertullian warns Scapula that it is inherent to Christianity for Christians to seek out persecution, for "[y]our cruelty is our glory."[4]

As we have seen repeatedly, Mark is insistent that following Jesus will involve suffering, and to give one's life on account of Jesus and the Gospel, will result in eternal life (8:34—9:1; cf. 10:29–30). To seek out and rush into persecution was an active way in which these early Christians followed Jesus. As is apparent in the quotes from Ignatius and Tertullian above, these Christians considered their persecutions to be a glorious way of proving their discipleship to Christ.

These radical martyrs also considered each of their deaths as a step closer to the victory of God in the cosmic battle against Satan, leading to the fullness of salvation.[5] Is this what Mark had in mind by portraying the suffering of the followers of Jesus as participating in God's work of salvation? To answer this question, we will need to compare the theology presented in Mark's Gospel with the theology behind radical martyrdom. For the theology behind radical martyrdom, Middleton's work will be used. However, the perspective of Candida Moss on martyrdom as *imitatio Christi* will also be considered. We will begin with a closer look at Mark's theology.

Mark's Theology and *Radical* Martyrdom

The Markan Jesus calls all who would follow him to deny themselves, to pick up their cross and to follow after him (8:34). That literal death is included in this call is made clear in the verses that follow: attempting to save one's life will lead to death, but losing one's life for the sake of Jesus and the gospel will ultimately save one's life. The scene is made even clearer in verse 38: "All who are ashamed of me and my words in this adulterous and sinful

---

3. Tertullian, "To Scapula," chapter V.
4. Ibid.
5. Middleton, *Radical Martyrdom*, 79–82.

generation the Son of Man will be ashamed of when he comes in his Father's glory with the holy angels." This possibility would be familiar to Mark's audience. In one of the letters of Pliny to the Emperor Trajan, he explains how he acted in trials of Christians. He would ask the person charged three times if they were a Christian; if they persisted, they were punished. Those, however, who denied,

> repeated after me an invocation to the gods, and offered religious rites with wine and incense before your statue (which for that purpose I had ordered to be brought, together with those of the gods), and even reviled the name of Christ: whereas there is no forcing, it is said, those who are really Christians into any of these compliances: I thought it proper, therefore, to discharge them.[6]

While this quote is from a later date, Mark's ideal audience is aware of a similar procedure. They would be asked if they were indeed Christians, and if they answered positively, they would likely be killed. If they could not stand strong enough under fear of suffering and death and they denied Christ, their life would possibly be saved. To die a Christian meant, however, to enter into eternal life with Christ. To deny Christ in an attempt to save one's life meant to forfeit this true life (Mark 8:35–38).

Mark's words would not be merely figurative language,[7] inferring a daily denial as in Luke 9:23, but for many Christians they would be a de-briefing before they faced their final persecution, encouraging them to choose true life. Just as Moses set before the people life and death, blessings and curses (Deuteronomy 30:19) before they entered the Promised Land, the Markan Jesus was setting the choice between life and death before all who would follow him. In both instances, the choice of true life entails obedience. Moses had given the people the laws of God to follow; Jesus presented the people with himself, and the way of suffering that he would go, as reflecting God's thoughts for their own obedience.

Of course, some may have preferred to be creative in avoiding persecution. Annemarie Luijendijk discusses two documents from the early fourth century CE in which it becomes clear that Christians at times found ways

---

6. Pliny, "To the Emperor Trajan," 10.96. Trajan was Roman emperor from 98–117 CE.

7. See also Collins, *Mark*, 408; Witherington, *Mark*, 244; Contra Robbins, "Intertexture of Apocalyptic Discourse." Combrink agrees with Robbins, and states that Jesus's "teaching on discipleship in 8:27—10:46 is also not related to martyrdom ("Salvation," 55).

to live a normal life despite measures taken to make it difficult for them.[8] One of these papyri is a letter from a man to his wife. He was on a journey to bring an issue involving several acres of land to court. Upon his arrival, he learned that he would need to make a sacrifice before being allowed to proceed in court. This, Luijendijk points out, was consistent with the decree issued in 303 described by Lactantius in his "Of the Manner in which the Persecutors Died": "an edict was published . . . ordaining also that, without any distinction of rank or degree, they [the Christians] should be subjected to tortures, and that every suit at law should be received against them; while, on the other hand, they were debarred from being plaintiffs in questions of wrong, adultery, or theft."[9] The demand that a sacrifice be made at the beginning of court proceedings would ensure that the plaintiff was not a Christian. This specific Christian, however, was creative in how he handled this. He writes to his wife that he found a friend whom he gave the power of attorney who made the sacrifice in his stead. After his friend made the sacrifice, he could go ahead with his own court issues.[10] This practice was known to Peter, Bishop of Alexandria, who wrote the following as to how these Christians were to be treated in the Church:

> And those who have not nakedly written down their denial of the faith, but being in much tribulation, as boys endowed with sagacity and prudence among foolish children, have mocked the snares of their enemies, either passing by the altars, or giving a writing, or *sending heathen to do sacrifice instead of themselves*, even though some of them who have confessed have, as I have heard, pardoned individuals of them, since with the greatest caution they have avoided to touch the fire with their own hands, and to offer incense to the impure demons; yet inasmuch as they escaped the notice of their persecutors by doing this, let a penalty of six months' penance be imposed upon them.[11]

Mark's message of embracing suffering in order to gain life would be pertinent to both deniers and those creative in avoiding punishment. According to the Markan Jesus, those who seek life in the face of persecution instead of carrying their cross and following Jesus would lose their life. Peter

---

8. Luijendijk, "Papyri from the Great Persecution."
9. Lactantius, "Of the Manner," ch XIII.
10. Luijendijk, "Papyri from the Great Persecution," 357, 360–62.
11. Peter of Alexandria, "Canonical Epistle," canon 5 (emphasis mine). See Luijendijk, "Papyri from the Great Persecution," 362.

of Alexandria's decree was more lenient, hoping to provide the impetus to repent so that in a future trial, they might stand firm.[12]

Persecution is presented as a given in all believers' experience. The Markan Jesus does not say, "if it happens that you are faced with death on account of me, be faithful, die and you will receive true life." He *assumes* the moment of choice will come, just as he presents his own pending suffering as "necessary" (8:31). This is also reflected in Mark 13: "You must be on your guard. You *will* be handed over to the local councils and flogged in the synagogues. On account of me you *will* stand before governors and kings as witnesses to them. . . . Brother *will* betray brother to death and a father his child. . . . Everyone *will* hate you because of me, but those who stand firm to the end will be saved" (13:9, 12a, 13). The disciples are not being told that this may happen to a few of them; these things are being presented as the future that they can expect.

Through Mark, the early Christians were enjoined to embrace suffering in order to gain entrance to true life. But does Mark foresee and suggest that his hearers actively seek out this suffering as soldiers rushing into battle at the sound of the battle-cry on the frontline? I think his message reaches deeper than ascribing an internal value to the mere suffering itself. There is a spiritual dimension that is important to Mark; the essence is not the loss of physical life.

The message of the three teaching moments reflects their narrative context, and has to do with relinquishing rights of status, identity, family and possessions, *as well as life itself*, in following Jesus and embracing suffering. Mark's narration of the moment in which the paths of Jesus and the disciples painfully part ways may also be pertinent to understanding the essence of this obedience. In Gethsemane, Jesus pulls himself aside from his disciples and prays. He does *not* want to suffer and die, yet he prays that God's will be done anyway. He also enjoins his disciples to pray so that they do not fall to temptation. But they do not pray. And they do fall away because they are not able to act against their desire to live. To Mark's reader this is a vivid illustration of the conversation that Jesus had with his disciples in chapter 10, immediately following the conversation with the rich man seeking the way to eternal life. Who can be saved? With man, it is impossible. But all things are possible with God (10:26–27). Jesus chose to pray, to ask God for help, and he remained faithful. The disciples did not, and they fell away.

We have discussed above (see especially chapter 4) Mark's choice to portray the depths of human suffering and fear in Jesus at this crucial moment. In doing so, Mark highlights his very basic human desire for life;

---

12. See Peter of Alexandria, "Canonicial Epistle," canons 6–8.

Jesus did not want to suffer and die. And yet, after praying, he was able to allow God's will to happen in spite of his own will. The essence of the Markan message of obedience to God is illustrated here: "not what *I* want, but what *you* want" (14:36). And this can only happen through the help of God. It was not for the sake of dying that Jesus was faithful; it was for the sake of doing God's will.

Mark's message of following Jesus has more to do with the outworking of the depths of obedience to God than with seeking death for the sake of martyrdom. To Mark, the Kingdom of God is the goal of salvation (cf 1:15). And the Kingdom of God is there where God's will is done. Mark tells his hearers that this obedience to God will lead to death for many, if not all, of those who wish to follow Jesus; and its true expression will be faithfulness at such a moment. But he does not line up his hearers to seek out martyrdom for the sake of martyrdom.

Mark and Salvific Suffering in the Cosmic Battle

According to Middleton, the Gospel of Mark lends itself to being interpreted in a way that is conducive to radical martyrdom. These radical martyrs, he says, saw their deaths as contributing to the cosmic battle between God and Satan. And Mark's theology emphasizes this cosmic conflict, encouraging the choice to position oneself on the side of God.[13]

In this cosmic battle, final victory would be contingent on a certain number of martyrs. This is reflected in Revelation 6:9–11:

> When he opened the fifth seal, I saw under the altar the souls of those who had been slain because of the word of God and the testimony they had maintained. They called out in a loud voice, "How long, Sovereign Lord, holy and true, until you judge the inhabitants of the earth and avenge our blood?" Then each of them was given a white robe, and they were told to wait a little longer, until the number of their fellow-servants and brothers and sisters who were to be killed as they had been was completed.

By purposefully seeking a martyr's death, each disciple would be adding to the number needed that would bring the time of persecution to an end and issue in the Day of Judgement. Each confrontation was seen as a contest with Satan; each death brought God's final victory one step closer.[14]

---

13. Middleton, *Radical Martyrdom*, 151.
14. Ibid., 128: "Some even desired to suffer hardship and death as a means of

Middleton's arguments rely heavily on what he sees as an indication of the cosmic war in Peter's rebuke of Jesus in 8:32. The Markan Jesus had just announced his impending death and resurrection when Peter took him aside and began to rebuke him, after which Jesus turns around and rebukes Peter, calling him "Satan." The Greek verb ἐπιτιμάω is used in the first half of the gospel in the context of rebuking demons and a storm. "Therefore," concludes Middleton,

> The verb appears to be used in the context of supernatural conflict, and at this crucial juncture in the Gospel—the point where Jesus declares his hand, embracing the way of suffering and death—Satan, through Peter, launches an assault against Jesus by attempting to 'exorcize' him. However, Satan . . . is thwarted by Jesus's counter-rebuke.[15]

Middleton interprets the opposition against the way of suffering and death as satanic, emphasizing the battleground of the cosmic battle between God and Satan. Jesus's response to Peter that he was thinking human thoughts and not God's thoughts aligns human thinking with Satan. The test of whether one is on God's side or Satan's side in the battle is the acceptance of the way of the cross set forth by Jesus.[16]

The question needs to be addressed whether Mark does indeed emphasize the idea of a cosmic battle between God and Satan, and place the deaths of Jesus and his followers within this context, portraying them as bringing victory to God's side of the battle. Mark uses very strong language in the incident of rebuke back and forth between Peter and Jesus, making very clear on whose side Peter's thoughts belonged. But is that Mark's emphasis?

Throughout Mark, Jesus has clear authority over all that is demonic. The first public miracle that the Markan Jesus performed was casting out a demon in 1:12. The crowds were amazed at his authority. Throughout the narrative, Jesus's authority over demonic activity is clear and decisive. In the confrontation with the teachers of the law from Jerusalem in 3:22–30, the Markan Jesus indicates that he has bound Satan—the strong man— and entered his house. Now he is taking his possessions.[17] That Jesus is the stronger one as opposed to Satan, is emphasized again when the Markan

---

defeating Satan, and help bring about God's eschatological Kingdom."

15. Ibid., 150–51.

16. Ibid., 151.

17. See also Hooker, *Mark*, 116; Witherington, *Mark*, 157–58; and Guelich, *Mark*, 176–77. France, *Mark*, 338; and Lane, *Mark*, 143, however, suggest that there is an ongoing conflict in which Jesus, as the stronger one, is able to attack and defeat Satan in each confrontation.

Jesus encounters a demon-possessed man in the region of the Gerasenes (5:1–13). With a word, he casts out a legion of demons from a man who had inhuman strength and whom no chains could hold down. Jesus is incomparably stronger.

This power over Satan, however, runs parallel in the narrative to an increasingly clear misunderstanding by humans as to Jesus's identity and mission. While those not following Jesus thought he might be John the Baptist, Elijah, or one of the prophets (6:14–16; 8:27–28), the development of the perception of the disciples is portrayed as especially clumsy. They are terrified when he calms the wind and the waves (4:40–41) and after the miraculous feeding of the four thousand, while in the boat on the way to Bethsaida, they again dreadfully misunderstand the meaning of Jesus as he warns them against the yeast of the Pharisees and of Herod: "Do you not yet perceive or understand? Have your hearts been hardened? Having eyes, do you not see and having ears, do you not hear?" (8:17b–18). As they arrive in Bethsaida, a blind man is brought to Jesus for him to heal (8:22–26). Jesus attempts to heal him, but it does not work in one try. Only after Jesus touches his eyes a second time does the man begin to see clearly. Immediately after this gradually opening of the eyes, Jesus has a conversation with his disciples as to who the people in general think he is, and who *they* think he is (8:27–30). The disciples begin to understand that Jesus is the Messiah, but they still do not see clearly. As Jesus goes on to speak of his impending suffering, Peter tries to rebuke him for doing so. He does not understand. Just as the blind man was healed slowly and in stages, the eyes of the disciples begin to see, but are not yet fully open.

This struggle within Mark's Gospel with humans is striking in the face of the ease with which Jesus is victorious in the context of demonic battle. Mark aligns the human thoughts of Peter against those of God. The struggle that Mark draws up is played out in the hearts of Jesus's disciples. The key to Mark's focus is reflected in the Gethsemane scene (14:32–40). Jesus exhibits terrible fear and emotional suffering. He does not *want* to suffer and die. But in choosing for God's will in spite of his own fear, God's Kingdom and salvation purposes were served. When a disciple follows Jesus, they follow in the same pattern of choosing God's will in spite of their own—even unto death. The way of salvation is indeed through literal suffering and death, for Jesus first and then for all who would follow him. But the nuance of Mark's emphasis is not a cosmic battle won by martyrdom, but a cosmic battle won by the step that comes before the actual death: the choice to have God's will be done, not one's own will.

James Hanson understands the combination of "Satan" and the "rebuking" between Peter and Jesus (8:32–33) as providing the scene with an "aura of an exorcism".[18] According to him, the inability of the disciples to accept the way presented by Jesus is caused by "Satan's grasp on their minds" as opposed to the "'possession' by the Holy Spirit (1:10)" through whom Jesus is able to go the way of giving his life.[19] And indeed, as we have seen in the discussion on the failure of the disciples in chapter 3 above, it will be the "'possession' by the Holy Spirit" as described in 1:8 that will enable the disciples to go this way as well. As has been discussed earlier, the moment of the cross is depicted in Mark as the moment of greatest power of God's Kingdom (cf. 9:1). And this is also the decisive moment in which the Spirit is made available to others to embrace the way of the cross in following Jesus.

Middleton is right to suggest that Mark's emphasis on the way of suffering for Jesus and for the disciples is placed in context of the cosmic battle. The battle is won, however, not at the moment of death, but when the martyr has prayed to God, as Jesus did in Gethsemane: "but not what I want, but what you want" (14:36b). Mark did not intend that his audience actively seek death as Tertullian, in his letter to Scapula, suggests that some did. But he did intend that his audience understand that their own faithfulness in the face of persecution, by the Spirit of God, would make a salvific difference in the cosmic battle. While they were mistaken in their fierce actions, the radical martyrs understood well that the Gospel of Mark portrays faithfulness unto death as helping to "bring about God's eschatological Kingdom."[20]

Mark and Salvific Suffering as *Imitatio Christi*

Candida Moss also finds a belief in a salvific value to the suffering of martyrs in her study of the Early Church's martyrdom literature. The salvific value lies in what she terms *imitatio Christi*.[21] In both martyrdom literature as well as New Testament texts, she finds an attitude of encouraging the emulation of Christ's suffering. It is not difficult to see this in regards to the Gospel of Mark.

Moss takes this emulation, however, a step further than I think is warranted. According to her, Mark insists that the disciples not only walk their own path in the pattern that Jesus had set for them. They are to go the *same* path that Jesus went. Their suffering and death are presented as *synonymous*

---

18. Hanson, *Endangered Promises*, 240.
19. Ibid., 241.
20. Middleton, *Radical Martyrdom*, 128.
21. Moss uses a simple definition of *imitatio Christi*: "the idea that Jesus's followers should seek to imitate him" (*Other Christs*, 23).

to the suffering and death of Jesus—a re-enactment of the suffering of Jesus.[22] While she infers that this message of *imitatio Christi* is to be understood soteriologically,[23] she unfortunately does not explain *how* Mark sets this emulation in a salvific context.[24]

Moss does show that the martyr narratives interpreted the deaths of the martyrs as salvific, basing their interpretations on New Testament texts. While these martyr narratives vary individually, one of the more consistent features is that they *function* the same as Jesus's death.[25] The salvific aspect was found in the idea that the martyrs would share in the status of the exalted Christ. "Even if ancient Christians interpreted the death of the martyr in individual and diverse ways, they agreed that it was a special salvifically valuable death. The death of the martyr—as sacrifice, example, or victory—meant that the martyr enjoyed an unusual and highly privileged experience of the afterlife."[26]

Mark's notion of salvation, however, has little to do with the attainment of the status of exalted Christ. Mark consistently pours God's salvific intervention into the mold of the Kingdom of God. Jesus is indeed the Messiah, the anointed King. But he is first the suffering Son of Man. This approach does not contradict the exaltation of Jesus as King, but places it in context of the suffering and persecution that happen first. Moreover, Mark re-interprets leadership in the Kingdom of God in terms of service. Mark does not allow room for an interpretation of martyrdom as personally salvific *in order to reach a higher status in the afterlife*. Salvation in the Gospel of Mark is found in terms of service to others. There is no indication that the service of the leaders in the Kingdom of God (cf. 10:42–45) would be transformed into status in the afterlife. Indeed, Mark's narrative is written to an audience who does not want to suffer, encouraging them to pray for the enabling to accept what God wants, even when they do not want to. There is no room for a promise of a personal reward in Mark's Gospel.

Moss might find support for her ideas of personally salvific suffering in James Kelhoffer's ideas of the status that suffering brings. According to Kelhoffer, suffering serves to provide legitimacy and standing as a

---

22. Ibid., 28–33.

23. Ibid., 22.

24. Although her purpose is to show that her interpretation is merely *possible*, Moss chides others for stopping just short of using the term "imitation" in their own interpretation of Mark's theological message. The inference is that they do so out of non-scholarly motivation. See ibid., 21, 29n58 (on 218).

25. Ibid., 110.

26. Ibid., 111. See also 164.

disciple in the Gospel of Mark.[27] A major problem with his thesis is that Mark defines *suffering* in terms of losing, or giving up, status. The disciple is called to become as a child (10:15), to become the "last" and "servant to all" (9:35). While the Markan Jesus recognizes the fact that James and John would indeed suffer for him (10:39), he cannot promise them that this would bring the status that they ask for (10:40). He continues with a teaching moment comparing the lust for power over others that the leaders of the nations exhibit, with the giving up of status that characterizes a true leader in God's Kingdom: "Instead, whoever wants to become great among you must be your servant, and whoever wants to be first must be slave of all. For even the Son of Man did not come to be served, but to serve, and to give his life as a ransom for many" (10:43–45). Mark's message is not about future exaltation. It is about giving up status and rights, and one's own will (cf. 14:34–36) in this life.

The three references to the future coming of the Son of Man in 8:38; 13:6–27; and 14:62 might bring a tension into this argument. However, they must also be heard in context of a leadership that is expressed in service, not in status. There will be a time of vindication for God's people who have suffered and died on account of Jesus. The purpose of this time of judgement/vindication is not to gain status, but to right what has gone wrong.

Moss's work points to a possibility of finding salvific value in the suffering of the disciples in Mark, as does my thesis. However, her observation that in the martyrdom literature, the salvific aspect is to be found in the reward of status that is given to the disciple who is faithful unto death, does not hold true for Mark. It may appear to be merely a slightly different nuance, but the focus in Mark is on letting go of status and securities, not on securing one's own salvation. The message that to save one's life (8:35) or receive eternal life (10:17, 30) comes through giving one's life, does not make ordinary sense. The teachings in Mark that insist upon service, even slavery, and becoming as a child, preclude status or security as motivation for this very action and attitude. A person must give up one's life (expressed in selling all they own, giving up family, house, and fields to follow Jesus) to gain life, or inherit eternal life. The essence, as seen above, is that they choose for God's will and not their own. Only this "suffering" and "dying" that goes the way of giving up power and privilege is to be understood as salvific in Mark's Gospel.

---

27. Kelhoffer, *Persecution, Persuasion and Power*, 183–225.

Conclusions

It is not difficult to see how Mark's gospel may have fed into a culture or theology of radical martyrdom. Mark's ideal hearers would have been familiar with persecutions for a variety of reasons—especially for not taking part in all the Roman laws. Mark's message of the salvific nature of the path of discipleship as following Jesus unto death could have formed an encouragement to hasten the process and give oneself to be killed. However, in doing so, they would step beyond Mark's purposes.

Mark's message is not about a specific number of martyrs needed for salvation to be complete. The scene on which Mark's cosmic battle is fought is in the understanding of the disciple. God's thoughts must be thought, and his will must be chosen above one's own. And in order to do so, God's Spirit will be given. But to choose to have his Spirit enable one to follow is not easy. The key is found in Jesus and his obedient death on the cross. The Markan Jesus provides the positive illustration for how the battle is to be won: by prayer and asking God to do his will, despite what one wills for oneself. In Mark, the great battle with Satan is fought and won by Jesus. And yet, persons must still choose for themselves if they are to align themselves with Satan or Jesus. The only way to join the winning side is through faithful obedience unto death, made possible through God's Spirit. Each time a person does so, a cosmic struggle is won. The path of discipleship in Mark is salvific. Perhaps this is why Mark opens with the words, "The beginning of the good news of Jesus Christ." He shows the beginning, the way forward, and invites his audience to follow the path that he describes. The rest of the story must be written through the lives of those who follow.

Mark's reception history includes those who wrote about martyrdom. This indicates that his message included a deep relevance for those facing persecution. This message, however, did not insist upon martyrdom in such a way as to encourage a radical martyrdom, or as to promise special heavenly status to the martyrs. The giving up of one's life that Jesus taught should be understood as consistent with the teachings of giving up status. The disciples understand their role in God's Kingdom as one of leadership. And Jesus re-interprets this leadership in terms of being a status-less slave to those being led. The disciples are given the status of Jesus's family in Mark 3, but Mark proceeds to define this status in terms of giving up all rights and privileges.

Middleton and Moss both agree, that Mark's message of giving up life in the pattern that Jesus set for them indicates a salvific nature of the suffering of the disciple. However, the way in which each interprets that salvific nature is decisively different. Moss suggests that it refers to a special bonus, reward or status in the afterlife, given to the one who was faithful unto death. This interpretation has been shown to be incompatible with Mark's message. Middleton's interpretation, however, provides support to my thesis in his recognition that Mark places significant emphasis on the cosmic struggle in his narrative. The Kingdom of God is near, and that encounters resistance from Satan and those aligned with him. Each time martyrs align themselves with God, choosing God's will rather than their own, this has cosmic significance. It does not attain a special treat for the disciple, but is salvific in the sense that it furthers God's Kingdom.

The various backgrounds to Mark's narrative flow together to form Mark's message. We have looked at socio-historical aspects of Mark's culture, and observed that these reveal that God brings salvation through his family as each member follows him, choosing his way above their own. Another important aspect of Mark's background that must be discussed is formed by intertextuality with Scripture. Mark's places his narrative from the start (1:2) in the context of God's salvation story. In part 3, we will look at this background and how it enlightens Mark's message of salvation and the salvific way of the cross.

Part Three: Relevant Intertextual Background to Mark 8:22—10:52

In Part Three, we will be looking at three groups of intertextual themes that Mark incorporates into his narrative. As we saw in the previous investigation, Mark's narrative is thoroughly Jewish. An aspect of this Jewishness that must not be underestimated is formed by the sacred texts that formed and defined the people in their relationship to God.

Mark's narrative is colored profusely by themes he takes from Isaiah: salvation, blindness, and the suffering servant. These themes and their relevance to my research will be discussed in chapter 7. Chapter 8 will discuss Mark's use of the term Son of Man as an allusion to Daniel 7. Mark employs this term in each of the passion predictions, but also at other key moments throughout his narrative. Our discussion will then proceed, in chapter 9, to the climactic suffering of Jesus on the cross. At the most intensely painful moment of the narrative, the Markan Jesus calls out loudly with words from Ps 22: "My God, my God, why have you forsaken me?!" This will need to be investigated as an important part of Mark's commentary on Jesus's death.

Our investigation of the connection between the suffering of Jesus and the suffering of the disciples will be informed throughout each chapter by the dimension that these texts bring to Mark's narrative.

7

Mark's Use of Isaiah's Salvation Narrative

*"As is written in Isaiah the prophet, behold,
I send my messenger before you"*

MARK 1:2AB

ALERT AND SEASONED HEARERS might realize that not all that follows the above introductory statement is actually written in *Isaiah* the prophet, but they will know that what follows comes from the scriptures, and at least some of it comes from Isaiah. With the conflated quote which follows, Mark places his entire narrative in the context of God's whole story of salvation. This salvation is reflected in Exodus as well as in the prophets Isaiah and Malachi. It is well known that Morna Hooker argues against a specific allusion to Isa 53 in the ransom statement of Mark 10:45. What is not often noted is her remark that "the theology of Isa 40–55 as a whole is certainly an important part of its background."[1] Indeed, Isaiah as a whole is an important part of the background to Mark's whole story.[2] Mark's opening statement and the quotation(s) that follow provide the hearer with an important hermeneutical hint. What follows is in line with God's story of salvation as portrayed in, among other texts, the book of Isaiah. And a close look at how Isaiah forms much of Mark's background and informs much of his narrative will help us to understand the salvation context that my thesis ascribes to the connection between Jesus's suffering and discipleship.

According to J. Ross Wagner, Isaiah embodies "the 'story' of Jewish Restoration Eschatology," which he explains as "a narrative whose basic outline is clear—God will restore his covenant people as promised—but whose

---

1. Cf. Hooker, *Mark*, 249.

2. According to Jeremias, one should not interpret the use of the Servant Songs of Isaiah in isolation from the entire book. In the time of Mark, Isaiah was not divided into "Proto-, Deutero-, and Trito-Isaiah," but was in the form that we find it today ("παῖς θεοῦ," *TDNT* 5:682). See also Hengel, "Effective History of Isaiah 53," 79.

detailed plotline is developed in diverse ways in the surviving literature."³ One of Isaiah's features of this "plotline" is the role, or roles, of the Suffering Servant.⁴ With Mark's emphasis on suffering, and the divine necessity of suffering (Mark 8:31), the link is quickly made, at least by modern readers.⁵ Does Mark, however, make this link?

Rikki E. Watts also suggests an Isaianic background to the whole of Mark, concentrating on the New Exodus theme.⁶ Thomas Hatina, while not denying Isaiah's influence on Mark, has suggested an important corrective to Watts's interpretation, and emphasizes the need to consider Mark's own narrative as programmatic to understanding his theology above that of a metanarrative from outside.⁷ Mark uses Isaiah through quotations and various allusions and echoes to place his narrative in a context of a story that has been going on for centuries. He understands his narrative about Jesus to be the continuation and fulfilment of this greater story of God. And while it consists of elements—specifically the cross—that might find resistance to both Greco-Roman and Jewish ears, he presents it as being completely in line with the understanding of God's continuous story of salvation.⁸

In the interpretation of Mark's use of Isaiah, his own narrative will provide the clues to understanding the allusions. As he uses and refers to various aspects of Isaiah's story, his ideal audience makes the connection that these stories are consonant with each other, and that God is bringing his age-old promises of salvation to fulfilment. Three important aspects of Mark's narrative are: he sets his story firmly in the context of God's story of salvation; he uses a motif of seeing and hearing to coax his hearers forward to understand Jesus's identity of a suffering Messiah and the role of the Spirit of God in going this way of suffering; and he insists upon a faithful obedience for disciples of Jesus that reaches to the depths of human suffering. As

---

3. Wagner, *Heralds of the Good News*, 29, n. 103. "Eschatology" in this sense does not refer to some other-worldly salvation, but to God's purposefulness in accomplishing this cumulative restoration.

4. This suffering motif is not necessarily unique to Isaiah. See, for example, the faithful in Dan 7 who suffer much before vindication, as well as the Maccabean martyrs, especially in 2 and 4 Macc. Also: *The Assumption of Moses*, 3.11–13. In this text, Moses is portrayed as having suffered many things in his attempt to keep the Israelites from sinning. The exodus is a key motif in the Jewish salvation history, forming a mold for the "new exodus" that is reflected in Isaiah.

5. See Lane, *Mark*, 300 (also n. 84); Evans, *Mark*, 120–23; France, *Mark*, 420–21.

6. See Watts, *Isaiah's New Exodus and Mark*.

7. Hatina, *In Search of a Context*, 22–23.

8. Collins has suggested that the passion narratives form their own genre, which she describes as "a narration of the fulfilment of prophetic oracles" ("From Noble Death," 487).

we will see in this chapter, Mark employs Isaiah to inform his message in each of these aspects.

Hatina's method of interpreting all quotations and allusions in line with Mark's own narrative has inspired the method employed in this study.[9] The context within Mark's message will be considered for each quotation or allusion. I will also consider the simple, atomistic, meaning of the alluded to text within Mark's narrative as well as considering how its context within Isaiah might affect Mark's message.[10]

The General Salvation Context to Mark's Gospel

The following chart demonstrates the verbal parallels between the text of Mark 1:2–3 and Exod 23:20, Mal 3:1, and Isa 40:3.

Mark 1:2a	
Καθὼς γέγραπται ἐν τῷ Ἡσαΐᾳ τῷ προφήτῃ . . .	
(As is written in Isaiah the prophet . . .)	

1:2b	Exod 23:20
ἰδοὺ ἀποστέλλω τὸν ἄγγελόν μου πρὸ προσώπου σου.	Καὶ ἰδοὺ ἐγὼ ἀποστέλλω τὸν ἄγγελόν μου πρὸ προσώπου σου, ἵνα φυλάξῃ σε ἐν τῇ ὁδῷ, ὅπως εἰσαγάγῃ σε εἰς τὴν γῆν, ἣν ἡτοίμασά σοι.
(behold, I send my messenger before you)	("And behold I send my messenger before you, to guard you on the way, so that he brings you into the land, which I have prepared for you.")

---

9. The method I employ will of necessity be simpler than Hatina's, however. Neither space nor purpose will permit the in-depth collaboration of critical methods he considers and uses.

10. See Ben-Porat: "It is possible to read and understand the alluding text (AT) without actualizing the allusion. The actualization of the allusion is a step towards a richer interpretation" ("The Poetics of Literary Allusion," 115).

1:2b,c	Mal 3:1
ἰδοὺ ἀποστέλλω τὸν ἄγγελόν μου πρὸ προσώπου σου, ὃς κατασκευάσει τὴν ὁδόν σου[11]	ἰδοὺ ἐγώ ἐξαποστέλλω τὸν ἄγγελόν μου, καὶ **ἐπιβλέψεται ὁδὸν** πρὸ προσώπου μου, καὶ ἐξαίφνης ἥξει εἰς τὸν ναὸν ἑαυτοῦ κύριος, ὃν ὑμεῖς θέλετε· ἰδοὺ ἔρχεται, λέγει κύριος παντοκράτωρ.
(behold, I send my messenger before you, who will **prepare your way**)	("Behold, I send out my messenger, and he will **prepare the way** before me, and suddenly/unexpectedly the Lord will come into his own temple, which you seek, and the messenger of the covenant, which you want, behold, he comes, says the Lord Almighty.")
1: 3	Isa 40:3
Φωνὴ βοῶντος ἐν τῇ ἐρήμῳ ἑτοιμάσατε τὴν ὁδὸν κυρίου, εὐθείας ποιεῖτε τὰς τρίβους αὐτου,	Φωνὴ βοῶντος ἐν τῇ ἐρήμῳ ἑτοιμάσατε τὴν ὁδὸν κυρίου, εὐθείας ποιεῖτε τὰς τρίβους τοῦ θεοῦ ἡμῶν·
(A voice of one crying out in the wilderness, Prepare the way of the Lord, make straight his paths.)	(A voice of one crying out in the wilderness, Prepare the way of the Lord, make straight the paths of our God.)

We have already discussed Mark's prologue extensively; it is not necessary to repeat that discussion here. What we have noted is that it centers around the promise given by John the Baptist that Jesus (the one "coming after" him) would baptize in the Holy Spirit, thereby fulfilling the eschatological hope of the Holy Spirit as expressed in Ezekiel 36:27.

Mark begins this prologue with the conflated quote from Exodus, Malachi and Isaiah. If it was Mark's purpose to use the words of these passages without reference to their own contexts, they merely point to John the Baptist whose ministry led the way for the ministry of Jesus. They do clearly point to the Baptist. However, they do more than that. The contexts of these older texts provide depth and meaning in their function as background to Mark's message.

---

11. The emphasized phrase refers to a parallel in meaning, though not a word for word match in the Mark and Malachi (LXX) texts.

Exodus 23:20

The context of the quoted text from Exodus is the first exodus, as Moses leads the Israelites out of slavery in Egypt towards the Promised Land. God has brought the Israelites into the wilderness, where he takes the time to give his laws to them through Moses. He teaches them how to live as his people. He tells them that he will send an angel ahead of them to guard them and to make sure that they arrive at the place that God has prepared for them. They are admonished to listen to the angel because God's own Name is in him, and he will not forgive their rebellion. If they do listen to him, God will be with them and help them.

The reference to the first exodus places Mark's narrative within the saving context of God's relationship with the Israelites. The first exodus was a great act of salvation, and a crucial moment in the forming of the identity of the Israelites as God's people. They would be God's people if they lived as God described to them, according to the laws he gave them. If they did this, God's messenger would go with them and would bring them in safety to the land promised them. Though without verbal parallel, this idea is echoed in Mark 3:35, where Jesus makes a statement that functions as a radical redefinition of the people of God, but with the context of Exod 23:20 in mind, is merely a re-statement of what should have been common knowledge: the people of God are those men and women who obey him. John's ministry is as the ministry of the angel in Exodus. He is to go before Jesus (cf. 1:7 ἔρχεται ὁ ἰσχυρότερός μοθ ὀπίσω μου), *and* to go before the people of God in this new act of salvation and formation of identity as God's people. He does this by bringing people to a renewed obedience through baptism and forgiveness of sins.[12] And as we have noted in chapter 3 above, he goes before God's people in the pattern of obedience that leads through rejection and suffering (cf. 9:11–13).

Malachi 3:1

The context of Mal 3:1 is eschatological salvation. God promises his coming with reference to the covenant, signifying his relationship with his people. The emphasis here is also on (dis)obedience. God will come in judgment. He will painfully purge his people and refine them with fire. It is not clear if the promise/warning is to purge individuals of sin, or to purge the group of sinfulness, which might include getting rid of "sinners" themselves. In any case, the result is a people who serve God in righteousness. This coming of

---

12. See also Stock, *Mark*, 47.

God in judgment in order to purify his people will also be prepared by the coming of a messenger (3:1).[13]

While the Exodus allusion makes reference to the way *of the people of God* within the act of salvation, the Malachi quote makes reference to the way *of God* as he brings judgment leading to salvation. Mark's adjustment of the pronoun μου (Malachi, *LXX*) to σου (Mark 1:2c) doesn't bar either emphasis from having a bearing on the meaning of his narrative, but brings the "your way" (1:2c) grammatically in line with "before you" (1:2b), indicating that the one who has a messenger sent out before him is the one whose way is being prepared.[14] Salvation is God's work, and yet also entails his people walking a certain way. Mark doesn't reveal yet what that way is, but it begins with repentance and obedience. This Malachi quote provides a fitting background, which places the baptism of John in a salvific context.

Isaiah 40:3

The context of Isa 40:3 is again salvation. Although God's people had experienced suffering, more than what would be expected for her sins, God had not forgotten them. He would definitely come and continue his work of salvation for and through them (cf. Isa 42:6), bringing it to fullness as described in Isa 35. In Isa 40:3, the messenger is a figure announcing the coming of God himself. The calling out for preparations as well as the announcement of his coming evoke images of a messenger sent ahead to announce the coming of a king. The focus is not on the messenger, but on the king.

As Mark uses the quote, he draws from the words announcing the messenger of Isa 40:3 to announce the ministry of John the Baptist. According to Hatina, this "change of referent also affects a change of sense," neutering or at least subduing the original context of the coming of God to bring salvation. Hatina states that the quotation is used by Mark to

---

13. In Mal 4:5–6 this messenger is *Elijah*. Mark alludes to this identification through his allusion to 2 Kgs 1:8 in his description of John's clothing in Mark 1:6, but does not specifically identify John as Elijah, however, until Mark 9:9–13. Lane, *Mark*, 51.

14. France states in answer to the question of *whose* way it is that John comes to prepare, that as Mal 3:1 and Isa 40:3 both speak of the coming of the Lord, there seems to be "no room for a human figure in the eschatological drama other than John himself, the forerunner sent to prepare for the eschatological coming of God" (62). Although Malachi clearly uses the first-person pronoun to refer to God, Mark changes the pronoun "to some unspecified third person, 'you'. In Ex. 23:20 the 'you' was Israel; here we are left to assume, with Christian hindsight, that it is Jesus" (France, *Mark*, 64). Hooker remarks that the minor changes have been made "in order to make them appropriate.... The messenger who is sent to prepare the way (v.2) is thus more closely defined as the voice crying 'prepare the way of the Lord' (v.3)" (*Mark*, 36; emphasis in original).

indicate that the coming of John the Baptist was in line with Scripture, and thus also in line with God's will.[15] His interpretation is atomistic, and denies Mark's intention that the quoted texts bring a broader context to the meaning of his narrative.

Hatina's interpretation encounters a problem when we look at the narrative of Mark as a whole. In his interpretation, Mark begins his story with a major emphasis on the fact that John the Baptist and his ministry were according to God's will. John the Baptist is important to Mark, but only as messenger of one greater than he. As Mark tells us, his message is: "One stronger than I am is coming after me, I am not fit to bow down and loosen the tie of his sandals. I baptize you with water, but he will baptize you in the Holy Spirit!" (1:7-8). Mark does indeed use Isa 40 to announce John the Baptist. But the context of Isa 40 creates the expectation that this story is not about John, but about God himself, coming with salvation.

The pertinence of the theme of coming salvation, which is present in the contexts provided by all three of the quoted/alluded to passages in our conflated quotation, is reinforced in the allusion which introduces the first revelation of Jesus's true identity as the Son of God. As we have discussed earlier, the tearing of the heavens likely alludes to Isa 64:1. The context within Isaiah is an intense lament, expressed in this cry longing for a new and decisive salvific act of God on behalf of his people. Mark's narrative shows Jesus seeing the heavens open, the Holy Spirit descending upon him, and hearing God's voice refer to him as God's beloved Son. The allusion to Isa 64:1 brings with it the sense that God is now indeed responding to this cry for salvation by rending the heavens, coming down in his Spirit upon Jesus, his beloved Son, hereby bringing the salvation described in the Isaianic narrative in Isa 65 and 66.

As Hooker points out, hearing and seeing in Mark are "ways of comprehending the truth."[16] Jesus is the one who sees the heavens open and Spirit descend, and who hears the voice of God claiming him as his beloved Son. The Markan Jesus understands his mission, and he understands it in context of God's great new act of salvation. The context of the quotations used by Mark in 1:2-3 elicits the expectation of God's arrival to bring salvation, with the need for his people to repent and to begin to live as his people, obeying his laws. That which Jesus saw and heard as he rose out of the water after baptism also indicated a context of salvation for the mission of Jesus. Mark's audience is enticed to begin to look for *the* ultimate, great salvific act of God.

15. Hatina, *In Search of a Context*, 182.
16. Hooker, *Mark*, 46.

To See or Not to See

Mark 4:12 provides its interpreters with an enormous challenge. After a long day of teaching in parables, the Markan Jesus, paraphrasing Isa 6:9–10, tells his disciples who are wondering about the parables, "The mystery of the Kingdom of God has been given to you. But to those on the outside everything is said in parables so that, 'they may be ever seeing but never perceiving, and ever hearing but never understanding; otherwise they might turn and be forgiven'" (4:11–12). This is a potentially daunting announcement; Mark tells his audience that Jesus continues by pointing out the lack of understanding on the side of even these privileged to have received the "mystery of the Kingdom of God" (4:13)! Is Mark telling us that God purposefully bars some from understanding and thus from participating in his salvation?

This passage is strategically placed within a larger unit (4:1–41, or perhaps even including 3:20–35) which, from a hearer's perspective, begs to be wrestled with. As Elizabeth Struthers Malbon says, "Like the Marcan Jesus with the disciples, the Marcan implied author with the implied reader works hard—doubly hard—to make himself understood."[17]

If we were to interpret Mark's use of Isa 6: 9–10 atomistically, it would indicate harsh judgment. Jesus tells a parable to the crowds, which his disciples have difficulty understanding. As they question Jesus about it, he tells them that only they have been given the mystery of the Kingdom of God. To those outside it has not been given. To these, Jesus speaks in parables, wishing to harden their hearts even more, keeping them from understanding and repenting and being forgiven. This would come close to, if not being equal to, pronouncing God's judgment over "those on the outside" (4:11). But is this what Mark is really saying? Who are those on the outside? There must be more going on here than meets the eye (or ear).

The use of the term in 4:11 reflects its use in 3:20–35, where the Markan Jesus provides a contrast between on the one hand Jesus's family members who were standing outside and the Jerusalem scribes who neither believe in him nor "do God's will," and on the other hand those inside, sitting around him who are obedient to God.[18] Mark does indeed judge the outsiders harshly (3:28–29). In 4:11, however, the category "outsiders" is broadened to include any who persist in their deafness and blindness. The outsiders are not necessarily the crowds on the seashore. Mark's emphasis in 4:11 does not permit a reading that seals their fate. Though seemingly harsh, the Isaianic

---

17. Malbon, "Echoes," 227.
18. See the discussion on Mark 3:20–35 above in chapter 5.

context provides hope of a redemption brought about by God himself which will enable a healing of their blindness and deafness.[19]

In Mark's narrative of this day by the sea, Jesus continues speaking, presumably to the crowds (cf. 4:34), with the encouragement that a lamp is not brought out only to be concealed, for all that is hidden will be revealed. This does not sound as though he wishes to keep their eyes blind or their ears deaf. They must *consider carefully* what they hear [βλέπετε τί ἀκούετε]. Mark, moreover, notes that Jesus would only teach the crowd in parables as to how much they could understand (4:33). The narrative does not show Jesus actively hindering the crowds from understanding. The Markan Jesus encourages the crowds to listen carefully so that they will understand. The truth may be hidden now, but only so that it will be revealed (4:22).

Rather than providing extra information (e.g., as if the Markan Jesus were saying: "I do not want those outside to understand and thus take part in salvation"), the purpose of the Isaiah quote here is to make his audience aware that the Kingdom of God is not as they thought it might be. It is difficult to understand; however, if they do consider carefully what they hear and see, they will understand. While Malbon does not specifically interpret the meaning of Isa 6:9–10 in the context of Mark 4:11–12, her intratextual interpretation of the echoes and foreshadows in the Markan narrative of 4:1–34, 7:14–23, and 4:35—8:21 shows a similar interpretation pointing to the dire need to listen well and look carefully in order to understand.[20]

If we consider the Isaianic context of the quote, there is a negative relation between understanding and judgment. Isaiah 5:13a states "Therefore my people will go into exile for lack of understanding" (cf. Isa 27:11). When the prophet asks the Lord for how long the eyes and the ears of the people will be closed to understanding, the Lord answers "until the cities lie ruined and without inhabitant, until the houses are left deserted and the fields ruined and ravaged, until the LORD has sent everyone far away and the land is utterly forsaken. And though a tenth remains in the land, it will again be laid waste" (Isa 6:11–13a).

While "seeing and hearing though not perceiving and understanding" has to do with judgment and destruction, the opposite has to do with salvation and healing.[21] We have already noted that Isa 35 should be understood

---

19. See also Brower, *Mark*, 126–29.

20. Malbon: "Understanding and understanding more are what is at stake for both the implied reader and the characters of Mark's narrative at 4:1–34 and 7:14–23" ("Echoes," 217).

21. Hooker: "Although the quotation's function is negative, however, the reference to 'turning' and to 'forgiveness' points to the fact that the *primary* purpose of the Lord's coming is to bring salvation" ("Isaiah in Mark's Gospel," 39; emphasis in original).

as a background to Isa 40:3. It also forms part of the context of Isa 6:9–10. When God does bring salvation, he will open the eyes and ears of those not understanding: "Then will the eyes of the blind be opened and the ears of the deaf unstopped" (Isa 35:5; cf. Isa 32:3–4a).

The theme of understanding and salvation continues throughout Isaiah's narrative. The relation between salvation and understanding is seen in Isa 42:5–7:

> This is what God the LORD says—
> He who created the heavens and stretched them out,
> Who spread out the earth and all that comes out of it,
> Who gives breath to its people, and life to those who walk on it:
> "I, the LORD, have called you in righteousness;
> I will take hold of your hand.
> I will keep you and will make you
> To be a covenant for the people
> And a light for the Gentiles,
> To open eyes that are blind,
> To free captives from prison
> And to release from the dungeon those who sit in darkness.

Here salvation is offered to the Gentiles who are blind and deaf. But not only the Gentiles need their eyes opened:

> Hear, you deaf; look, you blind, and see! Who is blind but my servant, and deaf like the messenger I send? Who is blind like the one committed to me, blind like the servant of the LORD? You have seen many things, but have paid no attention; your ears are open, but you hear nothing" (Isa 42:18–20).

In Isa 44, the LORD explains that he has redeemed his people himself, and so now they can return to him (44:22b–23). This is again repeated in 46:12–13: "Listen to me, you stubborn-hearted, you who are far from righteousness. I am bringing my righteousness near, it is not far away; and my salvation will not be delayed. I will grant salvation to Zion, my splendor to Israel" (cf. Isa 48:8–11). Deutero-Isaiah provides a narrative of God bringing salvation which, opening their eyes and ears to see and hear, will result in understanding and righteousness to the Jews and to the Gentiles alike.

By quoting Isa 6:9–10 Mark brings his audience to an intense awareness of their own lack of proper understanding together with a just-as-intense expectation that God himself will provide the solution. God will provide the solution, as we have seen in chapter 3 above, through his Holy Spirit (cf. Mark 1:8). The outsiders are not all who are blind or deaf, but, looking back to 3:29, they are those who blaspheme the Holy Spirit, who persist in disobedience, and who will not come inside.

Mark embeds his quotation of Isa 6:9–10 in a segment of his narrative in which he also speaks of the mystery of the Kingdom of God having been given to those who are on the inside. What is this "mystery"? Mark makes it clear that the ones who reject God's Spirit are those on the outside. The ones surrounding Jesus, who do the will of God, are the insiders. Could it be that Mark intends his audience to understand that this mystery has something to do with Jesus and doing the will of God? Further on in the narrative, the Markan Jesus will tell his disciples that the Son of Man must die, and that all who would follow him, must give their lives if they wish to save them. This is the way of obedience. Mark insinuates that the mystery will be revealed—"for things are not hidden except to be made visible" (Mark 4:22). This whole segment is surrounded by an *inclusio* of Jesus being in the boat. It may even form a sandwich. Either way, the inner parable section should be understood in relation to the outer section. In 4:1, he is said to have stepped into the boat, sitting out on the lake, to teach the crowds. In 4:36, we read, "Dismissing the crowd, they took him with them like he was, in the boat." While crossing the lake, a storm breaks out, and the disciples fear for their lives. In contrast, Jesus sleeps through it, resting peacefully until woken rudely by the disciples. Jesus chides them for their fear, and stills the wind and the sea. The question posed by the Markan disciples provides the direction Mark's audience must look for understanding this little story: "Who then is this? Even the wind and the sea obey him!" (4:41). This is authority that belongs to God: "You rule over the surging sea; when its waves mount up, you still them" (Ps 89:9). The ideal hearer will have been listening carefully, still considering what the mystery of the Kingdom of God might be, and will take this question ("Who is this Jesus?") to lead their listening and looking as the narrative continues. As Mark's audience continues to follow his clues of listening and looking, they will finally be led to the cross. And at the cross, if they continue to follow the lead of this seeing motif, they will find the mystery of their own obedience, as we have seen above, in the Holy Spirit.[22]

One other aspect of this segment in Mark 4 is the parable of the sower, or perhaps more accurately, of the various types of ground. It is not mere coincidence that Mark intertwines these. The parable foreshadows the failure of the disciples in the rocky ground which gladly received the seed at first, but could not bear fruit when the riches and cares of the

---

22. See chapter 3 above.

world overtook it.[23] This also foreshadows the conversation of Jesus and his disciples about the fate of the rich: it is very difficult for them to enter into God's Kingdom. The disciples are astonished, asking, "Who can be saved?" And Jesus answers them, "With people, it is impossible, but not with God; all things are possible with God" (10:23–27). The Isa 6 quotation in its context, with the baggage it takes with it from the whole Isaianic narrative, provides Mark's audience with the same message. Humanly, it is impossible; but do not fear, for God will open the seeing eyes that are blind, and the seeing ears that are deaf, allowing his people to understand, repent, obey (cf. 3:35), and be saved.

God's Servants in Mark and in Isaiah

"Καὶ γὰρ ὁ υἱὸς τοῦ ἀνθρώπου οὐκ ἦλθεν διακονηθῆναι ἀλλὰ διακονῆσαι καὶ δοῦναι τὴν ψυχὴν αὐτοῦ λύτρον ἀντὶ πολλῶν."
Mark 10:45

The influence of the theme of the Servant in Isaiah on Mark's Gospel is a debated issue. For reasons of space, and because it is highly relevant to our subject, I will concentrate on one text: Mark 10:45. The concentration on this one text, however, will necessitate an awareness of its context in the narrative.

Much has been debated over the background to Mark 10:45 focusing on whether or not it contains an allusion to Isa 53. Nestle-Aland 27 and several commentators agree that the reference to "a ransom *for many*" in Mark 10:45 alludes to Isa 53:12: "for he bore the sin of many...."[24] C. K. Barrett and Morna Hooker see no reason to assume Isa 53 behind the "ransom for many" saying.[25] The temptation while looking and listening for allusions is to isolate the text. But Mark 10:45 is the conclusion to a longer conversation, and ought not to be interpreted apart from the rest.

---

23. Tolbert, "How the Gospel, of Mark" 353, and *Sowing the Gospel*, 171.

24. See Collins, *Mark*, 500; France, *Mark*, 420, 421; Evans, *Mark*, 120–23; Donahue and Harrington, *Mark*, 315.

25. Hooker, *Mark*, 248–49. According to Hooker, the only word the two passages share in common is the word "many." This is far too slight a foundation on which to base an allusion. C. K. Barrett comes to the same conclusion on the basis of limited linguistic connection in his article "The Background of Mark 10:45": "Not even two swallows make a summer; two words . . . do not prove the use of the Song as a whole" (2). See, however, Collins (*Mark*, 500) who says that the passages share "important similarities."

Hooker does see the broader background of Isa 40–55 as "certainly an important part of its background."[26] In her understanding of the term "ransom for many," the ransom refers to the general term of "redemption," though it is not spelled out exactly how; the "for many" indicates that somehow all God's people are benefited. According to her, what the Markan Jesus would be saying in Mark 10:45 is that "suffering and victory belong to each other, and that it is only through the former that the latter is achieved."[27]

I agree with Hooker that this important, though unpopular, sense is included in the saying. However, if we take a closer look at both the Markan context of the saying and the Isa 40–55 background, a deeper interpretation rises to the surface. The saying forms the climax to a conversation that begins with just two of the disciples, the brothers James and John. They understand that one day Jesus will lead the Kingdom, and they ask for privileged leadership spots beside him when this comes to be. One can almost hear Jesus sigh as he responds to them, asking if they are able to suffer as he will. Oh, indeed, we are! is the answer.[28]

Perhaps realizing that this problem of misunderstanding the situation might not be isolated to James and John, Jesus calls the rest of the disciples to him and explains, "You know that those who are regarded as rulers of the Gentiles lord it over them, and their high officials exercise authority over them. Not so with you. Instead, whoever wants to become great among you must be your servant, and whoever wants to be first must be slave of all. For even the Son of Man did not come to be served, but to serve, and to give his life as a ransom for many" (10:42–45). The disciples had previously heard Jesus tell them something similar: "Anyone who wants to be first must be the very last, and the servant of all" (9:35). But this time he added more to the statement.

The statement about the Son of Man has tended to receive more attention than its context, as a proof text regarding the meaning of the death of Jesus. Yet, the καὶ γάρ with which the statement is introduced puts it clearly in conjunction with the preceding statement. The γάρ is an explanatory conjunction, explaining the sense or the reason for what precedes it. The καὶ can be best explained in this text as an ascensive conjunction, indicating the extent to which the preceding applies. Understood in this way, our attention shifts to the preceding statement: "Whoever wants to become great among you must be your servant, and whoever wants to be first must be slave of

---

26. Hooker, *Mark*, 249. Cf. France (*Mark*, 420–21), who suggests that Mark 10:45 summarizes the whole sense of Isa 53.
27. Hooker, *Mark*, 251.
28. See Brower, "'We Are Able.'"

all." Even in this sentence, Mark uses καὶ as an ascensive conjunction: the disciples, of which it has become painfully clear that they all want to become great and the first, must not only be each other's servants, but be slave of all. But Jesus is not done yet. He goes on to explain what he means even more deeply: to be truly great and truly first, they must not only be servants of each other and even slaves to all, but even give their lives in this service following the Son of Man who took this to its absolute limit in giving his life as a ransom for many.[29]

As we will see in the following chapter, the Son of Man allusion to "one like a son of man" in Dan 7:13 indicates that the Markan Jesus speaks here about a representative figure. The type of representation which Mark means to present is one in which those who are represented are included somehow. The representative has gone to the limits of this principle in giving his life as a ransom for many, and this is thus the type of servitude and slavery of which the Markan Jesus speaks. But what could the "ransom for many" mean, then, if this statement is given as example of the outer limits of what the disciples are called to do?

Isa 40–55 is pregnant with language similar to the "ransom for many" language in our statement. The *LXX* uses the noun λύτρον and its cognate verb λυτρόω eight times in various forms in this section. The agent is always the Lord God. The object, those who have been redeemed, is his people, Israel. The setting is the intense suffering that the people of God have experienced on account of their stubborn sinfulness, and the words of hope that God himself has not forgotten them, but will bring salvation (Isa 40:2); he has ransomed them (43:1). The situation might *resemble* that of family members who have been sold off because of the father's debt, who are now being ransomed back to the family, but actually it is because of their own sin that they have been suffering (Isa 50:1); God has no creditors nor is his "arm too short to save" (Isa 50:2). The word "ransom" is used, but not because something is owed. In fact, God's people are ransomed without ransom (52:3)! Referring to Cyrus, whom has been called and enabled by God to be the instrument of setting his people free, God says, "καὶ τὴν αἰχμαλωσίαν τοῦ λαοῦ μου ἐπιστρέψει οὐ μετὰ λυτρων οὐδὲ μετὰ δώρων, εἶπεν κύριος σαβαωθ" (Isa 45:13 *LXX; emphasis mine*).

My purpose is not to provide a commentary on Isaiah. An interpretation of the Isaiah passages would necessitate a more complex study of the texts. While God is said not to redeem with pay in Isa 45:13, he is said to give "Egypt for your ransom, Cush and Seba in your stead" in Isa 43:3. After God has promised to ransom without pay, the prophet draws a picture of

---

29. See also Green and Baker, *Recovering the Scandal of the Cross*, 41.

Egypt, Cush and Seba coming to him or them (it is not clear to whom[30]), as slaves, bowing down and pleading with them, saying, "Surely God is with you, and there is no other; there is no other god" (45:14). Although in Isa 45:13, it is said that God would redeem without pay, the parallel of Isa 45:14 with Isa 43:3 should be taken into consideration in an interpretation of Isaiah's purposes. Klaus Baltzer suggests the possibility that it is the Israelites who do not have to pay for their redemption, but that God does pay a price. But he also suggests the possibility of hearing this as an "admonition to the Persian administration. You have received enough compensation—now set the prisoners free!"[31]

According to John Watts, Yahweh's speech in Isa 45 "is a *tour de force*. Israel is reluctant. Cyrus does not even know God's name.... But God proclaims his sovereign right and will to make them all work together to produce the results that he wants: a restored Jerusalem and a free exilic community." His goal is that all will know that "Yahweh alone is God."[32] Through this activity he intends that Cyrus will know (45:3) that Yahweh is God, that all his empire will know (45:6) that Yahweh alone is God, and that Israel will acknowledge God as the one who has accomplished this goal (45:11–13)." When Mark speaks of ransom in the sense of Isaiah's story of redemption, he is affirming that God guarantees that he will redeem his people, and that there is no other god or person to whom Yahweh owes anything.

Within this context of restoration and ransom, God uses servant(s) to help his purposes come about. Though there has been much debate about the identity of the servant(s) of the Lord in Isaiah,[33] one thing is certain: what God's servant accomplishes, God himself accomplishes (Isa 46:11–13). The prophet leaves no doubt about the author of the redemption that occurs. God may call a servant, even Cyrus ("though you have not acknowledged me," Isa 45:4), to play a part in his salvation plan. The salvation, however, is accomplished by no less than God himself.

Another thing that can be said about the context of God's salvation plan in Isaiah, is that it entails suffering. In Isa 49, the servant does not recognize any fruits of his labor, yet trusts in God to bring about his purposes (Isa 49:4). God promises to not only restore Israel, but also to make them a light to the Gentiles so that they would bring God's salvation to the ends of the earth (Isa 49:6). In Isa 50, the suffering is clear: "I offered my

30. Baltzer, *Deutero-Isaiah*, 238–40.
31. Ibid., 240. See 237–41.
32. Watts, *Isaiah*, 157.
33. Donahue and Harrington, *Mark*, 315.

back to those who beat me, my cheeks to those who pulled out my beard; I did not hide my face from mocking and spitting" (Isa 50:6). Again, the servant trusts that God will bring the final vindication and bring about his purposes (Isa 50:8–9).

Isaiah 52–53 gives a sort of climactic re-cap. God's people are called to get up, to shake the dust of themselves, and to free themselves from the chains around their necks, because they will be restored (52:1–2). It had seemed as though they had been taken captive for nothing; God is the one who was orchestrating what was happening, though no one saw his hand (52:5). God declares that he will now show his people that he is in control (52:6). The prophet continues by breaking out into a song of praise to God who will now, in the sight of all the nations, bring his salvation to the ends of the earth. At first the nations jeered at the sight of the servant, but he will now cause kings to be silent, "for what they were not told, they will see, and what they have not heard, they will understand" (52:15; cf. 6:9). These kings and Gentile nations will see and understand God's salvation, and the role of Israel.

The song in Isaiah continues with the well-known words of Isa 53. The suffering that the servant bears has to do with the sin of "us" (why the sudden switch from God's perspective in 52:13–15 to the first person plural is not clear, although it may indicate that 53:1–12 is what the kings of 52:15 finally come to see and understand). The suffering that the servant experiences is deep and even leads to death (53:12), yet it has to do with the coming of peace and salvation for "us" (53:5, 10, 11 12c). This is the way in which God himself has ransomed his people.

Now we return to Mark 10:45, with its language of service, suffering, and giving one's life. These themes are all three connected in Isa 40–55 to God's work of salvation. The ransom language in Mark 10:45 hints of the ransom language in Isa 40–55. As we have seen, ransom in context of God's salvation means that God himself has dedicated himself to bring salvation and restoration. It does not mean that God owes something. If Mark is purposefully alluding to Isaiah then his use of λύτρον is in the sense in which Isaiah speaks of God ransoming his people, without pay, through servants who meet with suffering, and with a personal dedication to bring his promised salvation.

Mark 10:43–45, taking an allusion to Isa 40–55 into consideration, has Jesus enjoining his disciples to give themselves to God's great plan of salvation. The mystery of which Mark speaks is the same which the kings and the nations finally understood and saw: that the culmination of suffering of the servant of God leads to God's great work of salvation and healing and freedom for all the nations. The Markan Jesus understands this. In Mark 10:43–45, he enjoins his disciples to follow him in service, in being slave, in even giving their lives.[34] For in doing so, God will bring his salvation.

Conclusions

Taking the narrative of Deutero-Isaiah as the background to Mark's story enlightens various aspects, especially the otherwise puzzling use of Isa 6:10 and the debated understanding of the ransom statement in 10:45.

From the beginning of his book forward, Mark portrays a story of God's salvation in line with Isaiah. The quotations and allusions used in his prologue create an expectation in Mark's ideal hearers that the story that follows will show God's great act of salvation begin.

Mark's use of the theme of "seeing, hearing, and understanding" from Isaiah, marked by his quotation of Isa 6:10 at Mark 4:12, is reflected at both story level and discourse level. His use of the difficult quotation does not indicate that the Markan Jesus purposed to keep the eyes of his disciples or even the crowds closed to understanding, but rather Mark employs it to coax his audience into listening carefully. The Isaianic resolution of the problem of seeing yet *not* perceiving and hearing yet *not* understanding is the promise of God finally to provide understanding. This background encourages Mark's hearers to accept that they have difficulty hearing and seeing, and to listen carefully while expecting God's resolution to their problem. As he brings salvation, he will enable their understanding.

The salvation that God brings is, according to Mark, difficult to understand. As we have seen in the context of Mark 10:45, God's servants in his work of salvation are enjoined to give themselves in service, in slavery, and even to follow Jesus in giving their lives. The ransom of which Mark speaks is not payment of a debt due, and not even a full commentary on the meaning of the death of Jesus. It alludes to God as redeemer, just as in Isaiah. He owes nothing, yet he stands as guarantor to restore his people, and through them, to restore all the nations of the earth. It is difficult to understand, but this is his way.

The Markan Jesus has given himself to be a servant of God to the point of giving his life in God's salvation narrative. This way of service to God is presented by Mark as serving the least and being a slave to all. While some

---

34. Stuhlmacher suggests that while the suffering servant of Isa 53 is commonly interpreted in ancient Jewish and early Christian sources as an individual, this must not be opposed to a communal understanding: "The dichotomy is, however, a false one. In Judaism the individual figure of the Servant-Messiah is the prince . . . who rules over the people of God and simultaneously represents them before God. So also with Jesus. He is the Son of God who leads the people of God" ("Isaiah 53," 147).

would consider this a dichotomy,[35] it is not different from Isaiah's presentation of the service of God's servant who gives even his life in God's salvation for all nations (Isa 52:13—53:12). God's work of salvation is accomplished through the suffering and even death of his servants.

This understanding of Isaiah's message of God's salvation and the way in which blindness figures in Isaiah is found to be essential to understand how Mark moves his narrative forward in communicating his message as an outworking of the narrative described in Isaiah. God himself stands as guarantor to provide sight to the blind and eschatological salvation. In Mark this is apparent as the ideal reader is moved to discover that God finally provides for the ability to follow truly, as a servant, in the death of Jesus and the baptism in the Holy Spirit.

Mark alludes to another text from Scripture in his teachings about God's salvation narrative. It is as the Son of Man that Jesus will be rejected and will suffer and die before rising again. In the following chapter we will look at Mark's use of this term, and how he intends an allusion to Daniel 7 to elucidate his message.

---

35. Cf. Hooker, *Jesus and the Servant*, 74.

8

Mark's Use of Daniel's *One Like a Son of Man*

> *"And he began to teach them that the Son of Man must suffer much and be rejected by the elders, high priests and the teachers of the law, and be killed and after three days rise again."*
>
> (MARK 8:31)

IN EACH OF THE three passion predictions in Mark (8:31; 9:31; 10:33–34), it is said that the Son of Man must suffer, be killed and after three days rise again. Although these three passion predictions are not the only places that the Markan Jesus uses the term,[1] by using the term at these important points in his narrative, Mark wants his hearers to understand that as Jesus suffers and dies, he does this as the Son of Man. Why does the Markan Jesus use this term to express his death? What does this mean to my thesis that within Mark's narrative, the death of Jesus is connected to the way of the cross for the disciples to follow? Does the term *Son of Man* shed any light on this connection? This chapter will attempt to address these questions.

Review of Relevant Scholarship

In order to understand the meaning of the suffering of Jesus and the suffering of his disciples, we must understand Mark's meaning of the term Son of Man. Scholars from the early centuries CE on have attempted to find the true meaning behind this phrase. The Gospel writers all note Jesus using this phrase to identify himself. In Acts, Stephen uses the term to describe Jesus

---

1. In Mark, the term *Son of Man* occurs in 2:10, 28; 8:31, 38; 9:9, 12, 31; 10:33, 45; 13:26; 14:21, 41, 62.

seated at the right hand of God (Acts 7:56). Yet beyond these references, the term is not found in the New Testament writings as a common title. This has prompted so much study that Collins begins her 1987 article with the recognition that "taking up this well worked problem in New Testament scholarship may seem audacious to some, futile to others."[2] To catalogue all the work done on the subject would not be possible for reasons of space and relevance. Only what is relevant to this study will be briefly traced.

Much of the Son of Man scholarship in the past fifty or so years has been driven by the concern to understand if and why the historical Jesus might have used this term to refer to, or at least through which to understand, his own mission. Until the 1950's most scholars assumed uncritically that the Son of Man was a recognized title in the first century CE referring to an apocalyptic figure "identical with the Messiah."[3] This assumption was founded on the basis of the *Similitudes of Enoch* and IV Ezra.[4]

Since then, however, a consensus has formed within scholarship that Son of Man was not an apocalyptic title.[5] This was quickly nuanced by Barnabas Lindars who has insisted that there did exist a general idea of a messianic figure who would act as God's agent at the end of time, and that this idea may have influenced the use of Son of Man by Jesus.[6] Others do not go so far as Lindars in stating that Jesus's use of the term implicated a messianic figure, but insist rather that there is evidence that Dan 7 was an "object of reflection in that period."[7] An allusion to Dan 7 ought to be taken into consideration in the Gospels' use of the term.

In our narrative study of Mark's use of the term, some of the historical debate is helpful. Geza Vermes, Barnabas Lindars and Maurice Casey have approached the subject from the Aramaic use of the term. Vermes suggested that the term is an idiom, used as a circumlocution in instances when it is desirable to soften the effect, enhance tact or communicate an appropriate humility. The Son of Man is thus an "indirect reference to the self."[8] According to Lindars, the term could be used by a speaker to refer to himself, but including a class of people with whom the speaker identifies himself: "a

---

2. Collins, "Origin," 391.
3. Bornkamm, *Jesus of Nazareth*, 175.
4. Burkett, *Son of Man Debate*, 70. See also Bultmann, *Theology*, 26–32.
5. See Leivestad, "Exit the Apocalyptic Son of Man"; Bock, " Use of Daniel 7," 89.
6. See Lindars, "Re-Enter the Apocalyptic Son of Man," 65.
7. Bock, "Use of Daniel 7," 90.
8. Vermes, "'Son of Man' Debate," 23. See also Vermes, *Jesus the Jew*; and "Use of בר נש\בר נשא in Jewish Aramaic."

man in my position."⁹ According to Maurice Casey, this idiom is a "general term for human beings as a whole."¹⁰ It can, however, be also used as a self-reference, in reference to a sub group of which the speaker is a part, or in reference to "someone else made obvious by the context."¹¹

While Vermes stressed the self-reference aspect of the term, Casey stresses this important general meaning to the term that cannot be avoided. In reference to the ransom saying in Mark 10:45 he says:

> The general level of meaning of the term בר [א]נש[א] further reinforces Jesus's assertion that they will share his fate, and it is clear that death is included. The general level of meaning is also sufficiently loose to include the other members of the twelve. At the same time, it idiomatically refers primarily to the speaker, whose leadership in the whole incident was decisive. This general meaning is not only unavoidable in Aramaic, it is available only in Aramaic.¹²

The studies of the Aramaic use of the term Son of Man are especially helpful to this study.¹³ They have indicated the communal nuance to the term that must not be forgotten. While the written Gospel of Mark is in Greek, and not Aramaic, the language of the setting of the narrative is Aramaic. Mark notes this himself at a few important places within his narrative.¹⁴ Of course, however, if Mark intended to communicate this communal nuance in Greek, he would have to make this clear in other ways. I think that he does this through the use of an allusion to the *one like a son of man* in Dan 7.

Morna Hooker, in her book *The Son of Man in Mark*, does see an allusion to Dan 7 in the passion predictions. According to Hooker, Dan 7 provides a way to understand how it could be that Jesus would suffer. Mark places the suffering of the Son of Man in the context of conflicting authorities. Just as in Dan 7, where true authority was rejected by the beasts and caused to suffer terribly before finally being vindicated, Jesus's authority was rejected by the Jewish leaders who would cause him to suffer and die before he was finally vindicated. Jesus's suffering is, thus, not

---

9. Lindars, *Jesus Son of Man*, 23.
10. Casey, *Solution*, 80.
11. Ibid., 80.
12. Ibid., 134.
13. Some other studies of the Son of Man in Mark from a narrative perspective: Kim, "*Son of Man*" *as the Son of God*; Chronis, "Reveal and to Conceal"; Snow, *Daniel's Son of Man*.
14. Mark 3:17; 5:41; 7:34; (14:36); 15:34.

an inevitable part of his Messiahship, but an inevitable consequence of his true authority being rejected.[15]

Another scholar from the 20th century whose work ought to be mentioned is T. W. Manson. Manson argued in 1931 for an interpretation of the term the Son of Man that included a communal aspect. Aware of the Aramaic idiom meaning *the man*, with the possibility of use as a self-reference, he also pointed out the frequent symbolic use of the word *man* in apocalyptic literature.[16] According to Manson, the Son of Man in the gospels "stands for the manifestation of the Kingdom of God on earth in a people wholly devoted to their heavenly King."[17] With this figurative use of the Son of Man, the OT ideas of the remnant, the righteous sufferer of the Psalms, and the suffering servant of Isaiah, are all brought together in the gospel sayings. According to Manson, the idea of a remnant that would "save by self-sacrifice and suffering" was embodied "in the figure of the Son of Man in the teaching of Jesus."[18] This Son of Man figure, however, encompassed both Jesus and his disciples. The passion predictions are much more than predictions of the impending suffering of Jesus.[19] They speak of a culmination of a biblical ideal that includes all who would follow Jesus, yet, that finds its ultimate expression in Jesus himself.

Manson's idea of a communal Son of Man is instructive and finds unexpected support from Casey's work.[20] An understanding of the Aramaic idiom as Casey suggests provides the room to interpret the Son of Man texts in a communal or general way, while not letting go of the self-reference aspect.[21] It is, however, not unproblematic. Manson's thesis that the word *man* represents an apocalyptic idea rests on shaky ground. It may be used in apocalyptic texts in the examples Manson cites: Daniel, the *Similitudes of Enoch* and *IV Esdras*.[22] However, Casey has shown us extensively that the

---

15. Hooker, *Son of Man*, 109–12.

16. Manson, *Teaching of Jesus*, 212. Regarding its use in Dan 7:13 he says, "There we find the expression 'one like a son of man,' that is 'a human figure': and this phrase is not to be understood literally, but as an ideogram, if one may so describe it, meaning 'the people of the saints of the Most High'" (212).

17. Ibid., 227.

18. Ibid., 230.

19. Ibid.

20. I say unexpected because Casey, unlike Manson, does not agree with a *suffering* Son of Man, whether or not corporate. See the discussion below in this chapter.

21. See also Casey, "Corporate Interpretation." Casey shows that where there were various ways of interpreting the *one like a son of man* in Jesus's time, a corporate interpretation did also exist (179).

22. Manson, *Teaching of Jesus*, 212.

term the Son of Man was used commonly in varied situations in Aramaic in the time of Jesus.[23] That such a common term could also be used with an apocalyptic tint provides us with no extra information. A more helpful approach would be to establish whether Mark intends an allusion to the *one like a son of man* symbol of Dan 7:13 in his use of the term.

Mark's Use of *Son of Man* to Allude to Daniel 7

The question now lies before us: Does Mark allude purposefully to Dan 7 when he uses the idiom *Son of Man* in order to enhance his own narrative? If so, what is it from Dan 7 that he especially wants his hearers to be aware of as they consider the suffering of Jesus and the suffering of those who would follow him?

From a narrative perspective, the Son of Man spoken of in Mark 2 will be the same Son of Man spoken of in Mark 8 and in Mark 14. We must be careful, however, while approaching the Son of Man in Mark in terms of characterization. The Son of Man is not a full character whose actions and speech we can follow throughout the narrative. The narrator tells us nothing about him. He is only spoken of through the mouth of the Markan Jesus. When Jesus speaks of him, Jesus is speaking of himself. We can say that what is true of the Son of Man within Mark, is true of the Markan Jesus. But we cannot turn it around and say that what is true of Jesus is true of the Son of Man. When we see Jesus walking on water in the narrative, we are not encouraged to see the *Son of Man* walking on water. Mark, by having Jesus calm his disciples with the words "I am" (6:50), is encouraging his hearers at that moment to sense that somehow God is present in Jesus. When Mark uses the term Son of Man, he is encouraging his hearers to understand another aspect of who Jesus is. While the Son of Man is not a full (or round[24]) Markan character, Jesus is. The term Son of Man, however, is a consistent aspect of the characterization of Jesus.

Though the term Son of Man does not provide an allusion *per se*, Mark's use of the term throughout his narrative may contain an allusion to Dan 7. As noted above, Casey has shown that an Aramaic usage of the term would hold a communal nuance. Yet, Mark did not choose to use the Aramaic term and then translate it for his hearers as he does at other parts in his narrative (5:41; 15:34). He has allowed the phrase in Greek to elicit its own

---

23. See Casey, *Solution*, throughout. See also Hurtado and Owen, *"Who Is This Son of Man?"* for recent discussions of the Son of Man from a historical perspective, including critiques of Casey's *Solution*.

24. See Rhoads, Dewey, and Michie, *Mark as Story*, 102.

response. He translated it literally into words that according to context were fairly obviously pointing to Jesus himself. However, they would also incite ears into listening more carefully and consciously searching the memory for other instances in which they had heard this term.

Rhoads, Dewey, and Michie, in *Mark as Story*, note that "Mark creates characters that are consistent.... [He] presents rich characterizations by being minimally suggestive. The narrator reveals these characters to the reader in a gradual process, guiding what readers know and when they know it."[25] The Markan Jesus uses *Son of Man* fourteen times. Although some scholars separate the sayings into different categories,[26] when studying the term through the perspective of characterization it is helpful to look at the contexts of all the sayings together and in order of appearance in the narrative. This will help us see the gradual process with which Mark develops the characterization of Jesus as the Son of Man.

Markan Contexts of the Son of Man Sayings

- 2:10 "But that you will know that the **Son of Man** has authority to forgive sins on earth—he says to the paralytic..."
- 2:28 "So the **Son of Man** is Lord even of the Sabbath."

In 2:10 and 2:28, the Markan Jesus refers to himself as the Son of Man in the context of authority. Both instances have to do with issues that are prerogatives of God. The teachers of the law take issue with his claiming authority to forgive sins in 2:10, and the Pharisees take issue with his claiming authority regarding what one could do on the Sabbath in 2:28. While these authority figures were acting as though they took God's side in the conflict, they are presented as being antagonists of Jesus. In extension of the Sabbath story in 2:28, Mark notes that Jesus healed a man with a shriveled hand on the Sabbath. Here the Markan Jesus asks the rhetorical question: "Which is lawful on the Sabbath: to do good or to do evil, to

---

25. Ibid., 99.

26. Hooker (*Mark*, 87) mentions three categories: present activity (2:10, 28), the impending suffering (8:31; 9:9, 12, 31; 10:33, 45; 14:21 [twice], 41), and future vindication (8:38; 13:26; 14:62). Yet she also recognizes that these categories "are not as clear cut as is often assumed, and that there is a certain overlap of ideas." Lane (*Mark*, 298–99) prefers to separate the sayings into four categories, following De Tillesse, *Le secret messianique dans l'Evangile de Marc*: (A) "to indicate the theological significance of an incident for [Mark's] Christian reader," (B) "announcing Jesus' suffering," (C) "allusions to the three prophetic announcements of the passion," and (D) "texts promising his parousia in glory".

save life or to kill?" (3:4), before proceeding to heal the man. After this the Pharisees immediately began to make plans to kill Jesus. The context in which Jesus is characterized as the Son of Man in both of these instances shows a conflict with the Jewish authority figures regarding the interpretation and implementation of God's authority.

- 8:31 *And he began to teach them that the **Son of Man** must suffer much and be rejected by the elders, high priests and the teachers of the law, and be killed and after three days rise again.*

- 8:38 *"For if one is ashamed of me and my words in this adulterous and sinful generation the **Son of Man** will be ashamed of them when he comes in his Father's glory with the holy angels."*

- 9:9 *And as they were descending the mountain, he gave them strict orders to recount to no-one what they had seen, until the **Son of Man** should rise from the dead.*

- 9:12–13 *Jesus replied, "To be sure, Elijah does come first, and restores all things. How is it written about the **Son of Man** that he suffer much and be rejected? But I tell you, Elijah has come, and they have done to him everything they wanted, just as it is written about him."*

The following use of *Son of Man* is in the first passion prediction. Narratively, this text should be interpreted within its context which includes the teaching moment following it and the transfiguration experience with the conversation afterwards of the Markan Jesus with his three disciples as they descend the mountain. Within this section, Son of Man is used four times. As a narrative unit, these ought to be considered together.

The first use notes that the Son of Man *must* suffer and be rejected by the authority figures, and be killed and rise again after three days. The conflict on the issue of authority is hinted at while the suffering theme takes precedence. The combination of the use of δεῖ with the mention of rising again after three days hints that even though this may seem not right (Peter's reaction is foreshadowed), God is somehow in control. He will not forsake Jesus, but will provide vindication at the proper time.[27] The second use, embedded in Jesus's speech to those who would follow him, refers to his coming in glory in a context of judgment. Those who are ashamed of him, and by implication do not give their lives, but attempt to save them, will experience

---

27. Casey, *Solution*, 207, quotes Esther Rabbah IX,2 commenting on Esth 5.1: "Israel are never left in dire distress for more than three days ... of Jonah it says, 'And Jonah was in the belly of the fish three days and three nights' (Jon. 2.1). The dead also will come to life only after three days, as it says, 'On the third day he will raise us up, and we shall live before him' (Hos. 6.2)."

shame by the Son of Man when he comes in glory. This implies that they would not be following Jesus (8:34). To follow him would mean to suffer and endure rejection by the authority figures, just as he would.

The following uses are in an eschatological context, immediately following the transfiguration experience on a high mountain. They occur in conversation as Jesus and Peter, James, and John descend the mountain. The disciples are not to speak of what they have seen until the Son of Man rises again. This gives us no new information, but does echo back to 8:31. The question this prompts within the story is not about the Son of Man, but about the order in which things will happen in the last days: "Why do the teachers of the law say that Elijah must come first?" (8:11). Answering them, Jesus respects this teaching of the authority figures, adding that Elijah has indeed come, but they have done to him "everything they wished" (8:13), referring to the death of John the Baptist (6:14–29).

Sandwiched within this short discussion of Elijah, however, is a question back to his disciples: "Why then is it written that the Son of Man must suffer much and be rejected?" This use of the term Son of Man is again embedded in the ideas of rejection and suffering as in 8:31. This time, the context also hints at an eschatological importance of the suffering.[28] The sandwich construction indicates that the suffering of both Jesus and John the Baptist have something to do with each other. John the Baptist, as Elijah, came first and suffered and was rejected (cf. 6:17–29). Jesus, as the Son of Man, was going to suffer much and be rejected, and all who would follow Jesus were expected to follow on the same way, also experiencing suffering and rejection. But this way of suffering and rejection was to be interpreted in an eschatological context in which God was present and would provide vindication at the proper time.

While each of these four usages are clearly self-references, they also hint at a wider interpretation with a corporate nuance. Not only must Jesus be rejected and suffer and die before rising again, but all who would follow him must deny themselves and pick up their cross and follow him. When the Markan Jesus says both that he must suffer and die, and that those wishing to follow must follow the same pattern, Mark reflects the Aramaic sense of the term as a self-reference with a communal sense. By embedding the latter two sayings in the conversation regarding Elijah, Mark furthermore indicates the eschatological significance of the pattern of suffering and rejection.

28. Cf. Mal 3:1. See also Brower, "Elijah."

- 9:31 *For he taught his disciples and said to them, "The **Son of Man** is betrayed into human hands and they will kill him. And having been killed, after three days he will rise."*

- 10:33–34 *"Behold, we are going up to Jerusalem and the **Son of Man** will be betrayed to the high priests and teachers of the law and they will condemn him to death and will hand him over to the Gentiles, and they will mock him and spit on him and flog him and kill him and after three days he will rise."*

- 10:45 *"For even the **Son of Man** did not come to be served, but to serve, and to give his life as a ransom for many."*

This eschatological significance continues to be hinted at in these three instances. Mark 9:31 and 10:33 are both passion predictions, similar in form and context to 8:31. Both refer again to the rejection, suffering, death and resurrection of the Son of Man. Both are followed by discipleship teaching moments. The teaching moment in 9:33–50 speaks of the importance of service, foreshadowing the more extensive teaching moment in 10:35–45. The importance of the content of this teaching moment to the understanding of Mark's use of the term Son of Man is indicated by the inclusio formed by the Son of Man texts in 10:33 and 10:45. The first instance is a descriptive prediction of the passion, in which the steps of suffering that are narrated in Mark 14 and 15 are laid out. The second instance is part of the discipleship teaching moment which indicates the extent of the servant leadership required of the disciples as the ultimate sacrifice of the Son of Man as ransom for many.[29]

The text within the Son of Man inclusio in 10:33–45 shows James and John coming to Jesus with a request to sit on both sides of him in his glory. Jesus informs them that these seats are not his to give, and asks them if they are able to undergo the suffering that he must undergo. They answer positively. The Markan Jesus goes on to differentiate between the leadership style of the rulers of the Gentiles who "lord it over them" and "exercise authority over them" (10:42) and the leadership style of God's Kingdom, where those who want to be great become the servants, and those who want to be first become the slaves of all, following Jesus's own leadership as the Son of Man who came to "give his life as a ransom for many" (10:45).

The context is eschatological hope of the coming of the Kingdom of God, with an emphasis on suffering and authority issues. By asking for the seats next to Jesus in his glory, James and John are asking for seats of honor next to Jesus in his Kingdom. Although Matthew (19:28) and

---

29. See chapter 7 above.

Luke (22:30) both report Jesus announcing to the disciples that they will sit on thrones in his Kingdom, "judging the twelve tribes of Israel," Mark does not specify the element of judgment. Rather, the flow of the narrative indicates that Mark wants to focus on the desire for greatness that the two sons of Zebedee exhibit.

Jesus juxtaposes the authority of the rulers of the Gentiles with the authority of the disciples within the Kingdom of God. The authority of the Gentiles is oppressive, whereas authority in God's Kingdom is exercised by service, even slavery, even giving one's life in God's salvation narrative. The fact that the Son of Man came to give his life as a ransom for many indicates that he is the true authority.

- 13:26–27 *"And then they will see the **Son of Man** coming in clouds with much power and glory. And then he will send his angels and will gather his elect from the four winds, from the ends of the earth to the ends of the heavens."*

This Son of Man saying occurs within one of only two speeches of any length by the Markan Jesus.[30] One of Jesus's disciples had openly admired the great temple building, to which Jesus had answered that it would be destroyed with not one of the stones left on the other. When alone with him, four of his disciples asked him about the time frame in which this would happen. His answer was a description of severe suffering. At the climax of this distress and suffering, "'the sun will be darkened, and the moon will not give its light; the stars will fall from the sky, and the heavenly bodies will be shaken'" (13:24b–25). At this point, the Son of Man will be seen "coming in clouds with great power and glory."

The context of this saying is suffering for the earth, and especially for the followers of Jesus. The saying gives information about the Son of Man: he will be seen coming in clouds with great power and glory, and will send his angels to gather his elect. The *will be seen* anticipates the reply of Jesus to Caiaphas in 14:62.[31] It also echoes the statement in 9:1 "I tell you the truth, some who are standing here will not taste death before they see the Kingdom of God come with power."

While the text here in 13:26 can appear to be a simple self-reference to Jesus, implying by the context a time when he would return to gather his followers to himself when we look closer this interpretation becomes less self-evident. As noted above, the statement is closely connected to both 14:62 and 9:1.

---

30. The other lengthy speech is in Mark 4.
31. Evans, *Mark*, 329.

In chapter 3 above, an interpretation of 9:1 was offered in which the moment of the coming of the power of the Kingdom is interpreted as indicating the crucifixion. In Mark, the heights of Kingdom power are found in the depths of human powerlessness. This has special significance to the disciples. The power of the Kingdom of God becomes the power to obey God. The disciples are given hope that before they need to die for Jesus, they will receive power to do so.[32]

Can the coming of the Son of Man in 13:26–27 feasibly refer to the crucifixion? In the context of 13:26–27, the Markan Jesus speaks of great tragedies and atrocities that will happen in the future, "the sun will be darkened, and the moon will not give its light; the stars will fall from the sky, and the heavenly bodies will be shaken." And that is when the Son of Man will be seen "coming in clouds with great power and glory" (13:26).

At first reading, this context does not seem to support a double equation: the coming of the Kingdom = the coming of the Son of Man = the crucifixion. But it may, however, do just that. Mark 9:1 says that some of those standing around Jesus would not taste death before they see the Kingdom of God come with power. We discussed above in chapter 3 that the death spoken of would be the death that was chosen as a result of not being ashamed of Jesus or the gospel; it would be death that leads to life. This is the death and suffering that has been associated throughout Mark as being a part of the role of the Son of Man. So then, if we understand 9:1 to mean "some of you will not be asked to die for me until you *see* (and thus understand) my death for you," this implies that when they do *see and understand*, the power of the Kingdom of God will become manifest in them, and they will be able to die for his sake.

In light of this reading, in 13:26–27 the disciples are being told that just at the time of the greatest distress imaginable for Jesus's followers, the Son of Man will be seen coming in clouds with great power and glory. This *seeing* refers again to understanding. Just at this time of distress, when the suffering is most unbearable, people will see and understand (and experience) the power of the Kingdom of God through the crucifixion of Jesus as the Son of Man. The text states further that he (the Son of Man) will "gather his elect from the four winds, from the ends of the earth to the ends of the heavens" (13:27). This implies that although Jesus died alone as the Son of Man, without his disciples who ought to have been with him, the rest of the people of God will be gathered to him as they, too, experience the power to be powerless and to be faithful despite the most awful distress.[33]

32. See chapter 3 above.
33. cf. Dan 7:18, 22, 25–27.

The narrative plot supports this interpretation. The Markan Jesus consistently taught of his impending suffering and death as something that his followers could expect to share in. And yet, up until the actual crucifixion, Mark allows each one of Jesus's followers to fail at following him. Mark's audience, however, had been given the promise of the Holy Spirit in 1:8 as expectation that the ability to obey would come (see chapter 3 above). Moreover, they knew that Peter had become a great man of faith, one who had known suffering for the sake of Jesus and the gospel. Something had happened after the crucifixion of Jesus that made things different for Peter. The Kingdom of God had come with power.[34]

Mark 13:26 clearly alludes to Dan 7:13–14:

> In my vision at night I looked, and there before me was one like a son of man, coming with the clouds of heaven. He approached the Ancient of Days and was led into his presence. He was given authority, glory and sovereign power; all nations and peoples of every language worshipped him. His dominion is an everlasting dominion that will not pass away, and his kingdom is one that will never be destroyed.

Here we have several clear markers that indicate an allusion: Son of Man, coming with clouds, glory and power. Moreover, both texts narrate an intense period of suffering immediately prior to the "coming on the clouds," and both hint at a communal significance to the event. Mark 13 notes that the Son of Man sends his angels to gather his elect "from the ends of the earth to the ends of the heavens." The intense suffering of the elect will end and they will be brought to be with the Son of Man. The communal aspect of the one like a son of man in Dan 7:13–14 is to be found in its parallel in the interpretation of the vision in Dan 7:18, where it is shown that it functions as a symbol for the saints of the Most High. When Mark says that the Son of Man will "gather his elect from the ends of the earth to the ends of heaven," he is painting a picture of the formation of the saints of God by Jesus's own fulfilment of the role of the Son of Man. Jesus may be alone in his fulfilment of the role of the Son of Man at the moment of his death, but one day he will gather his elect and they will together fulfil this role as the holy people of God.[35]

---

34. Though not from Markan hand, the story of the stoning of Stephen in Acts also has Stephen, precisely at the moment when those in the Sanhedrin became "furious and gnashed their teeth at him," look up and *see* "the Son of Man standing at the right hand of God." After this, he forgave those who were stoning him (Acts 7:54–60), in the pattern that Jesus had given at his crucifixion (Luke 23:34).

35. See also Gray, *Temple in the Gospel of Mark*, who comes to the same conclusion that Mark intends the formation of the eschatological temple, or People of God, to be

- 14:21 "On the one hand, the **Son of Man** will go just as it is written about him. But on the other hand, woe to that man through whom the **Son of Man** is betrayed! It would be good for him if he had not been born."
- 14:41 And he came the third time, and said to them, "Sleep and take your rest. It is enough; the hour has come; behold, the **Son of Man** is betrayed into the hands of sinners."

These three instances of the Son of Man are in the context of suffering, and more specifically betrayal. The first of the three possibly indicates that the betrayal is written of in Scripture,[36] but the mention of betrayal by someone with whom the Markan Jesus is intimate (14:18, 20) also functions as an echo to the scenario described in Mark 13, where a major aspect of the suffering described is betrayal within the most intimate circles (13:12). While there the suffering and betrayal would be experienced by the followers of Jesus, after which the Son of Man would come in glory and power, here the betrayal is experienced by the Son of Man himself. As in the other passages discussed above, both suffering and glory are experienced by both Jesus and his followers. The Son of Man is part of Mark's characterization of Jesus. And Mark shows this Son of Man experiencing the same pain and excruciating suffering that his followers would experience.

- 14:62 Jesus said, "I am. And you will see the **Son of Man** sitting at the right hand of the Mighty One and coming with the clouds of heaven."

The final Son of Man statement within Mark takes place within the first trial narrative, after the arrest late at night, in the presence of "the high priest, all the chief priests, elders and teachers of the law." When the high priest asks him if he is "the Christ, the Son of the Blessed One," he answers with the words quoted above. The high priest immediately tears his garments and accuses him of blasphemy.

Regulations in the (much later) Mishnah (*m. Sanh* 7:5; cf. 7:4D1) suggest a narrowed down definition of blasphemy for which the death penalty could be given as the full pronunciation of "the divine Name." It is not clear if that is the reason that Jesus is accused of blasphemy in this instance. A. Y. Collins points to two instances in which Philo uses the term *blasphemy* in cases where a human claimed "a greater degree of authority and power than he has a right to do and, directly or indirectly, claim[ed] divine status

---

understood here (144–45). Also, Brower, "Holy One."

36. While Ps 41:9 provides scriptural background to the betrayal as described in Mark 14:18, another possibility of interpretation of this text could be that the fact that he must die is to be found in scripture, much the same as the use of δεῖ in 8:31. France, *Mark*, 567.

for himself."[37] Collins considers this broader definition of blasphemy likely to be the one used by the characters in this trial scene.

For either definition held of blasphemy, the issue is authority. The scene is poignant, as Jesus claims an authority, either that of God, or given by God. Darrel Bock suggests that the allusions to Ps 110:1 and Dan 7:13 infer together that Jesus "defines who the Messiah is in terms of the totality of the authority he possesses. This figure is so close to God that he possesses authority even over the nation's highest religious authorities. . . . Jesus claims total independence from the authorities of the day. He can be taken to Pilate."[38] The high priest, who ought to have been God's representative, proclaims him "worthy of death" (14:64).

This issue of authority is once again an important aspect of one of Mark's Son of Man sayings (cf. 2:10, 28). This is, however, not the only aspect of the context that is interesting to us. Through the use of a sandwich construction, Mark touches on the communal aspect as well.

Before the disciples had accompanied Jesus away from the city where they had eaten their Passover meal and towards Gethsemane where Jesus would be betrayed, Peter had insisted to him that he would even die with him if needed (14:31). On either end of the trial scene before the Jewish leaders, Mark tells the story of Peter's denial of Jesus. The first end of the sandwich is promising. Mark notes that Peter, in spite of having fled while in the garden, actually has followed Jesus (ἠκολούθησεν, 14:54; cf. ἀκολουθείτω μοι, 8:34) "right into the courtyard of the high priest" (14:54). It is as though he is giving himself a second chance. This Markan Peter knows that "all who would come after" Jesus, all who would join him in his mission as the Son of Man of Dan 7:13, would need to follow him to the point of death. So, Peter follows him. The second end of the sandwich, however, notes Peter failing. He is not able to attest to being one of those with Jesus. When he realizes what he has just done, he anguishes and breaks down, weeping.

All along we have noted that Mark includes a communal nuance to his portrayal of Jesus as the Son of Man. The Son of Man, who is given authority by God on earth (an authority which Jesus has shared with his disciples, 6:7–13), will face suffering and rejection before the time of vindication. Peter knows that he, too, has been invited to follow Jesus in his role as the Son of Man. At the *moment supreme*, when Jesus's fate was being sealed, and Jesus answered positively to the question set to him, Peter answered negatively, and refused to follow Jesus as the Son of Man.

37. Collins, *Mark*, 706. She refers to Philo, *Legatio ad Gaium*. 46.368 and *De Somniis* 2.18.130–32 (see 706n78).

38. Bock, "Blasphemy," 107–8. This article provides an overview of the complexity of historical and literary issues pertaining to the Jewish trial of Jesus.

This narrative sandwich reiterates the communal nuance to Mark's characterization of Jesus as the Son of Man. However, at the same time it also emphasizes the special role of Jesus within the communal role. Manson's description fits well:

> Jesus proclaims the Kingdom of God, he states the demands it makes, he declares the glories it promises. He calls men to receive it, to enter into it. He sets out to create in Israel that Son of Man. But not many can be found to go with him any part of the way, and none to follow him to the end. The last part of the way he travels alone: and at the cross he alone is the Son of Man, the incarnation of the Kingdom of God on earth. The Son of Man is rejected and slain.[39]

This describes well the situation painted by Mark at the moment that Peter exclaims his final denial. Manson knows how the story continues, as do Mark's hearers, and goes on in hope: "That ought to be the end of the story; but it is not. The sufferings and death of Jesus are the birth-pangs of the Son of Man. The cross proves to be the key that opens the Kingdom of God to men. The death of Jesus accomplishes what his teaching could not."[40] While Mark's hearers know that failure was not the end of the story for Peter, the focus here is on this failure. We have noted already the hopeful promise that Mark weaves through his narrative, beginning with 1:8, that Jesus will baptize in the Holy Spirit. This will enable the disciples to obey unto death, just as Jesus does. However, an important emphasis that Mark makes is that this obedience is *only* possible through the Holy Spirit. Only through the Holy Spirit, will it become possible for the disciples, or any other who wants to follow Jesus, to take part in the mission of being the eschatological people of God. Mark continues to stress the communal nuance to the Son of Man, but he also portrays the (initial) fulfilment of this role in the person of Jesus, without the disciples.

The Son of Man as Storytelling Device

What can we say about Mark's development of the characterization of Jesus as the Son of Man? Does his characterization constitute a consistent allusion to Dan 7?

If we were to take the Son of Man as a separate character in the Gospel of Mark, we would see a picture unfolding of a person who, having authority

---

39. Manson, *Teaching of Jesus*, 235.
40. Ibid.

on earth from God, comes into conflict with the ruling religious authorities, is rejected by them and sought after to be killed by them. He is betrayed by one in an intimate relationship with him, experiencing the depths of human suffering. But there is hope, for there is also promise of resurrection, and the prospect of sitting at the right hand of God in glory and power.

But we have also noted that the Son of Man is not a separate character in Mark. It is only a part of the characterization of Jesus. It is Jesus who uses the term about himself, but often in ways that invite others into this characterization. He uses it in ways that on the one hand repel the religious authorities of his day, and on the other hand invite his followers to see the power in the suffering that he must endure, and to join him on the same way of suffering and service. He uses it in ways that tell a story of redemption and vindication straight through rejection, suffering, and death. This story is not only the story of Jesus, but is presented as the story that Jesus is now experiencing *as the first* of all those who would follow. He is the ice-breaker on the way of God to redemption which leads through the depths of suffering.

Hooker suggests that Jesus did not use the term as a title, but to accept a role for himself "of obedient faith which the term evokes, and because he called others to share that calling with him."[41] My conclusion is that Mark uses Son of Man as a story-telling device that describes the way that Jesus *and those who would follow him* are to go in the coming of God's Kingdom. As a whole, it alludes to the dream and interpretation thereof that Daniel experienced in the vision recorded in Dan 7. The allusion may not be initially obvious to the hearers when they first hear it as the Markan Jesus announces "that you may know that the Son of Man has authority on earth to forgive sins" (2:10), but once they hear the words of 13:26, the allusion will be obvious to them and, as long as there is nothing that contradicts the process, they will automatically appropriate the new meaning to what they have already heard about the Son of Man. Once they realize that the Son of Man spoken of in Mark alludes to the story of one like a son of man in

---

41. Hooker, *Mark*, 93. My approach differs from hers in that she refers to the term as being of itself loaded with meaning, taken from both Ezekiel and Daniel: "The phrase was by no means a colourless way of referring to oneself: it conjured up all kinds of associations: the prophetic calling; the mission of God's obedient people; the possibility of suffering for those who were faithful to his will; the promise of final vindication" (92–93). My approach does not necessitate the phrase to already be loaded with meaning when Mark first chooses to use it. With each use, Mark gradually adds meaning to the term until 13:26 where it becomes clear that Mark does indeed intend for the reader to associate with the phrase all that is included in the vision and interpretation in Dan 7.

Dan 7, everything they have heard until then about the Son of Man will be colored by this new information.[42]

Mark's hearers will now understand that the clashes with authority in the beginning of the narrative were not only because that particular Pharisee or this teacher of the law did not like Jesus, but that the authority in the Kingdom of God has been given to Jesus—and not to the Pharisees and teachers of the law. This will not be a difficult step to make, as they have already been told that Jesus's message is about the coming of the Kingdom of God (1:15; cf. Dan 7:14, 18, 22, 27), that evil spirits recognize him as the Holy One of God (1:24; cf. Dan 7:18, 22, 27) and that his apparent authority is conspicuous (1:27-28; cf. Dan 7:14, 27). These references do not in themselves constitute allusions to Dan 7, but together they fit nicely in the context of an allusion to the vision.

A Suffering Son of Man?

Maurice Casey has insisted that the one like a son of man in Dan 7:13 is merely a symbolic figure who is on stage only in a moment of triumph.[43] For this reason, he claims it would be inappropriate to consider either the authority conflict situations in 2:10 and 28 or the references to suffering in 8:31; 9:(9), 12, 31; 10:33, 45; 14:21, 41 as allusions to Dan 7.[44]

Casey, however, is not considering Mark's narrative as a whole. And it is precisely the narrative as a whole that supports the allusion. In attempting to "find out whether the Gospel term 'the Son of man' was derived from Dan. 7:13,"[45] he approaches each saying individually. If the statement can be explained satisfactorily by the Aramaic use of the term, or translation processes leading from the Aramaic to the Greek, then an allusion is not in question. The result is that he finds no allusion to Dan 7 in most of Mark's uses of the term.[46] A narrative perspective on Mark, however, allows for a broader look at the term within the whole Gospel and leads to different conclusions.

---

42. An allusion to Dan 7 is clear at 13:26 and 14:62. See France, *Mark*, 534–35, 610–13; Lane, *Mark*, 329, 450–52; Collins, *Mark*, 615, 705n65; See also Casey, *Son of Man*, 163.

43. Casey, *Son of Man*, 39.

44. See also Hooker, *Son of Man*, 108: "The suggestion that the idea of the Son of man necessarily includes that of suffering seems at first absurd: he is a figure naturally associated with glory."

45. Casey, *Son of Man*, 157.

46. The only allusions to Dan 7 that Casey finds in Mark's use of the Son of Man would be in 13:26 and 14:62, and by derivation 8:38. Casey, *Son of Man*, 162–63; *Solution*, 192, 242–45.

Taking all of Mark's uses as a whole, as we have seen above, a comprehensive allusion to Dan 7 is likely. Secondly, Casey's observation that the one like a son of man in Dan 7:13 is merely a symbolic, triumphant figure does require his conclusion that it cannot have any reference to suffering.

According to Casey, the one like a son of man is purely a symbol of the triumph of the people of God.[47] It is not first of all a symbol of the saints, but of the *saints-in-triumph*. The suffering of the saints is only spoken of within the context of the interpretation of the vision;[48] it is not specifically mentioned in 7:2–13. The use of the symbolism of the human figure was in contrast to the beasts in order to emphasize the triumph of the true people of God. Casey says: the one like a son of man does not have

> independent experiences; he is a pure symbol with no experiences at all, other than the symbolic ones in vss. 13–14. To that extent he is a separate figure and he is to be dissociated from the sufferings of the Saints. The author's hope of deliverance by God was not 'based on the fact that Israel is already Son of man'. It was based on his faith in a reliable God who would deliver his people. Our author did not believe that Israel is, was, or would be 'the Son of man', he simply chose a man-like figure to symbolize Israel in triumph.[49]

The problem with Casey's argument is that he considers the symbols atomistically. Symbols, and even words, are communicated in context and are interpreted in context. Whether or not the Danielic figure like a son of man exists in technical words only in Dan 7:13–14, what is obvious to all hearers and readers of Daniel, is that the one like a son of man did represent Israel.[50] In Daniel's narrative, the one like a son of man who receives authority are the saints of the Most High who had earlier experienced extreme suffering.

The interpretation of the vision in Daniel is clear that *Israel in triumph* had first suffered greatly at the hands of the beastly kingdoms. Whether or not the symbol of this same Israel is seen suffering within the narrative of Daniel, that which is symbolized suffers greatly, and the memory of suffering does not easily fade. If this narrative was written in the time that Casey has

---

47. Casey, *Son of Man*, 164. See also 38, 39.

48. The dream technically includes both the vision described in Dan 7:2–14 and the interpretation described in Dan 7:15–27, but for the sake of clarity "vision" will be used to refer specifically to Dan 7:2–14.

49. Casey, *Son of Man*, 39.

50. I agree with Casey that the *Holy Ones of the Most High* in Dan 7 refer to *Israel* or *the true people of God*. See also, Poythress, "Holy Ones of the Most High." However, not all scholars share this view. See also Collins, "Son of Man and the Saints," who interprets the Holy Ones as Michael's angels (throughout).

suggested, namely between December 167 BCE and December 164 BCE,[51] and quickly gained popularity,[52] I find it difficult to imagine that its readers, whether in the second century BCE or in the first century CE, would be able to read or hear Daniel's vision without being intensely aware of the suffering of God's people as each beast arises from the sea, and the little horn arising from the fourth beast, "terrifying and frightening and very powerful" (Dan 7:7), boasted before even the Ancient of Days. As they hear of these beasts finally killed or stripped of power, and the one like a son of man receiving the authority, Daniel's audience will see God's people, having suffered and being vindicated. Whether or not we can say that Daniel offers us a suffering Son of Man figure, Daniel's hearers and readers are keenly aware that those represented by the one like a son of man in their moment of triumph had suffered greatly prior to this vindication. When Mark refers back to the vision in Daniel, it is natural for him to point to the suffering of God's saints, including and especially that of Jesus.

Conclusions

Mark employs the Son of Man phrase in a way that alludes to Dan 7. He invites the vision, as it were, looked at through the filter of his own story of Jesus and his followers, to elucidate the situation in his narrative.

The characteristics of the Son of Man in Mark that we have noted (conflicts with authority, suffering, vindication, coming on the clouds, authority, power and glory in the Kingdom of God) allude together to the dream and its interpretation in Dan 7. Mark portrays the whole story of the depths of suffering that Jesus experiences, and the depth of suffering his followers are enjoined to follow him through, in the context of Daniel's dream. The true saints of God are persecuted and overcome by evil leadership until the moment that God calls a halt to it and provides judgment in favor of the saints, giving them the sovereignty, power and greatness of the kingdoms under the whole heaven.

In his Gospel, Mark is not merely quoting or referring to Dan 7. He alludes to it in a way that provides a paradigm for understanding the suffering of both Jesus and his followers. It is as if Mark is saying to his audience that the vision of Dan 7 is happening in the narrative of Jesus and his disciples, and in the lives of his audience. Mark uses this paradigm to form his story-telling device of the Son of Man. In doing so, he adds his own unique elements to the story of Dan 7 to make his own narrative.

51. Casey, *Son of Man*, 10-11, 16.
52. Ibid., 11.

In portraying both Jesus and those who follow him as taking part in the story of the Son of Man, Mark signifies a unique role for Jesus. Within this story the Markan Jesus plays the role of ice-breaker, both going before and paving the way for those who would come after. Something happens in the crucifixion of Jesus that Mark points to almost mysteriously in 9:1 and 13:26 that has to do with the power of the Kingdom enabling those who would follow him *to be able* to follow him through suffering on his account and on account of the gospel.

We started this chapter with the question whether Mark's use of the term Son of Man allowed for the interpretation that Mark narratively connects the death of Jesus to the following of the disciples. In this chapter we have suggested that the term not only allows for it, but calls for it. The leadership involved in God's Kingdom includes the obedient service of both Jesus and those who would follow him.

Though at the crucifixion, Jesus fulfils the role of the Son of Man alone, at that very moment the power of the Kingdom of God is released which will enable those who follow him to one day join him as the holy people of God, giving their own lives in God's story of salvation.[53] In the following chapter, elements of Scripture will be discussed that Mark has woven into this crucifixion scene. Following Mark's lead, our concentration will be on Ps 22, but we will also discuss the implications of the Elijah misunderstanding centered around an allusion to Ps 69:21.

---

53. See especially chapter 3 above.

9

Mark's Use of Psalm 22's Righteous Sufferer

Καὶ τῇ ἐνάτῃ ὥρᾳ ἐβόησεν ὁ Ἰησοῦς φωνῇ μεγάλῃ·

Ελωι ελωι λεμα σαβαχθανι;

ὅ ἐστιν μεγθερμηνευόμενον· ὁ θεός μου ὁ θεός μου,
εἰς τί ἐγκατέλιπές με;

(Mark 15:34)

AT THE SCENE OF the crucifixion, Mark once again reaches into Scripture for words to describe the suffering of Jesus. Mark has used elements from Isaiah's narrative to remind his hearers that God himself is intimately involved in the bringing of salvation, and that the suffering of his servants contributes to this salvation. He has used an allusion to Daniel 7 to elucidate the relationship between Jesus's suffering and the suffering of his disciples by using the term *Son of Man*. And now, at the climax of the suffering of the Markan Jesus, it is Scripture that provides the only words with which he expresses himself in a deep, heart-felt cry: "ελωι ελωι λεμα σαβαχθανι;" (Ps 22:1).[1] Throughout his Gospel, Mark presents the various aspects of his theme of suffering as being consistent with Scripture. Until now we have emphasized Mark's connection between the suffering to Jesus to the suffering involved in discipleship. The Markan Jesus consistently pulls these two together. However, when Jesus dies, he dies alone. His suffering is not shared. Even after revealing the depths of his personal agony regarding the suffering that he knows lies before him, the disciples do not stand by him, let alone suffer with him. Mark takes from the Psalms to communicate the

---

1. See also France, *Mark*: "[Mark] wants us to feel Jesus' agony, not to explain it" (653). The words of Ps 22 quoted by the Markan Jesus do not provide a commentary on what was happening, i.e., as if God had truly abandoned Jesus at that moment; they give expression to his agony. I will be using the psalm numbering common to most English translations (for example, NIV). The *LXX* differs in chapter and verse number.

crucifixion to his audience. A look at Mark's use of Psalm 22 and 69 in relation to the death of Jesus may uncover the relation to discipleship that Mark intends his audience to understand.

Psalm 22 in Mark 15:33–39

What does Mark intend to portray about the suffering of Jesus on the cross through his use of Ps 22:1? Motifs from Isaiah throughout his narrative communicate the intimate presence and salvific purpose of God precisely in suffering. Could he intend these words to be taken literally to mean that God had actually abandoned him as he suffered on the cross? This suggestion was handled above in the discussion of the *pathos* of God. Instead of the "impersonal force of Scripture,"[2] it is precisely the relationship of God with Jesus as his Son that determines the plot (cf. 12:1–12). God does not recede from the stage. From the perspective of the motif of the divine *pathos*, Mark shows that as Jesus suffers and dies, God *goes with* his people in bringing them salvation.

Taking Mark's narrative as a whole, and in light of what we have already studied, it is unlikely that Mark intends this cry of dereliction from the cross to be understood literally as a moment when God actually abandons Jesus.[3] But if this is not so, why does he use it? Three important aspects of Psalm 22 shed light on Mark's usage: the Righteous Sufferer motif, a communal aspect to the individual lament, and an eschatological aspect of the psalm. Discussion of each of these aspects will be guided by Mark's own message and structure. Intertwined narratively by Mark, the Elijah misunderstanding belongs to any discussion of this heart-cry of the Markan Jesus and will be discussed before the conclusion of this chapter.

Psalm 22—Psalm of a Righteous Sufferer

Psalm 22 is an expression of deep suffering by one who considers themselves righteous and thus not deserving to be treated in this way. It is also a true lament—a cry to God as the One who ought to save them.[4] While there is debate within scholarly discussion regarding the existence of a cohesive

---

2. Collins, "From Noble Death," 485.

3. See also Carey, *Jesus' Cry*, 5–6. Carey also calls for an interpretation of the cry in light of Mark's whole narrative.

4. For the significance of the lament in the relationship of Israel to God, see Neary, "Importance of the Lament"; and Brueggemann, "Bounded by Obedience and Praise," especially 78–88.

tradition of a Righteous Sufferer motif,[5] it cannot be denied that the theme of the suffering of righteous people forms a recurring theme in Jewish ancient history. This is illustrated in the following story from 4 Maccabees.

The mother of the seven brothers who were brutally murdered by Antiochus, recalls to them how their late father used to remind them that suffering is part of their heritage:

> He taught you God's Law and about his prophets, about how Cain murdered his brother Abel, about Isaac who was placed on the altar to be sacrificed, and about how Joseph ended up in prison. Your father told you about the faith of Phinehas, and about Hananiah, Azariah, and Mishael in the flaming furnace. He praised and blessed Daniel, who was thrown into a pit of lions. He taught you this promise of God in the book of Isaiah: "When you walk through fire, you won't be scorched by the flames." You learned from him the songs of David, who sang, "The Lord's people will suffer a lot" (4 Macc 18:10–15).[6]

Not mentioned in the list provided in 4 Maccabees are the well-known righteous sufferers Job and the Servant in Isaiah. The list may not be complete, but narratively it is very effective in putting the suffering of these brothers into the context of the whole Jewish Story. Scripture often describes God's holy people in terms of their suffering as righteous people.

Mark's choice of Ps 22:1 on the lips of the dying Jesus is fitting. But in what sense? H. N. Roskam contends that Mark wrote his Gospel to encourage his community that Jesus was not a dishonorable criminal or a political traitor, but actually a righteous man.[7] Carey suggests that the tension implied in the righteous sufferer motif does justice to the depths of suffering that the Markan Jesus endured, and the Markan disciples are

---

5. Recent arguments: Carey, *Jesus' Cry*, finds the Righteous Sufferer motif present in Ps 22 as essential for interpreting Mark's message (see 126 and throughout); Ahearne-Kroll, *Psalms of Lament*, critiques especially the grouping of several Psalms of Lament in a category of "Psalms of the Righteous Sufferer," noting that this is a modern category and gives a pre-determined meaning to Mark's use of the Psalms of Lament in his passion narrative (see ch. 1, especially 13–18). While I agree that caution is needed when using such a modern construct as a given in interpreting Mark's use of a psalm, I do not agree with his observation that "in the case of Mark, there is little to indicate that Jesus dies as a righteous sufferer" (13). Jesus is portrayed throughout as being in right relationship to God *and* Jesus is portrayed as suffering greatly precisely because of this relationship. In other words, he is depicted by Mark as a righteous sufferer.

6. Elliot ("4 Maccabees," 791) dates 4 Maccabees to somewhere between 18–54 CE.

7. Roskam, *Purpose of the Gospel of Mark*, 190.

expected to endure, as well as the vindication that Mark's ideal hearers would expect to follow.[8]

The cry of the dying Jesus, "My God, my God! Why have you forsaken me?" is not the only reference to Ps 22 in the crucifixion narrative. An allusion to Ps 22:18 is present in 15:24, "Dividing up his clothes, they cast lots to see what each would get." Mark 15:29–32 provides a picture of the situation in Ps 22:7–8. All who see Jesus hanging on the cross mock him: those who pass by hurl insults and shake their heads; the chief priests mock him; those crucified with him heap insults on him.

By using various parts of Psalm 22 throughout the passion narrative, Mark places the suffering of Jesus in the context of the theme of the suffering of the righteous, found throughout the Hebrew narrative. As Hartmut Gese says, "What we have here is not a grasping back to the Old Testament in an attempt to clarify the Gospel account . . . it is more like the movement of the Gospel is being clothed here in Old Testament words, and what is more, through the voice of Jesus."[9] In 8:27–33, Mark shows Peter desperately not wanting suffering to be a part of Jesus's Messiahship. The Messiah should *end* the story of suffering. But Mark's Messiah instead *takes part in* the story of suffering. Mark takes words from the Jewish story and uses them to tell the story of Jesus's suffering.

But perhaps in some ways, the Markan Jesus does end the story of suffering precisely by taking part in it. Psalm 22 moves from intense suffering to a promise of salvation. Several scholars hesitate to include the context of Ps 22:22–31 as part of Mark's purposed intertextual allusion on the grounds that it would negate the intensity of the abandonment and despair voiced by quoting Ps 22:1.[10] However, a purposed allusion to the more victorious ending of the psalm need in no way retract from the intensity of the God-forsakenness of the quoted cry.[11] While Ahearne-Kroll includes the whole context of the psalm in his discussion of Mark's crucifixion narrative, he insists that its use does not "sidestep the horror by claiming that it is okay because God willed it or by making it the first episode in a divine plan of eschatological vindication of the Righteous Sufferer."[12] The atmosphere of the crucifixion is just as intensely painful as ever, which is made even more

---

8. Carey, *Jesus' Cry*, 5–6.

9. Gese, "Psalm 22," 180, *translation mine* (original: "Hier wird nicht zur Verdeutlichung des evangelischen Berichtes auf das Alte Testament zurückgegriffen . . . vielmehr kleidet sich hier der evangelische Vorgang selbst in alttestamentliche Worte, noch dazu in der Sprache Jesus"). See also Hays, "Christ Prays the Psalms," 106.

10. See for example Hooker, *Mark*, 376; France, *Mark*, 652–53.

11. See also Carey, *Jesus' Cry*, 5–6 and throughout.

12. Ahearne-Kroll, *Psalms of Lament*, 225.

excruciating, if possible, by the Elijah misunderstanding narrated immediately after the cry.

Mark's Gospel begins with planting a seed of hope for salvation (see 1:7–8). By taking from Ps 22 in his description of Jesus's terrible suffering, Mark keeps this seed of hope deeply buried, just as in the movement of the psalm itself, until the suffering has passed.[13] Not until Jesus dies does the confession of the Centurion, of whose presence the hearers were not yet aware, provide an allusion to the nations who will recognize and "bow down before [the LORD]" (Ps 22:27–28).

This eschatological aspect of Mark's use of Psalm 22 will be discussed more fully below. But first we will turn to the communal overtones of the psalm.

Psalm 22—The King's Communal Lament

Sigmund Mowinckel notes a pattern in Babylonian-Assyrian laments in which the king uses a royal "I" to express national misery. In these laments, the king identifies himself and his life with the life of the nation. He calls this the "oriental King-Ego style," and recognizes it in the Jewish laments expressed from the first-person singular perspective as well. When the nation is under attack, the king is personally under attack. When his people suffer, he suffers. For the king to pray for personal liberation from, or victory over, an enemy would be to pray for release or victory for the whole nation: ". . . the cause of people and state is looked upon as the personal—so to speak private—cause of the king himself."[14] We see this reflected in Ps 22 as well.

In the heading of Ps 22, both the Hebrew and the *LXX* note that this is a psalm of David. Reading Ps 22 from this perspective, we see a king lamenting the situation of Israel. The LORD is Israel's God, and he has shown himself powerful and faithful to deliver them in the past. Yet now he seems to have forsaken his people and left them to their own devices while they suffer at the hands of their enemies. The king describes their situation as if they were a helpless person, first coddled and nurtured as a child ("Yet you brought me out of the womb; you made me trust in you even at my mother's breast. From birth I was cast upon you; from my mother's womb you have

---

13. Ahearne-Kroll (*Psalms of Lament*, 101–7) insists that within the psalm, the victorious ending functions as a promise of praise as part of the petition to God to help the suffering psalmist.

14. Mowinckel, *Psalms in Israel's Worship*, 236 (see also 246).

been my God." Ps 22:9–10), then left alone in the midst of wild animals hungry for their prey.[15]

When any nation is surrounded by enemies and all hope is given up ("I can count all my bones; people stare and gloat over me. They divide my garments among them and cast lots for my clothing." Ps 22:17–18), it is a painful and terrifying experience for all involved. However, were *Israel* to die as nation, the stakes were even greater. God had promised that all nations would be blessed *through Israel*. God's salvation to all nations was at stake would Israel cease to exist. This is expressed in the thanksgiving portion of the psalm. Not only will the king exult in the LORD amongst his own people if the LORD hears and rescues them, but "all the ends of the earth will remember and turn to the LORD, and all the families of the nations will bow down before him, for dominion belongs to the LORD and he rules over the nations" (Ps 22:27–28). The act of saving would elicit praise from all nations and from all generations. All peoples of all times would be affected positively if the LORD would come and hear the cry of the king and rescue him and his nation.

It is the incipit of this psalm which the Markan Jesus shouts out loudly from the cross. He screams out the torture of the god-forsakenness which reflected his own emotion, yet included the experience of all his people. James L. Mays states that the words of Ps 22 can only be spoken by the Messiah: "Psalm 22 cannot be the prayer and praise of just any afflicted Israelite."[16] This may be so, in the sense that only the King or only the Messiah could be truly representative of the entire nation. However, I consider the very reason that Ps 22 is fitting for Mark to appropriate to the dying Jesus is that it *is precisely* the prayer of "*any* afflicted Israelite" (*my emphasis*). Each afflicted person of God finds his or her pain vocalized within this psalm. It is precisely this relationship between the individual and the corporate interpretation that provides the significance of the Messiah praying this prayer. In doing so, the Messiah is shown to be suffering the same suffering as the people. Each person could pray this prayer and find their own suffering expressed in it; when the Messiah prays this prayer, he is truly joining in the suffering of the people. And as he prays, each person could find their own prayer expressed in it. This reflects the solidarity expressed in the *pathos* of God who *goes with* his people while saving them.

Full of irony, Mark's crucifixion narrative presents Jesus as King of the Jews (15:2, 9, 12, 18, 26, 32) whose own personal cry is expressed as the cry

---

15. Imagery of wild animals representing national enemies is common in apocalyptic and poetic literature (i.e., in Daniel, cf. Isa 35:9).

16. Mays, "Prayer and Christology," 329.

of all God's people of all times and places. The narrative continues through the tearing of the temple curtain, signifying God's action of salvation,[17] to the confession of the centurion (15:39). Mark's hearers who have listened carefully are invited to discover the fulfilment of Psalm 22 as this representative of the nations now "recognizes and turns to the LORD and bows down before him" (see Ps 22:27–28) by acknowledging that Jesus was the Son of God.[18] God had indeed heard the cry of Jesus, and heeded his call for rescue. But just as his personal cry becomes the cry of all God's people, his rescue becomes salvation for all God's people. But his rescue is not in being taken down from the cross. Jesus dies. Ironically, it is in his dying—in embodying the lament of all God's people—that his cry is heard and heeded. It is precisely in his dying that the temple curtain is torn and the Centurion becomes convinced that he was the Son of God. It is significant that these two events are narrated immediately after Jesus's last breath. The death of Jesus, in which he joins in the depths of the suffering of God's people, is the decisive moment of the coming of God's great salvation.

In Mark, Jesus's death marks the decisive moment of God's salvation but it does not chronologically mark the end of all suffering. In 10:35–45, the Markan Jesus explains to his disciples that their own leadership in the Kingdom of God will be accomplished through their service, which will include suffering just as Jesus's own leadership meant giving his life.

Jesus's cry as King of God's people provides hope by embodying *their* suffering in the context of salvation. The Jewish story of salvation begins with the lament. In Exod 3:7–10, when God calls Moses to lead his people out of Egypt, he recalls to Moses twice that he has heard the lament of the people and has therefore come to save them. By placing the Ps 22 lament on the lips of Jesus at his moment of death, Mark communicates Jesus as the

---

17. The tearing of the curtain could signify several things at once. It forms an inclusio with the tearing open of the heavens in Mark 1:10 (see Ulansey, "Heavenly Veil"); it is an action of God forming a pair with the darkness of 15:33 (see Brower, "Elijah," 89–90, 92); it could indicate the opening of God's presence and salvation to all, without the levels of separation implicit in the temple system (Hooker, *Mark*, 378); and it could indicate God's judgment over the temple as Jesus becomes the new locus of God's presence on earth (Rossé, *Cry of Jesus on the Cross*, 71). None of these explanations need exclude the other.

18. Collins, *Mark*, 771; Brown, *Death of the Messiah*, 1149. Malbon, *Mark's Jesus*, 189: "Even if the Markan Jesus does not sense the presence of God in his death, the Markan narrator does. Even if the Markan Jesus is crying out only the first verse of Psalm 22, the Markan narrator seems aware of the entire Psalm—and is making sure that 'future generations will be told about the Lord.'"

embodiment of the lament that causes God to hear and see the suffering of his people, and the guarantee that God is accomplishing salvation.[19]

Eschatological Hope

As Richard Hays says, the royal psalms of lament would be read "as paradigmatic for Israel's corporate national sufferings in the present time, and their characteristic triumphant conclusions would be read as pointers to God's eschatological restoration of Israel."[20] The *LXX* includes the words εἰς τὸ τέλος in the heading of Ps 22 (in the *LXX*: Ps 21), reflecting this eschatological hope. The sufferings of the Jewish people longing for ultimate salvation became the womb of this cry for God's intervention and this expression of hope that God would indeed hear and come to their rescue.

As we have seen above, Mark uses Ps 22 in exactly this manner. By crying out the excruciating pain of ελωι ελωι λεμα σαβαχθανι; the Markan Jesus expresses the cries of all the sufferings of God's people. At the same time, and without softening the misery represented in the cry, Mark's hearers are reminded of the eschatological comfort provided by Ps 22. The rejoicing will not only include God's people whose cries for help have been heard, but will extend to all the nations, and include even those who have gone "down to the dust" and the "people yet unborn."

Mark's narrative supports the inclusion of this promise of eschatological salvation in the allusion evoked by the incipit Ps 22:1. At the beginning of his story, Mark narrates the tearing open of the heavens while God speaks, announcing that Jesus is his beloved Son in whom he is well-pleased (1:10–11). As we have seen above, the tearing open of the heavens likely alludes to the cry for God's salvation in Isa 64:1, "O, that you would rend the heavens and come down!"[21] At the crucifixion narrative, Mark tightly sandwiches the tearing of the temple curtain (15:38) within the narration of Jesus's death (15:37 and 15:39). I have noted elsewhere the description that Josephus has given of the outer temple curtain: an embroidered version of the heavenly bodies.[22] The sandwich indicates that the tearing of this temple curtain, which at the same time indicates a tearing of the heavens, has everything to do with Jesus's death. But this also hooks back to the tearing of the heavens in 1:10–11, with its allusion to Isa 64:1. If we are right to find an

---

19. See the discussion above (chapter 7) regarding the ransom language of 10:45 indicating God's personal guarantee that he will accomplish salvation.
20. Hays, "Christ Prays the Psalms," 110–11.
21. Hooker, *Mark*, 46; Lane, *Mark*, 55; Guelich, *Mark*, 32. France, *Mark*, 77.
22. See chapter 2 above.

allusion to God's salvation in the tearing of the heavens, then Mark is telling his hearers that Jesus's death is to be interpreted as God's salvific action. Though Gese misses the significant sandwich construction,[23] he agrees that the death of Jesus marks the eschatological break-through of the Kingdom of God:

> It is not as in Isa 53 the sin offering of which is spoken, nor even of the Messiah, but of *the death which reached to the deepest experience of suffering* which together with the work of God saving from death leads to the invasion of the eschatological Kingdom of God. The one who had announced this Kingdom in his life, leads it on in his death.[24]

One lingering question remains, however. If Mark's Gospel is meant to portray the coming of God's salvation, why does he not give the resurrection more attention in his narrative?[25] Mark's emphasis, however, is on the suffering and death of Jesus as the decisive act of God's salvation.[26]

In his presentation of the resurrection, Mark seems to be careful not to emphasize it too greatly. Women discover the empty tomb, where they are spoken to by "a young man dressed in a white robe" (16:5). Mark's description of this messenger is merely a "young man dressed in a white robe." Mark does not often speak of clothing, and when he does it is significant. The fact that he describes the young man in a white robe, giving the women a message from the risen Jesus, most likely indicates that he is a heavenly messenger, though the meagre description of his clothing need not indicate this. Luke adds a bit of drama to the scene here and says that *two* men *suddenly* appeared dressed in clothes that *gleamed like lightening* (Luke 24:4). Matthew speaks of a violent earthquake "for an angel of the Lord came down from heaven" whose "appearance was like lightening, and his clothes were

---

23. See Gese, "Psalm 22," 196.

24. Gese, "Psalm 22," 196. *Emphasis mine* (original, including my emphasis: "Es ist hier nicht wie in Jes 53 vom Sühnopfer die Rede, ja noch nicht einmal vom Messias, sondern *der zur tiefsten Leiderfahrung gesteigerte Tod* führt mit dem aus dem Tod herausrettenden Gotteshandeln zum Einbruch der eschatologischen βασιλεία τοῦ θεοῦ. Derjenige, der diese βασιλεία in seinem Leben verkündet hat, führt sie in seinem Tod herbei").

25. For the prominence of the resurrection in the proclamation of the early church, see Hays, "Christ Prays the Psalms," 111. See also 1 Thess 4:13–18 as an example of the presentation of the eschatological resurrection as encouragement to believers in the early church.

26. Gese does combine the resurrection as the salvific act of God with the death of Jesus as the catalysts for coming of the eschatological Kingdom. It is the death of Jesus, however, that receives the emphasis in Mark, and Gese recognizes this as well (cf. "Psalm 22," 196).

white as snow" (Matt 28:2–3). Mark has no need to emphasize the splendor of this angel after his focus on the breakthrough of salvation on the cross. To Mark, the resurrection is an important, vital part of the narrative, but his priority is the crucifixion narrative.

When one text is called upon to illumine another text, neither text is left untouched. Mark's presentation of salvation is not the same after his allusion to Ps 22. Neither is his presentation of salvation exactly that of Ps 22. Psalm 22 reflects a hope of a realized eschatology—God will hear the King's cry and come to the nation's rescue. When God hears the cry of the King, his response will encompass the cries of all the people ("they who seek the LORD will praise him" Ps 22:26). The blessing will reach out to all the corners of the earth, beyond space ("all who go down to the dust will kneel before him—those who cannot keep themselves alive") and time ("Posterity will serve him; future generations will be told about the Lord"). While Mark does not negate this Jewish longing that had been expressed throughout the centuries, not in the least through the use of the psalms, he presents the reality of salvation more as a movement towards that moment in which there will be no more suffering. The decisive moment in this movement is the death of Jesus on the cross. This is indicated by Mark's entire plot which builds the tension up throughout the narrative towards the cross, and is underlined by the tearing of the temple curtain and the confession of the Centurion.[27]

But Mark has woven a second line of tension into his story that is not resolved within the narrative. We have seen that Mark provides a promise to his audience that Jesus would be the one who would baptize them in the Holy Spirit. God's Holy Spirit would enable all who would follow Jesus to do just that: to follow him—even to the cross. The disciples have a role to play in God's scheme of salvation, but they do not seem able either to grasp the significance or exhibit the ability to live up to their role, though Mark presents Jesus's teaching very clearly. Those who would follow Jesus the Messiah *must* deny themselves, pick up their crosses and follow after him. They would be leaders in Jesus's Kingdom, but their leadership would consist of serving and being a slave to the least. Mark's plot does not show the disciples responding to this teaching or fulfilling their role. The tension that builds up because of their continual lack of understanding is not resolved, though climaxed in their running away and leaving Jesus to suffer alone. The promise that was spoken to the crowds around John the Baptist in 1:8 was revealed in 9:1 to the Markan disciples. The Kingdom of God will

27. Weeden, "Cross as Power in Weakness," 115: "That the death scene is the climactic event toward which the entire Gospel points is an inescapable conclusion thrust upon the reader by the unfolding drama."

come with power at the moment of the cross enabling the disciples to give their lives for Jesus and the sake of the gospel. This indicates that even after Jesus's death on the cross, there still will be work to be done. In this movement beyond the cross, the disciples *will* exercise leadership in serving and giving their lives for others (10:42–45), for they will be empowered through Jesus Christ to do so.

In Mark's presentation of salvation, the death of Jesus on the cross is the decisive moment when the cry of lament of all God's people is heard, and the power of the Kingdom is released in response. Mark begins his narrative appropriately by calling it "the beginning of the gospel about Jesus Christ, Son of God" (1:1). The salvation that Mark presents is indeed eschatological, and is not to be forced into just one moment in time. It has a decisive moment: the death of Jesus the Messiah. But it is to continue to grow as Jesus's disciples respond to the power released in Jesus's death.[28]

A Meaningful Misunderstanding: Seeing Elijah at the Cross

We have discussed earlier Mark's theme of understanding-misunderstanding throughout the Gospel.[29] Mark uses misunderstandings creatively in the discourse with his audience. As the disciples misunderstand the Markan Jesus, the implied hearers are prodded to consider Mark's intended meaning. This is illustrated well by Jesus's exasperated remark to his disciples in 8:17–18: "Do you still not see or understand? Are your hearts hardened? Do you have eyes but fail to see, and ears but fail to hear? And don't you remember?" The attentive audience is guided to look for important truths. And shortly following this remark, the audience is led to agree with Peter's announcement that Jesus is the Messiah. But this is quickly followed by another misunderstanding. Jesus claims that he must suffer and die at the hands of the leaders. And Peter fails to understand that this is part of his being Messiah. And this leads Mark's audience once again on to discover that even all who want to be a disciple must go this way as well. Each misunderstanding is planned to lead the audience to a deeper and truer understanding.

---

28. Cf. 4:26–32. See also Gese, "Psalm 22," 201, *translation mine*: "We understand the announcement of the death of Jesus, which was originally drenched in Psalm 22, . . . as the founding of the new being, in which the Risen One is present" (original: "Wir verstehen den Bericht vom Tod Jesu, der ursprünglich ganz von Ps 22 geprägt wird, . . . als Stiftung des neuen Seins, in dem der Auferstandene da ist").

29. See especially chapter 7 above.

As Jesus hangs on the cross in the depths of his suffering, Mark again narrates a flagrant misunderstanding. And, as Mark does, he draws attention to the misunderstanding without spelling out exactly what his hearers ought to understand. Hints are given, however, of where to look and what to listen for. Jesus had just cried out, "ελωι ελωι λεμα σαβαχθανι;" and some people standing near *hear* him and think that he is calling to Elijah. Offering him some sour wine in a sponge on a stick, they sit back to *see* if perhaps Elijah might come and rescue him. These people who had been standing near, *heard* and *looked*. But they heard wrongly, and therefore understood wrongly—Jesus was not calling out to Elijah, nor was he crying out to be taken down from the cross—and therefore they also sought wrongly to see if he would be rescued. They did not seek to look and hear well and thoroughly, and therefore they failed to understand.

Mark makes it clear to his audience what the bystanders ought to have understood. He quotes Ps 22:1, first in Aramaic, then translating it into Greek. He makes certain that his own audience first of all *hears* correctly, emphasizing it by the translation so that they will understand its importance. We have discussed above what they would have been led to understand: that Jesus is crying out the lament of all God's people, in the context of eschatological salvation. Jesus is dying as a righteous sufferer, representing all those of God's people who have suffered unjustly, and God is hearing his cry.

But why would Mark add precisely *this* misunderstanding at this place? We don't even know who the people are who are standing nearby and who misunderstand his cry. Collins notes that the use of the words *to hear* and *to see* here reflect 4:11–12, indicating that these bystanders are the outsiders inferred in 4:11.[30] But Mark is more interested in teasing his hearers into listening and looking correctly than in judging those who do not.[31] The Elijah misunderstanding is placed here purposefully by Mark to encourage his hearers to understand something.

The misunderstanding is woven intricately into the moment of Jesus's death, immediately after Jesus's loud cry to God, and right before Mark tells his hearers that Jesus died with a loud cry. Notwithstanding the fact that it

---

30. Collins, *Mark*, 755.

31. Although, there is a consistent theme of the judgment which those who do not accept Jesus's authority call down upon themselves, as reflected in especially 3:22–30; 11:12–21; and 12:1–12. While there could be an element of judgment reflected in the reference to the darkness that came over the land in 15:33 and the tearing of the temple curtain in 15:38, the misunderstanding does not seem to be primarily about judgment. At this place in the narrative, Mark is more interested in luring his hearers into understanding that suffering is part and parcel of the story of salvation.

would physically be most unlikely that a crucified man could die with a loud cry, Mark notes this cry twice.[32] Between these two cries, in the center of this misunderstanding, we find an allusion to Psalm 69:21, another psalm of a righteous sufferer. This reinforces the depths of the suffering of Jesus that Mark would have his hearers understand—and the fact that Jesus died as a righteous sufferer.[33] With the second mention of the cry, he is pulling the attention of his hearer back to the words of the incipit Ps 22:1.[34] Mark wants his hearers to understand the death of Jesus from the context of Ps 22. Jesus's death embodies and expresses the suffering of all God's people, and has everything to do with the coming of God's salvation. In contrast to what the bystanders hear, Mark's audience is to *hear* Ps 22:1, and *understand* Jesus's death as an expression of the suffering of God's people (the righteous), and seek to *see* the coming salvation from God.

The misunderstanding itself is a tool that Mark uses to engage his audience into searching to understand, but the mention of Elijah is also significant. This was discussed earlier, in chapter 3 concerning the promise of the Holy Spirit who was in Jesus and enabled him to obey even in the deepest suffering. Mark has added a faint echo of the Elijah/Elisha narrative of II Kings 2:9–14, reminding his hearers that if they see correctly, this Spirit will be available to them as well.[35] But in addition to this aspect of the misunderstanding, Mark wants his audience to remember all they have heard up to this point of Elijah. In the words of Steichele: "When Elijah is mentioned in Mark 15:35f, it alludes immediately to all that has been said ... about this Old Testament prophet throughout the Gospel."[36] What has been said so far about Elijah in Mark's story?

As we have seen, Mark's narrative structure rests on the three statements that Jesus is the Son of God, in 1:11, 9:7, and 15:39. Elijah enters the narrative each time connected to one of these Son of God statements.[37]

In Second Temple Judaism, there was an expectation that Elijah would return as an announcement of the coming of salvation.[38] This expectation

---

32. Whether or not Mark is equating the two cries as one, his second mention of a cry at the actual moment of death echoes clearly the cry of Ps 22:1, creating the literary sandwich by bringing his hearers back to the excruciating suffering of Jesus's death.

33. Steichele, *Der Leidende Sohn Gottes*, 277.

34. See also Brown, *Death of the Messiah*, 1079.

35. See chapter 3 above.

36. Steichele, *Der leidende Sohn Gottes*, 278, *translation mine* (original: "Wenn Elija in Mk 15,35f erwähnt wird, klingt damit zugleich all das an, was im Laufe des Evangeliums von diesem atl Propheten ... erzählt worden ist.").

37. See also Witherington, *Mark*, 398.

38. See Steichele, *Der leidende Sohn Gottes*, 67–69; Jeremias, "Ηλ(ε)ίας," *TDNT*

is echoed in the opening of Mark's gospel. Mark quotes from Mal 3:1 ("See, I will send my messenger, who will prepare the way before me")[39] in his opening quotation (1:2–3) which places Mark's message in line with God's story of salvation. Interpreted in its own context of Mal 4:5 ("See, I will send you the prophet Elijah before that great and dreadful day of the LORD comes"), the messenger of Mal 3:1 would be Elijah of Mal 4:5.[40] Mark further describes John the Baptist as the forerunner of Jesus using words that were descriptive of Elijah (1:6, cf. II Kings 1:8).

Later on in the narrative, at the Transfiguration moment, Mark portrays Jesus speaking with Elijah[41] and Moses before Peter makes his awkward remark about wishing to put up three tents, when God's voice is heard from heaven claiming Jesus as his beloved Son and admonishing the disciples to listen to him. Directly afterwards, on the way down the mountain, Jesus and his disciples have an interesting conversation about Elijah (9:11–13). In this conversation, as we discussed in chapter 8 above, Mark intertwines statements about the coming of Elijah and the suffering of the Son of Man. Earlier Mark had placed the mission of the disciples (6:7–13, 30) in the context of the rejection and suffering experienced by John the Baptist, Elijah *redivivus*. Mark is establishing a pattern.

Suffering and rejection are the responses that God's people can expect as they exercise authority and leadership within God's Kingdom. But that is not the whole story. Elijah had come to *restore all things* (9:12; cf. Mal 4:5–6). Full restoration is coming. Yet, while there are still those who reject the authority that God has given to them, God's people can expect to be rejected and to suffer many things.[42]

When Mark refers to Elijah in the crucifixion narrative, it is a tightly woven reminder of both the pattern of suffering and rejection that has been

---

2:931; Öhler, "Expectation of Elijah," 461–62.

39. The conflated quotation includes Isa 40:3 and Exod 23:20.

40. The reference to Mal 4:5 in Mark 9:11–12 encourages this interpretation.

41. According to Öhler (*Elia im Neuen Testament*, 125–27, 135) the Elijah who appears with Moses on the mountain to speak to Jesus is the historical Elijah, and not Elijah *redivivus*. The significance of the appearance of these two heavenly citizens would be merely to emphasize the heavenly sphere, into which the disciples are given a peek (125: "Elia und Mose [erscheinen] vor allem als Bewohner des Himmels. Sie gehören in jene Sphäre, in die die Jünger schauen dürfen und zu der Jesus eigentlich gehört"). Narratively, however, this appearance of Elijah does prompt the question in Mark 9:11 regarding the return of Elijah.

42. See also Weihs, *Die Deutung des Todes Jesu im Markusevangelium*, 443–44. Weihs recognizes that Mark specifically brings the suffering of all three (Elijah *redivivus*, Jesus, and the disciples) together in this text under the umbrella of God's will and God's Salvation plan.

established in his narrative, and the importance of hearing and seeing the right things in order to understand properly. While those standing nearby could only imagine that if some supernatural interference by Elijah were to come, perhaps then they would accept that Jesus was someone special, Mark indicates that the suffering of Jesus is only truly to be understood in the context of the suffering of Elijah (John the Baptist).[43]

The Markan Jesus dies as a righteous sufferer as is indicated by Mark's use of Ps 22:1 at the height of the suffering of Jesus. Though popular belief would say that Elijah would come to help the righteous in their suffering, Mark had already conditioned his hearers to understand that the way of rejection and suffering of the Son of Man had been prepared by Elijah. This is what Mark's ideal audience will realize as they hear the reference to Elijah in this emotion-filled scene.

But Mark is a master storyteller. This misunderstanding will continue to irritate his hearers, probing them to think further. We have already discussed the possibility of the Elijah/Elisha narrative as background to Mark's narrative, in which Elisha is given a double portion of Elijah's spirit after *seeing* him taken up.[44] Perhaps Mark is using irony here to allude to this historical Elijah, whose story may indeed help the righteous in their suffering, though perhaps differently from what those standing near expected? If so, then Mark's ideal audience will look more closely to the dying Jesus in order to understand and receive power to follow him when the time comes to pick up their own cross (9:1).

Conclusions

In this chapter, three implications have been drawn out of Mark's use of Psalm 22 in his crucifixion narrative. The first implication is that Jesus is described as dying as a Righteous Sufferer. Mark uses this Ps 22 as a portrayal of the depths of unjust suffering. This suffering is common to the Jewish people; their texts are full of stories of God's righteous people suffering unjustly. Mark portrays Jesus as taking part in this suffering.

The second implication is a communal nuance given to the death of Jesus. Ps 22 is a lament of King David. Such a lament of a king gives words to the suffering of the entire nation. These are words which any one of God's people could cry out in their own suffering; because they are spoken by

---

43. See Brower, "Elijah," 95: "The crowd is right in noting that Elijah does not come but it is radically wrong in its understanding of why he does not. . . . Elijah embodies the righteous sufferer motif in the same fashion as does the Son of Man."

44. See chapter 3 above.

Jesus, the King of God's people, they are at once the cumulative cry of all the people. In chapter 5 above, we discussed Jesus's suffering as an expression of the Pathos of God. By invoking Ps 22, Mark shows Jesus joining in the suffering of God's people as God moves his salvation story forward through this suffering and death of Jesus. The Markan Jesus is a reflection and expression of the God who goes with his people while saving them.[45]

The third implication is its eschatological aspect. The psalmist promises that praise to God will arise from all corners of the earth, as well as throughout generations, if and when the cry for help is answered. Jesus dies embodying the lament of all righteous sufferers, the excruciating pain of felt-abandonment by God. While he does so, God remains active behind the scenes. God carries the story from Ps 22:1 to the end of the psalm, and no sooner had Mark mentioned the cry for a second time than salvation had come to the ends of the earth (cf. Ps 22:27). The temple curtain was torn from top to bottom, and the Gentile centurion recognized, "ἀληθῶς οὗτος ὁ ἄνθρωπος υἱὸς θεοῦ ἦν" (Mark 15:39).

But Mark shows through the Elijah misunderstanding that something else is going on as well. The death narrative is centered around Ps 69, also a psalm of a Righteous Sufferer. The next layer, between the cry of Jesus and his last breath, is the Elijah misunderstanding. This functions in two ways. First of all, it reminds Mark's audience of the pattern of suffering that was set forth in the rejection and death that John the Baptist experienced. Jesus's death is part of this pattern, and their own rejection and suffering as God's people will also be part of this pattern. They know, however, that they cannot do this on their own. This misunderstanding might also remind them of the Elijah and Elisha narrative. Elisha receives double the spirit that was in Elijah after *seeing* him taken up. Mark coaxes his audience into *looking* so that they can truly *see* as Jesus dies. If they truly *see* and understand Jesus's death, they will receive God's Spirit to enable them to obey in their own suffering.

The discussion of Mark's passion narrative and his use of the Psalms 22 and 69 has shown that Mark indeed presents salvation in a way that includes not only the death of Jesus but the faithful following of disciples as well. Even though the incipit Ps 22:1 describes an experience of intense loneliness, it also provides a communal nuance that reminds Mark's readers of the pattern of suffering, which is to include them, that he has already set out in his narrative.

The intertextual investigation of Mark's use of Isaiah, the phrase Son of Man and its allusion to Daniel 7, and the allusions to Psalms 22 and 69

---

45. See also chapter 5 above.

in the crucifixion narrative, have each emphasized the pattern of suffering along which the way of salvation lies. It is not surprising then that Mark introduces the coming passion of Jesus with the little word δεῖ (8:31). It is not that God demands such suffering (or that such suffering would be demanded of him), but suffering of the righteous is the pattern that Mark has found in Scripture. And this is the way that Jesus must go. In Part Two, we saw that Mark has drawn upon his Jewish culture in portraying the way of Jesus in terms of the *pathos* of God, and the solidarity that binds God's family. The way that God goes, is the way that Jesus goes, is the way that Jesus's brothers and sisters and mother will go.

10

Conclusions

*Salvation in the Gospel of Mark as the Cross
of Jesus and the Path of Discipleship*

THIS STUDY BEGAN WITH an observation that Mark couples teaching about the death of Jesus to teaching about the necessity for the disciples to give their lives as well. These moments of double teaching are highlighted by their placement at the center of Mark's narrative, surrounded by an inclusio of blind healings, suggesting that the content of these teachings are of immense importance to Mark's message. The blind healings surrounding these teachings encourage Mark's audience to seek to see in a way that will lead to repentance and salvation (Mark 4:21–23; cf. 4:12). Furthermore, Mark's entire narrative is built upon three foundational pillar moments, in which Mark establishes his focus on salvation, and in which Jesus is recognized as the Son of God. This foundational structure was found to support and underline the teaching section, providing a context of salvation in which the teaching is to be understood.

The question that arises from this observation has to do with the significance of the suffering, or the cross, of the followers of Jesus in relation to that of Jesus. Does Mark put these on the same level of being necessary to God's story of salvation? How does the death of the disciples relate to that of Jesus according to Mark?

One aspect of Mark's narrative that seems on the surface to contradict, or at least to subdue, the teachings of the Markan Jesus is the failure of the disciples truly to understand and follow Jesus to the end in giving their lives. But did Mark intend to subdue the teaching of Jesus by portraying the failure of the disciples so vividly? In order to come closer to understanding the relationship between the death of Jesus and the suffering of the disciples, we have looked at motifs from Mark's socio-historical background that may have influenced Mark's message. Various allusions to Scripture that Mark has woven into his narrative have also been discussed, and these have indicated that Mark presents his narrative, in which the coupling of this suffering is central, as the fulfilling of hopes of eschatological salvation evoked by God's work of deliverance in Israelite history. The insights gleaned from Mark's background have been found to emphasize and support the message taught by the Markan Jesus: true discipleship entails a faithful following of Jesus even in the face of death.

We will now summarize these different insights into Mark's narrative with the goal of describing their cumulative effect on an understanding of the relationship of the suffering and death of Jesus and the giving of their lives of those who follow him in respect to salvation.

Sociohistorical Background

In the Greco-Roman world in which the Gospel of Mark was written, it was a common thing to lift up the death of a hero as something to emulate in similar circumstances. Admonitions to do so were written up in Noble Death accounts. The question arises: is Mark a sort of Noble Death account in which the audience is encouraged to face death with the same courage as the hero, Jesus? A reading of the martyrs' stories of the early Church gives one the impression that the Gospel was used in this way.

Mark's story, however, has a remarkable difference from these Noble Death accounts. Mark shows Jesus suffering in the deepest fear (14:34), falling to the ground to beg God repeatedly to allow his suffering to pass by (14:35–36, 39, 41). On the cross, he screams out, feeling that God had abandoned him (15:34). This is not Noble Death behavior. In the Noble Death accounts, the heroes were those who had conquered their fear and faced death with head held high, without a trace of emotion. This is the attitude these writings encouraged their audiences to emulate. For Mark to choose a completely different route was potentially shaming to his hero. And yet, he did this. There must have been a good reason for portraying Jesus with the common human emotions related to suffering: deathly fear and desperation.

In the Jewish literature depicting the character of God, we found a pattern that may very well have formed a background to Mark's portrayal of Jesus in the *pathos* of God. God is affected by the obedience or lack thereof from his people. He hates injustice, and is pleased with righteousness and compassion. His *pathos* moves him to choose faithfulness to his people, even in the depths of the pain caused by their unfaithfulness to him. When his people call out to him, he hears them, forgives their wanderings and goes with them to save them.

But to say that Jesus reflects God's *pathos* calls for a deeper look at the relationship between Jesus and God in Mark's Gospel. Mark portrays Jesus as Son of God, claimed so by God himself. He also portrays Jesus with divine qualities. He exerts authority that can only come from God; he calms storms and a raging sea; he walks on water. And Mark has him call out in comfort to the disciples who think he may be a ghost with the pregnant words, "I am." Mark does not say straight out that Jesus is God; he *says* that Jesus is God's Son. But in being God's Son, Jesus is *shown* to live out the authority and presence of God. A revised understanding of the corporate personality that is inherent in a Scriptural (especially in Ezekiel) understanding of the family helps to elucidate Mark's family language. Jesus, as God's beloved Son reflects God. When Jesus exorcises an evil spirit, God has healed the person. When Jesus gives his life, God has brought salvation. What his Son does, God does. Mark enhances this when he shows the Holy Spirit descending on Jesus at his baptism. It is no surprise, then, that when Jesus moves and speaks and does, God is moving, speaking and doing.

But Jesus is not meant to remain an only child. All who obey his Father are his mother and brothers and sisters. Jesus is the first, and brings others into his role. Together they exhibit God's *pathos* in their role of bringing salvation to all the nations. Whether Mark intends that the high Christological characteristics that are given to Jesus are to be shared with the faithful "brothers and sisters and mothers" (3:34–35) is not clear. Neither is the complete implication of the Markan Jesus's use of the "I am" clear: does Mark intend to portray Jesus *as God*, or that God is seen and experienced in Jesus? Perhaps human words fail in the expression of the mystery of God expressing himself as a human being. Perhaps this is why Mark continuously urges his audience to look and listen carefully in order to understand so they might repent and be saved (cf. 4:12). There are mysteries implied in Mark's message that go beyond what his words can accomplish.

Intertextual Background

This aspect of God doing what actors on earth work out is also reflected in Mark's use of Isaiah as a background to his narrative. Mark provides his audience with several allusions to the narrative of Isaiah. The first is found right at the start by including Isa 40:3 in his opening quotation. The *way of the Lord* is prepared by John the Baptist, understood as Elijah *redivivus*, who later lays out the pattern of giving his life which Jesus then follows, and which is presented as the way the disciples are to follow. Mark quickly goes on to portray God's act of salvation coming as Jesus rises from the baptismal waters, the heavens open and God's Spirit descends upon him. This act does not stand alone, but forms an *inclusio* together with the tearing open of the temple curtain in 15:38, just as Jesus breathes out his spirit. This indicates that Mark's whole narrative is to be understood in the context of God's decisive, salvific action.

Mark alludes to the Servants of God from Deutero-Isaiah in the Markan Jesus's discipleship teachings. Although it is difficult to prove a specific allusion to Isa 53 in the ransom saying at Mark 10:45, as Hooker suggests, taken broadly, the Servant Songs seem to be in the background of all the discipleship teaching of the Markan Jesus. God stands as guarantor to bring salvation to his people. He does this through his servants. He can work through anyone. His servants, however, give themselves to God's salvation to the point of giving up their own lives.

Leadership in God's Kingdom is practiced in the form of service, of being a slave to the least and giving one's life for others. Suffering as par for the course in this pattern of service in God's Kingdom is brought into focus by Mark in his use of the term *Son of Man*. Current scholarship has come to the consensus that first century CE Judaism did not use the term as a title to denote a Messiah-like figure. What scholarship has taught us is that the term was used as a self-reference with a communal overtone. When the Markan Jesus uses this term, the various contexts indicate together a likely allusion to Daniel 7. In the vision recorded in Daniel 7, the righteous people of God suffer greatly under rulers who persecute them and mock God. But then God calls a halt to the situation, and the time comes for judgment of the evil and vindication of the righteous. Daniel sees one like a son of man approaching God, and being given "authority, glory and sovereign power" (Dan 7:14). In the interpretation of the vision, Daniel is told that authority in God's Kingdom is given to the saints of the Most High. The one like a son of man is a vision-figure representing God's holy people.

Mark uses the term the Son of Man, not as a title, but as a story-telling device alluding to this vision in Daniel. When Mark speaks of Jesus's suffering, he does so in terms of the Son of Man. This reminds his audience immediately of what they already know from Daniel: that all God's people will suffer before the time of vindication comes. In a few instances, Mark speaks of the Son of Man in terms of glory and vindication before God. This reminds his audience that to the obedient, faithful people of God, vindication will come, and the Kingdom will be given to them. At the same time, Mark uses the term only through the mouth of Jesus. It is Jesus who goes before all in being this Son of Man who is faithful in suffering and vindicated by God. But the story in Daniel informs the audience's understanding that this is the path that follows for all God's people.

Mark's narrative shows Jesus paving the way, as an icebreaker would, for all God's people to follow. At the moment of deepest suffering, on the cross, in the midst of mocking from all who see him, the Markan Jesus cries out. This time Mark puts words in his mouth from a psalm of a righteous sufferer, Ps 22. The psalm describes the depths of pain that the righteous experience as enemies torture them to death, while God is nowhere to be seen. This is not how life should be for the righteous, for those living according to God's ordinances. The faithful people of God should live in the land in safety and abundance, but the righteous experience depths of physical suffering together with the excruciating experience of God-forsakenness at moments when they might expect to experience God's comfort and protection. Mark portrays Jesus as coming right into the depths of this experience in his obedience to God. His cry of abandonment on the cross reflects the cries of all the suffering righteous.

As Jesus lets out a loud cry and breathes his last, the temple curtain is torn from top to bottom, and a centurion who sees Jesus die, acknowledges that he must surely be God's Son. Mark's audience remembers the tearing of the heavens and the descent of God's Holy Spirit at the beginning of the narrative, and knows that salvation has come. For even a representative of the leaders of the Gentile nations acknowledges Jesus as God's Son.

Mark's audience will remember the suffering of the servant in Isaiah as they listen intently to the scene of the crucifixion and the death of Jesus. They will remember God's promises of being the guarantor of their salvation. Mark's audience will remember the story from Daniel, and how God's Kingdom would be given to *all* the saints of the Most High. And they will remember the words of Jesus, told to them by Mark, that they, too, must pick up their cross and give their lives if they do not want to lose them. God will vindicate, but before that happens, there will be suffering. They will see in Jesus's suffering the path that they are to follow. Obedience to God will lead them in ways that bring resistance from those not following God, who will torture and kill them. Mark's audience will see this happening in Jesus. And this will remind them of their own path in God's way of salvation.

Mark tells this passionate story of the Son of God sharing in the depths of human suffering, preparing and going the way that all God's holy people will go as God's servants in his bringing salvation. But this leaves his hearers with an uncanny feeling. The group closest to Jesus, his disciples, were not able to go to the cross with him. They had wanted to, had even thought they could, but they could not and did not. The disciples had abandoned Jesus; how could Mark's hearers ever remain faithful? Does Mark torture his audience with his story when they could never attain to its standards? To Mark's hearers, God's salvation takes on extra dimensions.

To join in God's Kingdom, they *must* obey God. But they *cannot*, so even to take part in salvation, they are led by Mark to entreat God to make them able to obey. Salvation begins to mean the basic ability to obey, in order to join in God's salvific movement.

Woven into his narrative, Mark provides hope that it is precisely in this death of Jesus that the key to one's own obedience will appear. The prologue is built up around the promise from John the Baptist that Jesus will baptize the repentant in the Holy Spirit. Immediately following this promise, Mark's audience is shown Jesus himself being baptized in the Holy Spirit, and the story of the Kingdom of God begins. The story that follows is one of a human being obeying God fully, and living out God's presence on earth. Jesus calls people to be his followers, and to share in his mission. Together they preach about God's Kingdom; they cast out evil spirits, and heal the sick. This ministry eventually leads to the cross, and that is where the paths of Jesus and of his disciples diverge. Jesus, full of God's Holy Spirit, is faithful to the end; the disciples, forgetting to ask God for help, abandon Jesus in an attempt to save themselves.

Salvation in the Gospel of Mark: The Cross of Jesus and the Path of Discipleship

We have shown how Mark has built reminders of the promise of the Holy Spirit into his narrative at crucial points. Mark promises that Jesus will provide baptism in the Holy Spirit to those longing to obey God (the ones John the Baptist spoke to were those who had come to him in repentance). In Mark 4, themes of obedience, the difficulty of understanding, and the hope of salvation are masterfully woven together.

The parable of the Sower provides the background: there is good ground that yields great amounts of fruit, and there are all sorts of ground that do not yield fruit. The description of the rocky ground fits the unfolding characterization of the disciples: they want to follow, but the troubles and persecutions are too much for them and they fall away. Tied to this parable, inserted in the center between its telling and its explanation, the Markan Jesus tells the disciples that they have the secret of the Kingdom, and those outside are kept in the dark so that they will not see and understand, hear and perceive, otherwise they might turn and be forgiven.

This sounds at first a bit fatalistic. However, the Markan Jesus continues immediately to reassure Mark's audience that a light is never brought out to be kept hidden, but to give light. Those who can hear, must do their best to listen carefully. The groups to whom Jesus speaks seem to overlap.

Mark seems purposefully vague about when Jesus is inside speaking to the disciples, and when he is outside speaking to the crowds. His purpose is not to describe Jesus teaching a predetermined fate for insiders and outsiders, but to encourage his audience to seek actively with their eyes and ears for the secret of God's Kingdom and thereby come inside where they can see clearly. With the parable of the Sower, or rather of the ground sorts, at the background to these teachings, Mark's audience is conditioned to expect this secret of the Kingdom to be the key to obedient faithfulness. At the end of the section, the disciples and Jesus move out to sea, while still in the boat (4:35–36; cf. 4:1). A great storm picks up which Jesus then stills. The disciples are dumbfounded. Who is this man? Someone with ears to hear might consider that only the God who created the sea could still the sea (cf. Jonah 1:9–11). Mark's audience is given a hint at where to find the secret of the Kingdom of God: in Jesus.

As Mark continues his narrative, he consistently portrays Jesus together with his disciples. What Jesus does, the disciples do. They may not understand (cf. 8:14–21), but they do it. They proclaim the gospel, heal the sick, and cast out demons, just as Jesus does. And then, in the midst of the Markan Jesus's teaching to the disciples that they not only share in his authority but also will share in his suffering, he encourages them that they will see the Kingdom of God come with power before they taste death. We have discussed how this may also mean that they will finally perceive the true power of God's salvation at the moment of greatest powerlessness, at the cross of Jesus. And then, when their own time comes to choose death instead of life on account of Jesus, they will also know the power of the Kingdom of God within themselves, enabling them to follow Jesus even in death. But this death will lead to life (see 8:35—9:1).

At the moment of Jesus' death, Mark narrates a misunderstanding about Elijah. In doing so, he not only reminds his hearers that they are to join in the pattern of dying that John the Baptist set and Jesus followed, but he also alludes to the narrative of Elijah's assumption into heaven. In that story, Elisha *saw* Elijah and received a double portion of his spirit (see 2 Kings 2:9–12). This enabled him to do twice the miraculous works that Elijah had done as man of God. *Seeing* plays an important part in the crucifixion narrative. The temple leaders mockingly suggest that if they *see* Jesus get down from the cross they would believe; the one misunderstanding Jesus's cry suggests they *see* if Elijah comes to help. The Centurion *seeing* how Jesus dies is heard making a confession of faith. Those looking wrongly do not find what they are looking for. It is noted only of the centurion that he *saw* how Jesus *died*, and it is as if the Holy Spirit himself gives him the words, "Surely this man is a Son of God." Together with two sayings of the voice of God calling Jesus his Son (1:11 and 9:7), this confession forms a foundational pillar to Mark's narrative. It seems a bit strange that Mark would begin his pattern with God speaking these words twice, and then break the pattern to have a Roman centurion speak the words. But perhaps the third pillar moment is spoken by God, too. The Holy Spirit is given to even Gentiles if they *see and perceive*.

Mark's audience is comforted even further when the women who had stood near, watching the crucifixion, come to the grave where Jesus had been put. They wonder who will help them move the stone that stands between them and Jesus. Perhaps Mark's ideal audience will remember the words of Jesus (4:16–17): the soil filled with stones hindering the growth of the seeds has begun to look very much like the disciples' reaction under persecution. Who will remove the stone(s)? Though Mark uses different words in 4:5 and 16:3, his ideal audience is visually oriented, and will make the connection: who will remove the rocks from the soil? When the women arrive at the tomb, they find that the stone has already been removed. The implication is that God has done this. This is reinforced when the young man dressed in white, presumably an angel from God, speaks to them, announcing that Jesus has risen from the dead, and that he goes before the disciples and Peter to Galilee . . . where they will *see* him. God's Holy Spirit will descend on them, too, enabling them to live in obedience as Jesus did.

Salvific Implications

The purpose of this study has been to understand, through a narrative reading of Mark, the nature of the relationship between the suffering of Jesus and the way of suffering for the disciples in Mark's message of salvation. Mark describes the two as intimately entwined. They belong together. They are bound by a shared depth of obedience to God. Both are necessary acts of God bringing his great work of eschatological salvation. Both will be vindicated by God himself. Together, Jesus and "those who would follow" (8:34) are included in the story of the Son of Man who will be seen in glory at the appointed time, after the time of greatest distress (13:26). The relationship of the one to the other is significantly different than the emulation of a Noble Death. These deaths are both painful ramifications of obedience to God, and together are acts of God's salvation on earth.

There is, however, a difference between the two. The death of Jesus may follow the pattern that included John the Baptist first, but only in the death of Jesus does Mark suggest that the Holy Spirit of God is manifested in such power that all who see and understand, will receive the Spirit and be able to confess Jesus as Son of God, and by implication, take up their cross and give their lives. In the death of Jesus lies the secret of the Kingdom of God: the manifestation of God's Holy Spirit who enabled Jesus to go the way of obedience that led to resistance and excruciating death, and who will enable followers to follow on that same way. God's Kingdom implies that God is Ruler. This implies that justice is done, sickness is gone, and evil spirits have fled never to return. But it also implies that, within each person, God's will is chosen above one's own will. Mark portrays this as the most difficult of all. It is impossible for humans, but, with God it is possible. God effects the enabling to do so himself, through his Spirit. But to accept this Spirit, one must look and listen, and perceive and understand the death of Jesus.

Both disciples and Jesus participate actively as God works out his salvation, and in that sense the suffering of both are salvific. But the truly good news that Mark brings to his audience is that through Jesus this is made possible for the disciples. The disciples' suffering is only salvific as they stay connected to Jesus in his suffering and death.

Contribution to Research

Much has been written on the Gospel of Mark throughout the years. Since the advent of narrative studies, Mark's full use of literary techniques has inspired many scholars in their interpretation of his little Gospel. Can anything new be said?

The strength of this study lies in the cumulative effect of the background studies together with the narrative interpretation. Much attention has been given to single aspects of Mark's Gospel. But Mark was prepared to be delivered as a whole to his audience. In its interpretation, the various backgrounds should be taken into consideration together with his various narrative focusses. Studying his Gospel from this perspective has led to the conclusion that his message portrays both the passion of Jesus and the path of the disciples who follow him as necessary aspects of God's story of salvation.

Where this study adds most directly to scholarship will be in the discussion of discipleship failure in Mark. No scholars have yet stretched the tension created in Mark by the failure of the disciples beyond the suggestion that failure is par for the course and that reconciliation is always available after failure. My interpretation that the promise of the Holy Spirit in 1:8 is intended to provide hope to Mark's audience of enabled obedience should be a fruitful addition to the conversation about discipleship in Mark.

With this hope as a background, many aspects of Mark's narrative can be studied anew. Mark portrays, for example, a curious fascination for clothing. While he hardly mentions clothing at all, when he does, it is meaningful. But how meaningful is the sheet that fell off the young man as he fled naked on that fateful night in Gethsemane? Does this have anything to do with the garment that might tear if a new patch were to be sewn on it (2:21)? Or with the white robe of the young man at the tomb? Does Mark's use of clothing have a similar connotation as of the wedding clothes told of by Matthew (Matt 22:11) or the robes of the saints in Rev 7:9–14?

Another issue that ought to be dealt with anew is a feminist understanding of the self-denial that Mark insists upon. Mary Vandenberg suggests in her article "Redemptive Suffering: Christ's alone" that no suffering of the disciples should be interpreted as redemptive because of a tendency for Christian women in abusive situations to conclude that their suffering is redemptive.[1] Her concern is legitimate, and the cross-bearing passages should never be used to justify abuse. The results of this research should be re-told with feminist concerns in mind, with special attention given to sensitive passages in Mark. A similar study could be attempted with the concerns of Liberation theologians in mind. Does Mark's message apply to those being forced into subservient positions by unrighteous politicians? It should not be forgotten that while Mark portrays the way of discipleship along the way of the cross that Jesus went, he also is clear that the message of this Kingdom of God is one that rebukes spiritual evil.

The message of following Jesus even unto death today is not popular. Yet for many believers it is a reality. There are many families who are not happy with members deciding that their loyalty to Christ goes beyond the loyalty to the family. There are many governments who do not want their citizens to follow Jesus. In some countries changing one's religion to Christianity is punishable with the death penalty or life imprisonment. Following Christ on this way is for them rebuking and overcoming evil in the way that Jesus did. The evil has no hold on them, not even in death. By giving their lives, they will gain their lives.[2]

Mark's Gospel is written as a Gospel of hope. It is the beginning of good news, and begs a response from its audience of looking intently and listening carefully. For this reason, a multi-discipline study of its theology with a contemporary pastoral emphasis might be a fruitful endeavor. Mark's little Gospel is, after all, pretentious in its implied pastoral purpose: to lead its audience to the place where they might find the heavens opening above them to see the Holy Spirit descend into them. Very rarely does a pastor preach of the Holy Spirit on Good Friday. Perhaps it would be a Markan thing to do.

1. See VandenBerg, "Redemptive Suffering."
2. See Thomas, *Unto Death*.

Bibliography

Achtemeier, Paul J. "*Omne verbum sonat*: The New Testament and the Oral Environment of Late Western Antiquity." *JBL* 109 (1990) 3-27.

Ahearne-Kroll, Stephen. *The Psalms of Lament in Mark's Passion: Jesus' Davidic Suffering*. Cambridge: Cambridge University Press, 2007.

———. "'Who Are My Mother and My Brothers?' Family Relations and Family Language in the Gospel of Mark." *JR* 81 (2001) 1-25.

Baltzer, Klaus. *Deutero-Isaiah: A Commentary on Isaiah 40-55*. Hermeneia. Translated by Margaret Kohl. Minneapolis: Fortress, 2001.

Barrett, C. K. "The Background of Mark 10:45." In *New Testament Essays: Studies in Memory of Thomas Walter Manson 1893-1958*, edited by A. J. B. Higgins, 1-18. Manchester: The University Press, 1959.

Barton, Stephen C. *Discipleship and Family Ties in Mark and Matthew*. SNTSMS 80. Cambridge: Cambridge University Press, 1994.

Bauckham, Richard. *God Crucified: Monotheism and Christology in the New Testament*. Didsbury Lectures 1996. Carlisle: Paternoster, 1998.

———. "The Son of Man: 'A Man in My Position' or 'Someone?'" *JSNT* 23 (1985) 23-33.

Beardslee, William A. "Saving One's Life by Losing It." *JAAR* 47 (1979) 57-72.

Bellinger, William H., and William R. Farmer, eds. *Jesus and the Suffering Servant: Isaiah 53 and Christian Origins*. Harrisburg, PA: Trinity, 1998.

Ben-Porat, Ziva. "The Poetics of Literary Allusion." *PTL* 1 (1976) 105-28.

Best, Ernest. *Disciples and Discipleship: Studies in the Gospel According to Mark*. Edinburgh: T. & T. Clark, 1986.

———. *Following Jesus: Discipleship in the Gospel of Mark*. JSNTSup 4. Sheffield: JSOT, 1981.

———. *Mark: The Gospel as Story*. Edinburgh: T. & T. Clark, 1983.

———. "Review of Wolfgang Roth, *Hebrew Gospel: Cracking the Code of Mark*." *SJT* 42 (1989) 575-76.

———. "The Role of the Disciples in Mark." *NTS* 23 (1977) 377-401.

Bird, Michael. "The Crucifixion of Jesus as the Fulfillment of Mark 9:1." *TJ* 24 (2003) 23-36.

Bligh, John. "Typology in the Passion Narratives: Daniel, Elijah, Melchizedek." *HeyJ* 6 (1965) 302-9.

Bock, Darrell. "Blasphemy and the Jewish Examination of Jesus." *BBR* 17 (2007) 53-114.

———. "The Use of Daniel 7 in Jesus' Trial, with Implications for His Self-Understanding." In *"Who Is This Son of Man?": The Latest Scholarship on a Puzzling Expression of the Historical Jesus*, edited by Larry Hurtado and Paul Owen, 78–100. LNTS. London: T. & T. Clark, 2011.

Boer, M. C. de. "Narrative Criticism, Historical Criticism, and the Gospel of John." *JSNT* 47 (1992) 35–48.

Bolt, Peter G. *The Cross from a Distance: Atonement in Mark's Gospel*. Downers Grove, IL: IVP, 2004.

Boomershine, Thomas E. "Audience Address and Purpose in the Performance of Mark." In *Mark as Story: Retrospect and Prospect*, edited by Kelly R. Iverson and Christopher W. Skinner, 115–42. Atlanta: SBL, 2011.

Boomershine, Thomas E., and Gilbert L. Bartholomew. "The Narrative Technique of Mark 16:8." *JBL* 100 (1981) 213–23.

Borg, Marcus J. "A Renaissance in Jesus Studies." *ThTo* 45 (1988) 280–92.

Boring, M. Eugene. "Markan Christology: God-Language for Jesus?" *NTS* 45 (1999) 451–71.

Bornkamm, Günther. *Jesus of Nazareth*. Minneapolis: Fortress, 1995.

Boyarin, Daniel. *Dying for God: Martyrdom and the Making of Christianity and Judaism*. Stanford: Stanford University Press, 1999.

Breck, John. "Biblical Chiasmus: Exploring Structure for Meaning." *BTB* 17 (1987) 70–74.

———. "Chiasmus as a Key to Biblical Interpretation." *SVTQ* 43 (1999) 249–67.

———. *The Shape of Biblical Language: Chiasmus in the Scriptures and Beyond*. Crestwood, NY: St. Vladimir's Seminary Press, 1994.

Broadhead, Edwin K. "Reconfiguring Jesus: The Son of Man in Markan Perspective." In *Biblical Interpretation in the Early Christian Gospels*. Vol. 1, *The Gospel of Mark*, edited by Thomas R. Hatina, 18–30. London: T. & T. Clark, 2006.

Brower, K. E. "Elijah in the Markan Passion Narrative." *JSNT* 18 (1983) 85–101.

———. "The Holy One of God and His Disciples: Holiness and Ecclesiology in Mark." In *Holiness and Ecclesiology in the New Testament*, edited by Kent E. Brower and Andy Johnson, 57–75. Grand Rapids: Eerdmans, 2007.

———. "'Let the Reader Understand': Temple and Eschatology in Mark." In *"The Reader Must Understand": Eschatology in the Bible and Theology*, edited by K. E. Brower and M. W. Elliot, 119–43. Leicester: IVP, 1997.

———. *Mark: A Commentary in the Wesleyan Tradition*. New Beacon Bible Commentary. Kansas City: Beacon Hill, 2012.

———. "Mark 9:1 Seeing the Kingdom in Power." *JSNT* 2 (1979) 17–41.

———. "The Old Testament in the Markan Passion Narrative." PhD diss., University of Manchester, 1978.

———. "'We Are Able': Cross-Bearing Discipleship and the Way of the Lord in Mark." *HBT* 29 (2007) 177–201.

———. "'Who Then Is This?'—Christological Questions in Mark 4:35—5:43." *EQ* 81 (2009) 291–305.

Brown, Raymond E. *The Death of the Messiah: From Gethsemane to the Grave*. 2 vols. New York: Doubleday, 1994.

———. "Jesus and Elisha." *Per* 12 (1971) 85–104.

Brueggemann, Walter. "Bounded by Obedience and Praise: The Psalms as Canon." *JSOT* 16 (1991) 63–92.

———. "The Costly Loss of Lament." *JSOT* 11 (1986) 57–71.

———. *Theology of the Old Testament*. Minneapolis: Fortress, 1997.

Bultmann, Rudolf. *Theology of the New Testament*. Vol. 1. Reprint, Waco, TX: Baylor University Press, 2007.

Burkett, Delbert. *The Son of Man Debate: A History and Evaluation*. Cambridge: Cambridge University Press, 1999.

Caragounis, Chrys C. *The Son of Man: Vision and Interpretation*. WUNT 38. Tübingen: Mohr Siebeck, 1986.

Carey, Holly. "'Is It as Bad as All That?' The Misconception of Mark as a *Film Noir*." In *Mark, Manuscripts, and Monotheism: Essays in Honor of Larry Hurtado*, edited by Chris Keith and Dieter T. Roth, 3–21. London: T. & T. Clark, 2015.

———. *Jesus' Cry from the Cross*. LNTS. New York: T. & T. Clark, 2009.

Carroll, John T., and Joel B. Green. *The Death of Jesus in Early Christianity*. Peabody, MA: Hendrickson, 1995.

Casey, Maurice. "The Corporate Interpretation of 'One Like a Son of Man' (Dan. VII 13) at the Time of Jesus." *NovT* 18 (1976) 167–80.

———. *The Solution to the 'Son of Man' Problem*. LNTS 343. London: T. & T. Clark, 2007.

———. *Son of Man: The Interpretation and Influence of Daniel 7*. London: SPCK, 1979.

Castelli, Elizabeth A. *Martyrdom and Memory: Early Christian Culture Making*. New York: Columbia University Press, 2004.

Chilton, Bruce, ed. *The Kingdom of God*. IRT 5. London: SPCK, 1984.

Chronis, Harry L. "To Reveal and to Conceal: A Literary-Critical Perspective on 'the Son of Man' in Mark." *NTS* 51 (2005) 459–81.

Chrysostom. "Homily IV on I Cor. 1.18–20." In vol. 12 of *Nicene and Post-Nicene Fathers*, edited by Alexander Roberts and James Donaldson; American edition, edited by A. Cleveland Coxe, 16–22. Translated by Hubert Kestell Cornish and John Medley. Reprint, Peabody, MA: Hendrickson, 1995.

Cobb, L. Stephanie. *Dying to Be Men: Gender and Language in Early Christian Martyr Texts*. New York: Columbia University Press, 2008.

Colijn, Brenda. *Images of Salvation in the New Testament*. Downers Grove, IL: IVP, 2010.

Collins, Adela Yarbro. "The Appropriation of Individual Psalms of Lament by Mark." In *The Scriptures in the Gospels*, edited by Christopher M. Tuckett, 223–41. BEThL 131. Leuven: Leuven University Press, 1997.

———. "Finding Meaning in the Death of Jesus." *JR* 78 (1998) 175–96.

———. "From Noble Death to Crucified Messiah." *NTS* 40 (1994) 481–503.

———. "The Genre of the Passion Narrative." *ST* 47 (1993) 3–28.

———. *Mark*. Hermeneia—A Critical and Historical Commentary on the Bible. Minneapolis: Fortress, 2007.

———. "Mark and His Readers: The Son of God Among Greeks and Romans." *HTR* 93 (2000) 85–100.

———. "Mark and His Readers: The Son of God Among Jews." *HTR* 92 (1999) 393–408.

———. "The Origin of the Designation of Jesus as 'Son of Man.'" *HTR* 80 (1987) 391–407.

Collins, J. J. "Cosmos and Salvation: Jewish Wisdom and Apocalyptic in the Hellenistic Age." *HR* 17 (1977) 121–42.

———. "The Son of Man and the Saints of the Most High in the Book of Daniel." *JBL* 93 (1974) 50–66.
Combrink, H. J. Bernard. *Die Diens van Jesus: 'n Eksegetiese Beskouing oor Markus 10:45*. Doctoral diss., Vrije Universiteit, Amsterdam, 1968.
———. "Salvation in Mark." In *Salvation in the New Testament: Perspectives on Soteriology*, edited by Jan G. van der Watt, 33–66. NovTSup 121. Leiden: Brill, 2005.
Culpepper, R. Alan. "Mark 10:50: Why Mention the Garment?" *JBL* 101 (1982) 131–2.
Daly-Denton, Margaret. "Early Christian Writers as Jewish Readers: The New Testament Reception of the Psalms." *RJ* 11 (2008) 181–99.
Daube, David. *The New Testament and Rabbinic Judaism*. London: Athlone Press, 1956. Reprint, Salem, NH: Ayer, 1992.
Davis, Ellen F. "Exploring the Limits: Form and Function in Psalm 22." *JSOT* 17 (1992) 93–105.
deSilva, David A. "X Marks the Spot? A Critique of the Use of Chiasmus in Macro-Structural Analyses of Revelation." *JSNT* 30 (2008) 343–71.
Dewey, Joanna. "'Let Them Renounce Themselves and Take Up Their Cross': A Feminist Reading of Mark 8:34 in Mark's Social and Narrative World." *BTB* 34 (2004) 98–104.
———. "Mark as Interwoven Tapestry: Forecasts and Echoes for a Listening Audience." *CBQ* 53 (1991) 221–36.
———. *Markan Public Debate*. SBLDS 48. Atlanta: Scholars, 1980.
———. "The Survival of Mark's Gospel: A Good Story?" *JBL* 123 (2004) 495–507.
Di Vito, Robert A. "Old Testament Anthropology and the Construction of Personal Identity." *CBQ* 61 (1999) 217–38.
Doble, Peter. *The Paradox of Salvation: Luke's Theology of the Cross*. SNTSMS 87. Cambridge: Cambridge University Press, 1996.
Donahue, John R., and Daniel J. Harrington. *The Gospel of Mark*. Sacra Pagina Series 2. Collegeville, MN: Liturgical, 2002.
Dowd, Sharyn Echols. *Prayer, Power, and the Problem of Suffering: Mark 11:22–25 in the Context of Markan Theology*. SBLDS 105. Atlanta: Scholars, 1988.
Dowd, Sharyn, and Elizabeth Struthers Malbon. "The Significance of Jesus' Death in Mark: Narrative Context and Authorial Audience." *JBL* 125 (2006) 271–97.
Driggers, Ira Brent. *Following God through Mark: Theological Tension in the Second Gospel*. Louisville: Westminster John Knox, 2007.
Droge, Arthur J., and James D. Tabor. *A Noble Death: Suicide and Martyrdom among Christians and Jews in Antiquity*. San Francisco: Harper, 1992.
Drury, John. "Mark." In *The Literary Guide to the Bible*, edited by Robert Alter and Frank Kermode, 402–17. Cambridge: Harvard University Press, 1987.
Edwards, James R. "Markan Sandwiches: The Significance of Interpolations in Markan Narratives." *NovT* 31 (1989) 193–216.
———. "The Servant of the Lord and the Gospel of Mark." In *Biblical Interpretation in the Early Christian Gospels*. Vol. 1, *The Gospel of Mark*, edited by Thomas R. Hatina, 49–63. London: T. & T. Clark, 2006.
Ehrman, Bart D., and Mark A. Plunkett. "The Angel and the Agony: The Textual Problem of Luke 22:43–44." *CBQ* 45 (1983) 401–16.
Elliot, David J. "4 Maccabees." In *The Oxford Bible Commentary*, edited by John Barton and John Muddiman, 790–92. Oxford: Oxford University Press, 2001.

Epictetus. *The Discourses as Reported by Arrian, the Manual, and Fragments*. Volumes I and II. Translated by W. A. Oldfather. LCL. Cambridge: Harvard University Press, 1959.

Ermakov, Arseny. "Holy Community in the Gospel of Mark." PhD diss., University of Manchester, 2009.

———. "Purity in the Synoptic Gospels." In *Purity: Essays in Bible and Theology*, edited by Andrew Brower-Latz and Arseny Ermakov, 89–113. Eugene: Wipf & Stock, 2014.

Evans, Craig. "The Function of Isaiah 6:9-10 in Mark and John." *NovT* 24 (1982) 124–38.

———. *Mark 8:27—16:20*. Word Biblical Commentary 34B. Nashville: Thomas Nelson, 2001.

Fleddermann, Harry. "The Discipleship Discourse (9:33–50)." *CBQ* 43 (1981) 57–75.

Fowler, Robert M. *Let the Reader Understand: Reader-Response Criticism and the Gospel of Mark*. Minneapolis: Fortress, 1991.

France, R. T. *Divine Government: God's Kingship in the Gospel of Mark*. London: SPCK, 1990.

———. *The Gospel of Mark: A Commentary on the Greek Text*. The New International Greek Testament Commentary. Grand Rapids: Eerdmans, 2002.

Fretheim, Terence E. *The Suffering of God: An Old Testament Perspective*. OBT. Philadelphia: Fortress, 1984.

———. "Theological Reflections on the Wrath of God in the Old Testament." *HBT* 24 (2002) 1–26.

Frey, Jörg, and Jens Schröter, eds. *Deutungen des Todes Jesu im Neuen Testament*. WUNT 181. Tübingen: Mohr Siebeck, 2005.

Garrison, Roman. *Why Are You Silent, Lord?* The Biblical Seminar 68. Sheffield: Sheffield Academic Press, 2000.

Geddert, Timothy J. *Watchwords: Mark 13 in Markan Eschatology*. JSNTSup 26. Sheffield: Sheffield Academic Press, 1989.

Gese, Hartmut. "Psalm 22 und das Neue Testament: Der älteste Bericht vom Tode Jesu und die Entstehung des Herrenmahles." In *Vom Sinai zum Zion: Alttestamentliche Beiträge zur biblischen Theologie*. BEvT 64. München: Chr. Kaiser, 1984.

Goulder, Michael D. "Those Outside (Mk. 4:10–12)." *NovT* 33 (1991) 289–302.

Gray, Timothy C. *The Temple in the Gospel of Mark: A Study in Its Narrative Role*. Reprint, Grand Rapids: Baker, 2010.

Green, Joel B., and Mark D. Baker. *Recovering the Scandal of the Cross: Atonement in the New Testament & Contemporary Contexts*. Downers Grove, IL: IVP, 2000.

Guelich, Robert A. *Mark 1—8:26*. Word Biblical Commentary 34A. Nashville: Thomas Nelson, 1989.

Gundry, Robert H. *Mark: A Commentary on His Apology for the Cross*. Grand Rapids: Eerdmans, 2000.

Hall, Douglas John. *God & Human Suffering: An Exercise in the Theology of the Cross*. Minneapolis: Augsburg, 1986.

Hanson, James S. "The Disciples in Mark's Gospel: Beyond the Pastoral/Polemical Debate." *HBT* 20 (1998) 128–55.

———. *Endangered Promises*. SBLDS 171. Atlanta: SBL, 2000.

Hare, Douglas R. A. *The Son of Man Tradition*. Minneapolis: Fortress, 1990.

Hartog, Paul. *Polycarp's Epistle to the Philippians and the Martyrdom of Polycarp: Introduction, Text, and Commentary*. Oxford: Oxford University Press, 2013. 171–86.
Hatina, Thomas R. *In Search of a Context: The Function of Scripture in Mark's Narrative*. JSNTSup 232. SSEJC 8. Sheffield: Sheffield Academic Press, 2002.
———. "Who Will See 'the Kingdom of God Coming with Power' in Mark 9,1— Protagonists or Antagonists?" *Bib* 86 (2005) 20–34.
Hay, Lewis S. "The Son of Man in Mark 2:10 and 2:28." *JBL* 89 (1970) 69–75.
Hays, Richard. "Christ Prays the Psalms: Israel's Psalter as Matrix of Early Christianity." In *The Conversion of the Imagination: Paul as Interpreter of Israel's Scripture*. Grand Rapids: Eerdmans, 2005.
———. *Echoes of Scripture in the Letters of Paul*. New Haven: Yale University Press, 1989.
Henderson, Suzanne Watts. *Christ and Community: the Gospel Witness to Jesus*. Nashville: Abingdon, 2015.
———. *Christology and Discipleship in the Gospel of Mark*. Cambridge: Cambridge University Press, 2006.
Hengel, Martin. *The Cross of the Son of God*. Translated by John Bowden. London: SCM, 1981.
Hengel, Martin, and Daniel P. Bailey. "The Effective History of Isaiah 53 in the Pre-Christian Period." In *The Suffering Servant: Isaiah 53 in Jewish and Christian Sources*, edited by Bernd Janowski and Peter Schulmacher, 75–146. Translated by Daniel P. Bailey. Grand Rapids: Eerdmans, 2004.
Henten, Jan Willem van. *The Maccabean Martyrs as Saviour of the Jewish People: A Study of 2 and 4 Maccabees*. SJSJ 57. Leiden: Brill, 1997.
Henten, Jan Willem van, and Friedrich Avemarie. *Martyrdom and Noble Death: Selected Texts from Graeco-Roman, Jewish and Christian Antiquity*. London and New York: Routledge, 2002.
Heschel, Abraham J. *The Prophets*. New York: Harper & Row, 2001.
Hester, J. David. "Dramatic Inconclusion: Irony and the Narrative Rhetoric of the Ending of Mark." *JSNT* 57 (1995) 61–86.
Heyer, C. J. den. "Jezus, de lijdende rechtvaardige en de Knecht des Heren." In *De Knechtsgestalte van Christus*, studies aangeboden aan Prof. Dr. H. N. Ridderbos, 54–64. Kampen: Kok, 1978.
Hezser, Catherine. "The Impact of Household Slaves on the Jewish Family in Roman Palestine." *JSJ* 34 (2003) 375–424.
———. *Jewish Slavery in Antiquity*. Oxford: University Press, 2005.
Hooker, Morna. "Beginnings and Endings." In *The Written Gospel*, edited by Markus Bockmuehl and Donald Hagner, 184–204. Cambridge: Cambridge University Press, 2005.
———. *The Gospel According to Saint Mark*. Peabody, MA: Hendrickson, 2005.
———. "Interchange in Christ." *JTS* 22 (1971) 349–61.
———. "Isaiah in Mark's Gospel." In *Isaiah in the New Testament: The New Testament and the Scriptures of Israel*, edited by Steve Moyise and Maarten J. J. Menken, 35–49. London: T. & T. Clark, 2005.
———. *Jesus and the Servant: The Influence of the Servant Concept of Deutero-Isaiah in the New Testament*. London: SPCK, 1959.

———. "Review of Casey, *The Solution to the 'Son of Man' Problem*." *JTS* 60 (2009) 639–43.

———. *The Son of Man in Mark: A Study of the Background of the Term "Son of Man" and Its Use in St. Mark's Gospel*. London: SPCK, 1967.

Hopkins, Keith. "Christian Number and Its Implications." *JECS* 6 (1998) 185–226.

Horbury, William. "The Messianic Associations of 'The Son of Man.'" *JTS* 36 (1985) 34–55.

Horsely, Richard A. *Hearing the Whole Story: The Politics of Plot in Mark's Gospel*. Louisville: Westminster John Knox, 2001.

Huntress, Erminie. "'Son of God' in Jewish Writings Prior to the Christian Era." *JBL* 54 (1935) 117–23.

Hurtado, Larry W. "Christology." In vol. 1 of *NIDB*, edited by Karen Doob Sakenfeld, 612–22. Nashville: Abingdon, 2006.

———. "Following Jesus in the Gospel of Mark—and Beyond." In *Patterns of Discipleship in the New Testament*, edited by Richard N. Longenecker, 9–29. Grand Rapids: Eerdmans, 1996.

———. "Jesus' Death as Paradigmatic in the New Testament." *SJT* 57 (2004) 413–33.

———. *Lord Jesus Christ: Devotion to Jesus in Earliest Christianity*. Grand Rapids: Eerdmans, 2003.

———. "The Women, the Tomb, and the Climax of Mark." In *A Wandering Galilean: Essays in Honour of Sean Freyne*, edited by Zuleika Rodgers, Margaret Daly-Denton, and Anne Fitzpatrick McKinley, 427–51. SJSJ 132. Leiden: Brill, 2009.

Hurtado, Larry W., and Paul L. Owen, eds. *"Who Is This Son of Man?" The Latest Scholarship on a Puzzling Expression of the Historical Jesus*. LNTS 390. London: T. & T. Clark, 2011.

Hyatt, J. Philip. "The Sources of the Suffering Servant Idea." *JNES* 3 (1944) 79–86.

Iersel, Bastiaan M. F. van. *Belichting van het Bijbelboek Marcus*. Boxtel: KBS, 1986.

———. "De Betekenis van Marcus vanuit zijn Topografische Structuur." *TvT* 22 (1982) 117–38.

———. "Concentric Structures in Mark 1:14—3:35 (4:1) with Some Observations on Method." *BibInt* 3 (1995) 75–98.

———. "Failed Followers in Mark: Mark 13:12 as a Key for the Identification of the Intended Readers." Translated by W. H. Bisscheroux. *CBQ* 58 (1996) 244–63.

Ignatius. "Letter to the Romans." In vol. 1 of *ANF*, edited and translated by Alexander Roberts and James Donaldson; American edition, edited by A. Cleveland Coxe, 73–78. Reprint, Peabody, MA: Hendrickson, 1995.

Italicus, Silius. *Punica in Two Volumes*. Vol 1. Translated by J. D. Duff. LCL. Cambridge: Harvard University Press, 1968.

Iverson, Kelly R., and Christopher W. Skinner, eds. *Mark as Story: Retrospect and Prospect*. SBLRBS 65. Atlanta: SBL, 2011.

Jackson, Howard M. "Why the Youth Shed His Cloak and Fled Naked: The Meaning and Purpose of Mark 14:51–52." *JBL* 116 (1997) 273–89.

Janowski, Bernd, and Peter Stuhlmacher, eds. *The Suffering Servant: Isaiah 53 in Jewish and Christian Sources*. Translated by Daniel P. Bailey. Reprint, Grand Rapids: Eerdmans, 2004.

Jeremias, Joachim. "Ἠλ(ε)ίας." *TDNT* 2:931.

———. "παῖς θεοῦ." *TDNT* 5:682.

Jervis, L. Ann. *At the Heart of the Gospel: Suffering in the Earliest Christian Message*. Grand Rapids: Eerdmans, 2007.
Josephus. *Complete Works*. Translated by William Whiston. Grand Rapids: Kregel, 1960.
Kaminsky, Joel S. *Corporate Responsibility in the Hebrew Bible*. JSOTSup 196. Sheffield: Sheffield Academic Press, 1995.
Kee, Howard Clark. "Review of Wolfgang Roth, *Hebrew Gospel: Cracking the Code of Mark*." *JBL* 109 (1990) 538–9.
Kelber, Werner. *The Oral and the Written Gospel: The Hermeneutics of Speaking and Writing*. Philadelphia: Fortress, 1997.
Kelhoffer, James A. *Persecution, Persuasion, and Power: Readiness to Withstand Hardship as a Corroboration of Legitimacy in the New Testament*. WUNT 270. Tübingen: Mohr Siebeck, 2010.
Kim, Seyoon. *The "Son of Man" as the Son of God*. WUNT 30. Tübingen: Mohr Siebeck, 1983.
Kingsbury, Jack Dean. "The Significance of the Cross Within Mark's Story." *Int* 47 (1993) 370–79.
Kittel, Gerhard, and Gerhard Friedrich, eds. *Theological Dictionary of the New Testament*. Translated by Geoffrey W. Bromily. 10 vols. Grand Rapids: Eerdmans, 1964–76.
Klauck, Hans-Josef. "Die erzählerische Rolle der Jünger im Markusevangelium: eine narrative Analyse." *NovT* 24 (1982) 1–26.
LaChance, Paul J. "Understanding Christ's Satisfaction Today." *SAJ* 2 (2004) 60–66.
Lactantius. "Of the Manner in Which the Persecutors Died." In vol. 7 of *ANF*, edited by Alexander Roberts and James Donaldson; American edition, edited by A. Cleveland Coxe, 301–22. Translated by William Fletcher. Reprint, Peabody, MA: Hendrickson, 1995.
Lane, William L. *The Gospel of Mark: The English Text with Introduction, Exposition, and Notes*. The New International Commentary on the New Testament. Grand Rapids: Eerdmans, 1974.
Lang, Friedrich Gustav. "*Sola gratia* im Markusevangelium: Die Soteriologie des Markus nach 9,14-29 und 10,17-31." In *Rechtfertung*, Festschrift für Ernst Käsemann zum 70. Geburtstag, edited by Johannes Friedrich, Wolfgang Pöhlmann, and Peter Stuhlmacher. Tübingen: Mohr Siebeck, 1976.
Larsen, Kevin W. "The Structure of Mark's Gospel: Current Proposals." *CBR* 3 (2004) 140–60.
Leithart, Peter. "I Don't Get It: Humour and Hermeneutics." *SJT* 60 (2007) 412–25.
Leivestad, Ragnar. "Exit the Apocalyptic Son of Man." *NTS* 18 (1972) 243–67.
Lentzen-Deis, Fritzleo. *Die Taufe Jesu nach den Synoptikern: Literarkritische und gattungsgeschichtliche Untersuchungen*. FTS 4. Frankfurt: Josef Knecht, 1970.
Lindars, Barnabas. *Jesus Son of Man: A Fresh Examination of the Son of Man Sayings in the Gospels in Light of Recent Research*. London: SPCK, 1983.
———. "The Place of the Old Testament in the Formation of New Testament Theology." *NTS* 23 (1976) 59–66.
———. "Re-Enter the Apocalyptic Son of Man." *NTS* 22 (1975) 52–72.
———. "Response to Richard Bauckham: The Idiomatic Use of Bar Enasha." *JSNT* 23 (1985) 35–41.

Luijendijk, Annemarie. "Papyri from the Great Persecution: Roman and Christian Perspectives." *JECS* 6 (2008) 341–69.

Lund, Nils Wilhelm. *Chiasmus in the New Testament*. Chapel Hill: The University of North Carolina Press, 1942.

Magness, J. Lee. *Sense and Absence*. Atlanta: Scholars, 1986.

Malbon, Elizabeth Struthers. "Disciples/Crowds/Whoever: Markan Characters and Readers." *NovT* 28 (1986) 104–30.

———. "Echoes and Foreshadowings in Mark 4–8: Reading and Rereading." *JBL* 112 (1993) 211–30.

———. "Fallible Followers: Women and Men in the Gospel of Mark." *Semeia* 28 (1983) 29–48.

———. "Galilee and Jerusalem: History and Literature in Marcan Interpretation." *CBQ* 44 (1982) 242–55.

———. "The Jesus of Mark and the Sea of Galilee." *JBL* 103 (1984) 363–77.

———. *Mark's Jesus: Characterization as Narrative Christology*. Waco: Baylor University Press, 2009.

Manek, Jindrich. "Composite Quotations in the New Testament and Their Purpose." *CV* 13 (1970) 181–88.

Manson, T. W. "The Son of Man in Daniel, Enoch and the Gospels." *BJRL* 32 (1950) 171–93.

———. *The Teaching of Jesus: Studies of Its Form and Content*. Cambridge: Cambridge University Press, 1963.

Marcus, Joel. *Mark 1–8: A New Translation with Introduction and Commentary*. The Anchor Bible. New York: Doubleday, 2000.

———. *The Way of the Lord: Christological Exegesis of the Old Testament in the Gospel of Mark*. Louisville, KY: John Knox, 1992.

Marshall, I. Howard. "Son of God or Servant of Yahweh? A Reconsideration of Mark i.11." *NTS* 15 (1969) 326–36.

Matera, Frank J. "The Prologue as the Interpretative Key to Mark's Gospel." *JSNT* 34 (1988) 3–20.

Mays, James L. "Prayer and Christology: Psalm 22 as Perspective on the Passion." *ThTo* 42 (1985) 322–31.

McCoy, Brad. "Chiasmus: An Important Structural Device Commonly Found in Biblical Literature." *CTSJ* 9 (2003) 18–23.

Menn, Esther M. "No Ordinary Lament: Relecture and the Identity of the Distressed in Psalm 22." *HTR* 93 (2000) 301–41.

Meyer, Marvin. "Taking Up the Cross and Following Jesus: Discipleship in the Gospel of Mark." *CTJ* 37 (2002) 230–8.

Middleton, Paul. "Christology, Martyrdom, and Vindication in the Gospel of Mark and the Apocalypse: Two New Testament Views." In *Mark, Manuscripts, and Monotheism: Essays in Honor of Larry Hurtado*, edited by Chris Keith and Dieter T. Roth, 219–37. London: T. & T. Clark, 2015.

———. "Noble Death or Death Cult: Pagan Criticism of Early Christian Martyrdom." In *People under Power: Early Jewish and Christian Responses to the Roman Empire*, edited by Michael Labahn and Outi Lehtipuu, 207–29. Amsterdam: Amsterdam University Press, 2015.

———. *Radical Martyrdom and Cosmic Conflict in Early Christianity*. LNTS 307. London: T. & T. Clark, 2006.

---. "Suffering and the Creation of Christian Identity in the Gospel of Mark." In *T. & T. Clark Handbook to Social Identity in the New Testament*, edited by J. Brian Tucker and Coleman A. Baker, 173–89. London: Bloomsbury, 2014.
Mol, Jurrien F. "Collectieve en Individuele Verantwoordelijkheid: een Beschrijving van Corporate Personality naar Ezechiël 18 en 20." English title: "Collective and Individual Responsibility: A Description of Corporate Personality According to Ezekiel 18 and 20." Doctoral diss., University of Utrecht, 2002.
Moloney, Francis J. *Mark: Storyteller, Interpreter, Evangelist*. Peabody, MA: Hendrickson, 2004.
---. "Writing a Narrative Commentary on the Gospel of Mark." In *Mark as Story: Retrospect and Prospect*, edited by Kelly R. Iverson and Christopher W. Skinner, 95–114. Atlanta: SBL, 2011.
Moss, Candida. *The Myth of Persecution: How Early Christians Invented a Story of Martyrdom*. New York: HarperOne, 2013.
---. "On the Dating of Polycarp: Rethinking the Place of the *Martyrdom of Polycarp* in the History of Christianity." *Early Christianity* 1 (2010) 539–74.
---. *Other Christs: Imitating Jesus in Ancient Christian Ideologies of Martyrdom*. Oxford: Oxford University Press, 2010.
Motyer, S. "The Rending of the Veil: A Markan Pentecost?" *NTS* 33 (1987) 155–57.
Moulder, W. J. "The Old Testament Background and the Interpretation of Mark x. 45." *NTS* 24 (1977) 120–27.
Moule, C. F. D. "'The Son of Man': Some of the Facts." *NTS* 41 (1995) 277–79.
Mowinckel, Sigmund. *The Psalms in Israel's Worship*. The Biblical Seminar 14. Sheffield: JSOT, 1992.
Moyise, Steve, and Maarten J. J. Menken, eds. *Isaiah in the New Testament: The New Testament and the Scriptures of Israel*. London: T. & T. Clark, 2005.
---. *The Psalms in the New Testament*. London: T. & T. Clark, 2004.
Musurillo, Herbert. *The Acts of the Christian Martyrs*. Oxford: Clarendon, 1972.
Neary, Micheal. "The Importance of the Lament in the God/Man Relationship in Ancient Israel." *ITQ* 52 (1986) 180–92.
Neusner, Jacob, trans. *The Mishnah: A New Translation*. New Haven: Yale University Press, 1988.
Öhler, Markus. *Elia im Neuen Testament*. BZNW 88. Berlin: Walter de Gruyter, 1997.
---. "The Expectation of Elijah and the Presence of the Kingdom of God." *JBL* 118 (1999) 461–76.
Origen. *Against Celsus*. In vol. 4 of *ANF*, edited by Alexander Roberts and James Donaldson; American edition, edited by A. Cleveland Coxe, 395–669. Translated by Frederick Crombie. Reprint, Peabody, MA: Hendrickson, 1995.
Owen, Paul, and David Shepherd. "Speaking Up for Qumran, Dalman and the Son of Man: Was Bar Enasha a Common Term for 'Man' in the Time of Jesus?" *JSNT* 23 (2001) 81–122.
Oyen, Geert van. *De Marcus Code*. Kampen: Kok, 2005.
Peacock, Heber F. "Discipleship in the Gospel of Mark." *RevEx* 75 (1978) 555–64.
Perkins, Judith. *The Suffering Self: Pain and Narrative Representation in Early Christianity*. London: Routledge, 1995.
Peter of Alexandria. "Canonical Epistle." In vol. 6 of *ANF*, edited by Alexander Roberts and James Donaldson; American edition, edited by A. Cleveland Coxe, 269–79. Translated by James B. H. Hawkins. Reprint, Peabody, MA: Hendrickson, 1995.

Pitre, Brant. "The 'Ransom for Many,' the New Exodus, and the End of the Exile: Redemption as the Restoration of All Israel (Mark 10:35–45)." *Letter & Spirit* 1 (2005) 41–69.

Plato. *Euthyphro, Apology, Crito, Phaedo*. Edited and translated by Chris Emlyn-Jones and William Preddy. LCL. Cambridge: Harvard University Press, 2017.

Pliny. *Letters and Panegyricus in Two Volumes*. Vol. 2. Translated by Betty Radice. LCL. Cambridge: Harvard University Press, 1969.

Plutarch. "On Tranquility of Mind." In vol. 6 of *Moralia: In Sixteen Volumes*, translated by W. C. Helmbold. LCL. Cambridge: Harvard University Press, 1970.

Porter, J. R. "The Legal Aspects of the Concept of 'Corporate Personality' in the Old Testament." *NovT* 15 (1965) 361–80.

Powery, Emerson B. "The Spirit and Political Dissent: Revisiting Mark 13:11." *JBPR* 2 (2010) 18–30.

Poythress, V. S. "The Holy Ones of the Most High in Daniel IV." *VT* 26 (1976) 208–13.

Puig i Tàrrech, Armand. "The Glory on the Mountain." *NTS* 58 (2012) 151–72.

Quintillian. *Institutes of Oratory or Institutes of an Orator*. In Twelve Books. Translated by John Selby Watson. London: George Bell and Sons, 1875.

Rahlfs, Alfred, and Robert Hanhart, trans. *Die Septuaginta*. Stuttgart: Deutsche Bibelgesellschaft, 2006.

Reumann, John H. "Psalm 22 at the Cross." *Int* 28 (1974) 39–58.

Rhoads, David. "Losing Life for Others in the Face of Death: Mark's Standards of Judgment." *Int* 47 (1993) 358–69.

———. "Narrative Criticism and the Gospel of Mark." *JAAR* 50 (1982) 411–34.

Rhoads, David, Joanna Dewey, and Donald Michie. *Mark as Story: An Introduction to the Narrative of a Gospel*. 2nd ed. Minneapolis: Fortress, 1999.

Riddle, Donald W. "The Martyr Motif in the Gospel of Mark." *JR* 4 (1924) 397–410.

Robbins, Vernon. "The Intertexture of Apocalyptic Discourse in the Gospel of Mark." In *The Intertexture of Apocalyptic Discourse in the New Testament*, edited by D. F. Watson, 11–44. SBLSymS 14. Atlanta: SBL, 2002.

Robinson, H. Wheeler. *The Christian Doctrine of Man*. Edinburgh: T. & T. Clark, 1920.

———. "The Hebrew Conception of Corporate Personality." In *Corporate Personality in Ancient Israel*. First published in *Werden und Wesen des Alten Testaments*, edited by P. Volz, F. Stummer, and J. Hempel. Berlin, 1936. Revised from 1964 edition. Edinburgh: T. & T. Clark, 1981.

Robinson, J. A. T. "Elijah, John, and Jesus: An Essay in Detection." *NTS* 4 (1958) 263–81.

Rogerson, J. W. "The Hebrew Conception of Corporate Personality: A Re-examination." *JTS* 21 (1970) 1–16.

Rosenzweig, Rachel. *Solidarität met den Leidenden im Judentum*. SJ 10. Berlin: Walter de Gruyter, 1978.

Roskam, H. N. *The Purpose of the Gospel of Mark in Its Historical and Social Context*. SNT 114. Leiden: Brill, 2004.

Rossé, Gérard. *The Cry of Jesus on the Cross: A Biblical and Theological Study*. New York: Paulist, 1987.

Roth, Wolfgang. *Hebrew Gospel: Cracking the Code of Mark*. Oak Park, IL: Meyer Stone, 1988.

Rowely, H. H. *The Faith of Israel: Aspects of Old Testament Thought*. London: SCM, 1956.

Ryou, Philip Ho-Young. "Apocalyptic Opening, Eschatological 'Inclusio': A Study of the Rending of the Heaven and the Temple Curtain in the Gospel of Mark with Special Reference to the Motif of 'Seeing.'" PhD diss., University of Glasgow, 2004.

Sabin, Marie Noonan. *Reopening the Word: Reading* Mark *as Theology in the Context of Early Judaism*. Oxford: Oxford University Press, 2002.

Santos, Narry F. "Jesus' Paradoxical Teaching in Mark 8:35; 9:35; and 10:43–44." *BSac* 157 (2000) 15–25.

———. *Slave of All: The Paradox of Authority and Servanthood in the Gospel of Mark*. JSNTSup 237. Sheffield: Sheffield Academic Press, 2003.

Schlimm, Matthew R. "Different Perspectives on Divine Pathos: An Examination of Hermeneutics in Biblical Theology." *CBQ* 69 (2007) 673–94.

Schmid, Wolf. "Implied Author." In *The Living Handbook of Narratology*, edited by Peter Hühn, Jan Christoph Meister, John Pier, and Wolf Schmid, n.p. Hamburg: Hamburg University. http://www.lhn.uni-hamburg.de/.

Schwarz, Günther. "ἀπαρνησάσθω ἑαυτὸν ...'? (Markus viii 34 Parr.)." *NovT* 17 (1975) 109–12.

Scott, M. Philip. "Chiastic Structure: A key to the Interpretation of Mark's Gospel." *BTB* 15 (1985) 17–26.

Seeley, David. *The Noble Death: Graeco-Roman Martyrology and Paul's Concept of Salvation*. JSNTSup 28. Sheffield: Sheffield Academic Press, 1990.

Seitz, Christopher. "Reconciliation and the Plain Sense Witness of Scripture." In *The Redemption: An Interdisciplinary Symposium on Christ as Redeemer*, edited by Stephen T. Davis, Daniel Kendall, and Gerald O'Collins, 25–42. Oxford: Oxford University Press, 2004.

Selvidge, Marla. "'And Those Who Followed Feared' (Mark 10:32)." *CBQ* 45 (1983) 396–400.

Seneca. *Ad Lucilium Epistulae Morales*. Volumes 1 and 3. Translated by Richard M. Gummere. LCL. Cambridge: Harvard University Press, 196–67.

Shiner, Whitney T. *Follow Me! Disciples in Markan Rhetoric*. SBLDS 145. Atlanta: Scholars, 1995.

Smit, Peter-Ben. "Review of *Philippians: Let Us Rejoice in Being Conformed to Christ*, by John Paul Heil." *RBL*, 2012. http://www.bookreviews.org.

Smith, Stephen H. *A Lion with Wings: A Narrative-Critical Approach to Mark's Gospel*. Sheffield: Sheffield Academic Press, 1996.

Snow, Robert S. *Daniel's Son of Man in Mark*. Eugene, OR: Wipf & Stock, 2016.

Standaert, Benoît. *Marcus Geweld en Genade: de Actualiteit van het Marcusevangelie*. Tielt en Weesp: Lannoo, 1985.

Steichele, Hans-Jörg. *Der Leidende Sohn Gottes: Eine Untersuchung einiger alttestamentischer Motive in der Christologie des Markusevangeliums*. Biblische Untersuchungen 14. Regensburg: Pustet, 1980.

Stein, Robert H. *Mark*. Baker Exegetical Commentary on the New Testament. Grand Rapids: Baker, 2008.

Sterling, Greg. "*Mors philosophi*: The Death of Jesus in Luke." *HTR* 94 (2001) 383–402.

Stock, Augustine. "Chiastic Awareness and Education in Antiquity." *BTB* 14 (1984) 23–27.

———. *The Method and Message of Mark*. Wilmington, DE: Michael Glazier, 1989.

Stuhlmacher, Peter. "Isaiah 53 in the Gospels and Acts." In *The Suffering Servant: Isaiah 53 in Jewish and Christian Sources*, edited by Bernd Janowski and Peter

Stuhlmacher, 147–162. Translated by Daniel P. Bailey. Grand Rapids: Eerdmans, 2004.

Tannehill, Robert C. "The Disciples in Mark: The Function of a Narrative Role." *JR* 57 (1977) 386–405.

———. "The Gospel of Mark as Narrative Christology." *Semeia* 16 (1979) 57–95.

Telford, William R. *Writing on the Gospel of Mark*. Guides to Advanced Biblical Research. Blandford Forum: Deo, 2009.

Tertullian. "Ad Martyras." In vol. 3 of *ANF*, edited by Alexander Roberts and James Donaldson; American edition, edited by A. Cleveland Coxe, 693–96. Translated by S. Thelwall. Reprint, Peabody, MA: Hendrickson, 1995.

———. "To Scapula." In vol. 3 of *ANF*, edited by Alexander Roberts and James Donaldson; American edition, edited by A. Cleveland Coxe, 105–8. Translated by S. Thelwall. Reprint, Peabody, MA: Hendrickson, 1995.

Thomas, Dalton. *Unto Death: Martyrdom, Missions, and the Maturity of the Church*. Tauranga, New Zealand: Maskilim, 2012.

Thomson, Ian H. *Chiasmus in the Pauline Letters*. JSNTSup 111. Sheffield: Sheffield Academic Press, 1995.

Tolbert, Mary Ann. "How the Gospel of Mark Builds Character." *Int* 47 (1993) 347–57.

———. *Sowing the Gospel: Mark's Work in Literary-Historical Perspective*. Minneapolis: Fortress, 1989.

Trocmé, Etienne. *The Formation of the Gospel According to Mark*. Translated by P. Gaughan. London: SPCK, 1975.

Trudinger, L. Paul. "'Eli, Eli, Lama Sabachtani?': A Cry of Dereliction? Or Victory?" *JETS* 17 (1974) 235–8.

Tuckett, Christopher. "The Present Son of Man." *JSNT* 14 (1982) 58–81.

Tyson, Joseph B. "The Blindness of the Disciples in Mark." *JBL* 80 (1961) 261–8.

Ulansey, David. "The Heavenly Veil Torn: Mark's Cosmic 'Inclusio.'" *JBL* 110 (1991) 123–25.

VandenBerg, Mary. "Redemptive Suffering: Christ's Alone." *SJT* 60 (2007) 394–411.

Vermes, Geza. *Jesus the Jew: A Historian's Reading of the Gospels*. London: William Collins Sons & Co., 1973.

———. "The 'Son of Man' Debate." *JSNT* 1 (1978) 19–32.

———. "The Use of בר נשא / בר נש in Jewish Aramaic." In *An Aramaic Approach to the Gospels and Acts*, by Matthew Black, 310–28. Oxford: Oxford University Press, 1967.

Wagner, Ross J. *Heralds of the Good News: Isaiah and Paul 'in Concert' in the Letter to the Romans*. NovTSup 101. Leiden: Brill, 2002.

Walton, John H. "The Imagery of the Substitute King Ritual in Isaiah's Fourth Servant Song." *JBL* 122 (2003) 734–43.

Watts, John D. W. *Isaiah 34–66*. Word Biblical Commentary 25. Waco, TX: Word, 1987.

Watts, Rikki E. *Isaiah's New Exodus and Mark*. WUNT II 88. Tübingen: Mohr Siebeck, 1997.

Weeden, Theodore J. "The Cross as Power in Weakness (Mark 15:20b–41)." In *The Passion in Mark: Studies on Mark 14–16*, edited by Werner Kelber, 115–34. Philadelphia: Fortress, 1976.

———. "The Heresy that Necessitated Mark's Gospel." In *The Interpretation of Mark*, edited by William R. Telford, 89–104. Edinburgh: T. & T. Clark, 2000.

Weihs, Alexander. *Die Deutung des Todes Jesu im Markusevangelium: Eine exegetische Studie zu den Leidens- und Auferstehungsansagen*. FB 99. Würzburg: Echter, 2003.

Welch, John, ed. *Chiasmus in Antiquity*. Hildesheim: Gerstenberg, 1981.

———. "Criteria for Identifying and Evaluating the Presence of Chiasmus." *JBMS* 4 (1995) 1–14.

Westermann, Klaus. "The Role of the Lament in the Theology of the Old Testament." *Int* 28 (1974) 20–38.

Witherington, Ben, III. *The Gospel of Mark: A Socio-Rhetorical Commentary*. Grand Rapids: Eerdmans, 2001.

Wright, N. T. *The New Testament and the People of God*. Minneapolis: Fortress, 1992.

Author Index

Ahearne-Kroll, Stephen, 91n22, 155n5, 156, 157n13

Baker, Mark D., 128n29
Baltzer, Klaus, 129
Barrett, C. K., 126, 126n25
Barton, Stephen C., 91n22
Bauckham, Richard, 90n18
Ben-Porat, Ziva, 117n10
Best, Ernest, 47–49
Bird, Michael, 57, 57n35, 60
Bligh, John, 62n50
Bock, Darrell, 134n5, 134n7, 146
Bolt, Peter G., 9–10, 82n50
Boomershine, Thomas E., 19
Bornkamm, Günther, 134n3
Breck, John, 22n54, 23n60
Brower, K.E., 3n4, 7, 15–16, 34n10, 57n35, 58n38, 60–61, 75n22, 82n50, 88n13, 89n15, 89n17, 92n26, 123n19, 127n28, 140n28, 145n35, 159n17, 167n43
Brown, Raymond E., 165n34
Brueggemann, Walter, 86–88, 98, 154
Bultmann, Rudolf, 134n4

Carey, Holly. xii, 154–55, 155n5, 156n11
Casey, Maurice, 134–37, 149–51, 149n42, 149n46
Chronis, Harry L., 135n13
Chrysostom, 74
Colijn, Brenda, 3n5
Collins, Adela Yarbro, 20n49, 21, 35, 54, 56, 60n45, 76, 80–84, 102n7, 116n8, 126n24, 126n25, 134, 145–46, 149n42, 154n2, 164

Collins, J. J., 150n50
Combrink, H. J. Bernard, 11, 102n7

Dewey, Joanna, 18n43, 19n45, 34, 49n19, 137n24, 138
Di Vito, Robert A., 94n27, 97
Doble, Peter, 79n39
Donahue, John R., 34n11, 35, 35n12, 89n17, 126n24
Droge, Arthur J., 75n20

Edwards, James R., 91n22
Ehrman, Bart D., 77
Elliot, David J., 155n6
Epictetus, 71–73
Ermakov, Arseny. 10n17, 38n21
Evans, Craig, 116n5, 126n24

France, R. T., 4, 89n17, 90n18, 91n19, 106n17, 116n5, 120n14, 126n24, 127n26, 145n36, 149n42, 153n1, 156n10
Fretheim, Terence E., 86n3, 87

Gese, Hartmut, 156, 161, 161n26, 163n28
Gray, Timothy C, 144n35
Green, Joel B., 128n29
Guelich, Robert A., 28n1, 89n17, 91n19, 106n17
Gundry, Robert H., 7–8

Hanson, James S., 49, 107–8
Harrington, Daniel J., 34n11, 35, 35n12, 89n17, 126n24
Hatina, Thomas R., 116–17, 120–21

Hays, Richard, 156n9, 160, 161n25
Hengel, Martin, 115n2
Heschel, Abraham J., 10, 80, 82n48, 85–87, 92n25
Hooker, Morna, 16n38, 20n49, 28n1, 32, 33n9, 35n15, 53–54, 55n31, 55n32, 59n42, 60n45, 67, 89n17, 90–91, 106n17, 115, 115n1, 120n14, 121, 123n21, 126–27, 126n25, 132n35, 135, 138n26, 148, 149n44, 156n10, 159n17, 173
Hurtado, Larry W., 7, 7n9, 14–15, 17, 31n7, 48n15, 88n14, 90n18, 137n23

Iersel, B. M. F. van, x, 28–29, 28n1
Ignatius, 100–101
Italicus, Silius. 71
Iverson, Kelly R., 19n45

Jeremias, J., 115n2
Josephus, 39n2, 161

Kaminsky, Joel S., 95n31, 96
Kelber, Werner, 45n3
Kelhoffer, James A., 109–110
Klauck, Hans-Josef, 46n9, 50n25

Lactantius, 103
Lane, William L., 37n19, 89n17, 91n19, 106n17, 116n5, 120n13, 138n26, 149n42
Leivestad, Ragnar, 134n5
Lentzen-Deis, Fritzleo, 40n24
Lindars, Barnabas, 134–35
Luijendijk, Annemarie, 102–3, 103n11
Lund, Nils Wilhelm, 22n54

Malbon, Elizabeth Struthers, 19n47, 28n1, 28n3, 29n5, 47, 49, 122–23, 123n20, 159n18
Manson, T. W., 12n24, 16n40, 97, 136, 136n16, 147
Marcus, Joel, 2n2, 35
Mays, James L., 158
McCoy, Brad, 21n52

Michie, Donald, 18n43, 19n45, 45n19, 137n24, 138
Middleton, Paul, ixn5, xin11, 7, 16, 24, 74, 100–101, 105–6, 108, 111–12
Mol, Jurrien F., 95–98
Moloney, Francis J., 25
Moss, Candida, ixn1, 24, 100–101, 108–111, 108n21, 109n24
Motyer, S., 35n12, 40n24
Mowinckel, Sigmund, 157

Neary, Micheal, 154n4

Öhler, Markus, 166n38, 166n41
Origen, 73–74, 76, 83

Peter of Alexandria, 103, 104n12
Pitre, Brant, 12
Plato, 70–71, 74–75, 75n20, 78–79
Pliny, ix, x, 102,
Plunkett, Mark A., 77
Plutarch, 73
Porter, J. R., 95
Powery, Emerson B., 51
Poythress, V. S., 150n50
Puig i Tàrrech, Armand, 57n34

Quintillian, 53n28

Rhoads, David, 6, 18n43, 19n45, 46–47, 49n19, 137n24, 138
Robbins, Vernon, 102n7
Robinson, H. Wheeler, 95–96
Rogerson, J. W., 95
Rosenzweig, Rachel, 81, 98
Roskam, H. N., 50, 155
Rossé, Gérard, 159n17
Roth, Wolfgang, 62n49
Ryou, Philip Ho-Young, 39n22

Santos, Narry F., 12–13, 13n26, 13n27
Schlimm, Matthew R., 86n3
Schmid, Wolf, 18n42
Scott, M. Philip, 23n60
Seeley, David, 69, 74–76, 76n25, 83
Seneca 69–71, 75, 75n20, 83
deSilva, David A., 23n59
Skinner, Christopher W., 19n45

Smit, Peter-Ben, 23n59
Snow, Robert S., 135n13
Steichele, Hans-Jörg, 165, 165n38
Stein, Robert H., 28n1, 75, 75n21
Sterling, Greg, 69, 76–79, 83
Stock, Augustine, 20n49, 21n53, 28n1, 119n12
Stuhlmacher, Peter, 131n34

Tabor, James D. 75n20
Tannehill, Robert C., 46
Telford, William R., 16n39
Tertullian, 74, 101, 108
Thomas, Dalton, 179n2
Thomson, Ian H., 21n53, 22
Tolbert, Mary Ann, 28, 48–49, 126n23

Trocmé, Etienne, 25
Tyson, Joseph B., 45

Ulansey, David, 35n12, 39, 159n17

VandenBerg, Mary, 179
Vermes, Geza, 134–35, 134n8

Wagner, Ross J., 115
Watts, John D. W., 129
Watts, Rikki E., 116, 116n6
Weeden, Theodore J., 45–46, 162n27
Weihs, Alexander, 8, 166n42
Welch, John, 22, 22n58
Witherington, Ben III, 89n17, 90n18, 102n7, 106n17, 165n37

Lightning Source UK Ltd.
Milton Keynes UK
UKHW022041141120
373401UK00009B/281